Using ACT and CFT for Burnout Recovery

Using ACT and CFT for Burnout Recovery: The Beyond Burnout Blueprint introduces an innovative approach to navigating burnout by integrating evidence-based strategies from Acceptance and Commitment Therapy (ACT) and Compassion-Focused Therapy (CFT).

Burnout is everywhere—especially in health care, education, and other demanding professions—and many solutions stop at surface-level fixes. This book offers an innovative, compassionate, science-based roadmap to build resilience and create responsive work cultures that not only address burnout but also prevent it from taking hold. The author presents *the Beyond Burnout Blueprint*: A six-step framework that moves people from depletion to sustainable burnout recovery. Through case stories, reflection exercises, and practical tools, readers learn how to craft a values-driven vision, welcome difficult emotions, defuse from unhelpful narratives, amplify unique strengths, practice fierce and restorative compassion, and let values guide their work and lives. The book bridges research and practice, applying psychological science not only to individual recovery but also to teams and organizations. Unlike quick-fix wellness guides, this book integrates ACT and CFT to tackle burnout at its roots both individually and systemically. It empowers readers to recover, prevent, and transcend burnout while shaping workplaces that are psychologically safe, compassionate, and resilient, offering enduring tools for personal renewal and organizational change.

With accessible writing and actionable strategies, this book equips clinicians, leaders, and professionals in high-stakes fields with skills that are both immediately useful and deeply transformative for helping those with burnout, and will appeal to anyone who may be suffering from burnout and looking for coping strategies to implement into their daily lives.

Shaina Siber, *LCSW,* is the founder of Affirm Mental Health and host of *The Affirming Minds Podcast.* An integrative therapist and educator with over 15 years of experience, she specializes in burnout recovery for high achievers, health care workers, and parents and champions trauma-informed, culturally humble, and LGBTQ-affirming care.

"*Using ACT and CFT for Burnout Recovery* is an exceptional and timely resource for anyone working in emotionally demanding roles. Shaina Siber weaves together science, story, and skill in a way that is both deeply compassionate and eminently practical. Rather than offering quick fixes, this book provides a clear roadmap that fosters recovery from burnout, increased resilience, and burnout-responsive workplaces. Whether you are a clinician, leader, or someone navigating burnout yourself, you will find wisdom, tools, and inspiration in these pages."

Dr. Simon A. Rego, *Chief of Psychology, Montefiore Medical Center, Bronx, New York, the United States; Professor of Psychiatry and Behavioral Sciences, Albert Einstein College of Medicine, Bronx, New York, the United States; and Co-Author of* The Cognitive Behavioral Therapy Workbook for Leaders: How Improving Your Mental Health Is Essential to Avoiding Burnout and Leading More Effectively

"Evidence-based and compassionate, *Using ACT and CFT for Burnout Recovery* brilliantly weaves together relatable storytelling and practical guidance for overcoming and preventing burnout. This book is exactly the book that I wish someone would've handed to me a few years ago when I personally was struggling with burnout. It's an invaluable resource for helping professionals and any person trying to find more meaning and stability at work and in life."

Dr. Kiki Fehling, *Co-Author of* Self-Directed DBT Skills: A 3-Month DBT Workbook – Regulate Intense Emotions and Create Lasting Change with Dialectical Behavior Therapy *and Author of* DBT Cards for Coping Skills: 125 DBT Skills and Strategies to Find Balance, Joy, and Purpose

"A wise and compassionate step-by-step guide to recovery from burnout. Easy to read and simple to apply. Highly recommended."

Dr. Russ Harris, *Author of* The Happiness Trap

Using ACT and CFT for Burnout Recovery

The Beyond Burnout Blueprint

Shaina Siber

 Routledge
Taylor & Francis Group

NEW YORK AND LONDON

Designed cover image: Cover Design by Cheakina

First published 2026
by Routledge
605 Third Avenue, New York, NY 10158

and by Routledge
4 Park Square, Milton Park, Abingdon, Oxon, OX14 4RN

Routledge is an imprint of the Taylor & Francis Group, an informa business

For Product Safety Concerns and Information please contact our EU representative GPSR@taylorandfrancis.com. Taylor & Francis Verlag GmbH, Kaufingerstraße 24, 80331 München, Germany.

ISBN: 978-1-041-07459-5 (hbk)
ISBN: 978-1-041-07430-4 (pbk)
ISBN: 978-1-003-64059-2 (ebk)

DOI: 10.4324/9781003640592

Typeset in Sabon
by Apex CoVantage, LLC

To M, with love and gratitude.

Contents

PART III
Broader Applications for the Beyond Burnout Blueprint   195

Acknowledgments

Thank you Routledge for your support in bringing this endeavor to life.

My deepest gratitude goes to Dr. Laurie Gallo, my colleague, friend, and the talented developmental editor of this book. I have been so fortunate to collaborate with you on clinical, educational, and program development throughout the years. I have always admired your ability to possess such a rich understanding of the scientific and academic foundations of this work while grounding it in applications that are compassionate, accessible, and transformative. That influence is woven throughout this book. You are an extraordinarily gifted teacher and clinician, and your insights have made this work immeasurably stronger. Thanks to Dr. Simon Rego and Dr. Kiki Fehling for generously lending your voices in support of this work through your blurbs. To Lyndy, my incredible operations and marketing coordinator at Affirm Mental Health: We are a small but mighty team, and you have been instrumental in supporting my ever-growing list of professional endeavors, including this book. Thank you for your flexibility, creativity, and kindness.

To the creators and contributors of the models that have deeply influenced this work—Steve Hayes, Paul Gilbert, Kristin Neff, Christopher Germer, Robyn Walser, Kelly G. Wilson, Kirk Strosahl, Russ Harris, Russel L. Kolts, Dennis Tirch, and Laura Silberstein Tirch. Although I have not met most of you, your work has profoundly shaped my life and practice, reverberating into the lives of my clients and now through the pages of this book.

To my family: My husband, Ismael, thank you for supporting me in writing this book, for creating the time and space I needed to prioritize it, and for believing that I could do bold and big things even when it was hard for me to see it myself. To my amazing children, Levi and Lily—you are the embodiment of the yin and yang of compassion. Levi, your kind, nurturing soul is an inspiration to all of us. Lily, your fierce love radiates through our home and hearts. Being your mother is the most incredible gift, and I will never take it for granted. I am so lucky to be your mom.

To my friends, new and old, who are endlessly supportive and encouraging. A special shout-out to Linda, who has been such an incredible cheerleader through this entire process. It has meant more than you will ever know.

To my clients: It has been one of the greatest honors of my life to be your therapist. Whether I worked with you as a trainee in graduate school or continue to work with you today, you have given my life purpose and meaning. To be entrusted with your stories and to walk beside you as you confront your pain and fight to create the lives you deserve are nothing short of miraculous. The therapeutic relationship is difficult to describe—bounded by ethical responsibility yet infused with profound care. Within those boundaries lie deep love, respect, and commitment I hold for every person I have had the privilege to work with.

And lastly, to myself. With this book so deeply rooted in self-compassion, I pause to thank me. Even if only my editor and I ever read these full pages, I am proud that I dreamed this up and dared to see it through. This book is part of my compelling vision and a true manifestation of the person I have been becoming. I promise to continue loving and caring for myself until the very end.

Introduction

How much of your life will you spend at work?

If you're anything like the average American worker, the answer is 90,000 hours, roughly one-third of your life (Pryce-Jones, 2010). That's more time than you'll spend with your partner, your children, or your closest friends. More time than you'll ever devote to hobbies, passions, or the dreams you keep promising yourself you'll get to "someday."

And yet, despite pouring so much of our lives into work, balance remains out of reach for most of us. The 40-hour workweek is now a relic. Nearly 40% of workers regularly clock more than 50 hours a week, and 1 in 5 of us will push past 60 (Saad, 2014). The United States remains one of the only developed nations without federally mandated paid vacations, and even when time off is offered, nearly half of employees don't take it (Dinesh & Parker, 2023) fearing they'll fall behind, appear replaceable, or drown under the avalanche waiting for them when they return.

Perhaps the most insidious part is this: Even when people aren't at work, work is still with them. Late-night emails. Weekend slack pings. The unspoken expectation to always be available. More than half of employees admit they cannot fully unplug (CNBC, 2022). "Time off" has become just another way of saying "working from somewhere else."

The consequences are staggering. Burnout is at an all-time high, with two-thirds of employees citing job burnout (Moodle, 2025). Overwork and chronic stress don't just drain our energy; they erode our health. Burnout increases the risk of depression and anxiety (Koutsimani et al., 2019), raises the likelihood of cardiovascular disease by 21%, and nearly doubles the risk of hypertension (John et al., 2024). Regularly working 55 or more hours per week increases stroke risk by 35% (Pega et al., 2021). In other words, burnout isn't just making us miserable; it's making us sick.

The term "burnout," coined by psychologist Herbert Freudenberger in the 1970s, described a state of physical and mental exhaustion among workers. Decades later, the World Health Organization (2019) formally acknowledged burnout as an "occupational phenomenon," characterized

DOI: 10.4324/9781003640592-1

by exhaustion, cynicism, detachment, and reduced effectiveness. While not classified as a medical disorder, the research is clear: Burnout contributes to a wide range of psychological and physical health problems (Salvagioni et al., 2017). Half a century after naming the problem, we are left collectivity scratching our heads on how to resolve it.

If you're experiencing burnout, chances are you've already tried to "fix" it. Maybe you leaned into conventional wisdom: More exercise, more sleep, more meditation, more sunshine, more kale. Maybe you bought into the idea that a vacation or spa day would reset your system. And maybe, like me, you walked out of more than one workplace wellness workshop mumbling expletives under your breath about the audacity of being told to "just drink more water" while drowning under impossible workloads.

Here's the truth: We cannot rely on "good vibes only" for finding our way out of burnout. There aren't enough green juices, yoga classes, or massages in the world to self-care burnout into submission. Even the most restorative vacation glow often evaporates before you've finished unpacking.

And we cannot ignore the systemic realities that drive burnout: Unsafe staffing, impossible workloads, workplace discrimination, bias, and harassment. These are real, pervasive, and damaging. This book will not ask you to deny them, minimize them, or pretend they don't matter.

But it will ask you to consider something that may feel counterintuitive: Burnout isn't something you can simply eliminate once your external circumstances change. Pain and challenge are inevitable in work, and in life. And your ability to meet difficulty with awareness, intention, and compassion is essential to moving beyond burnout.

If you're not convinced, I wonder if you have heard of an extremely rare genetic condition called *Congenital Insensitivity to Pain* (Schon et al., 2020). Affected individuals still have access to other physical sensations and can tell the difference between dull and sharp, or hot and cold, but pain goes undetected. For those of you who have been seriously injured, suffer from chronic pain syndrome, or even experienced the brief excruciation of a stubbed toe, this ailment may seem like a dream. A world without pain? Isn't this what we've hoped and prayed for as a society? Hasn't this largely been the aim of the medical, pharmaceutical, and mental health complex? It only takes a quick Google image search of this condition to experience a whole new appreciation for your pain receptors. You will see severely contorted broken bones, infected wounds, and burns. These individuals, mostly children, are severely vulnerable to repeated injury and illness and typically have a markedly stunted life expectancy due to this condition. Pain, it turns out, is protective. It teaches, it alerts, it sustains. Without it, we are profoundly vulnerable.

Burnout is much the same. Painful, yes. Exhausting, yes. But also, a signal, information that can guide transformation if we know how to listen. Just as physical pain protects the body, the distress of burnout can protect our lives from being lived out of alignment with our deepest needs and values.

That doesn't mean that the path forward is about eliminating pain, stress, or challenge. It means learning how to relate to these experiences differently. Growth is often born out of struggle. Transformation almost always comes tethered to discomfort. Eliminating pain may be impossible, but building the resilience to meet it with compassion and intention—that is within your reach.

What I can promise you is this: If you commit to the roadmap in these pages, you will start your process of burnout recovery not as a finish line, but as an embodied practice. You will cultivate burnout resilience by meeting stress with flexibility, presence, and compassion. Rooted in Acceptance and Commitment Therapy (ACT) (Hayes et al., 2012) and Compassion-Focused Therapy (CFT) (Gilbert, 2010), this blueprint empowers you to transcend symptoms rather than avoid them, reclaiming energy, purpose, and connection.

This is not about working harder to fix yourself. It's about learning to move through discomfort without losing sight of what matters most. Burnout resilience allows you to regulate, refocus, and rise when burnout shows up. Crucially, we will also cover systemic responsiveness, the changes needed at organizational and cultural levels to prevent and attend to burnout so that we're not carrying the burden alone. We need both.

Whether you feel lightly toasted or burnt to a crisp, your journey begins here. Take a moment. Let the word *burnout* linger in your mind. What comes up—memories, judgments, emotions, body sensations, urges? Whatever is there, let it surface. That's the raw material we'll be working with.

In this book, we'll explore burnout not as a fixed diagnosis, but as a collection of private experiences: Beliefs, emotions, expectations, and bodily responses tied to your professional identity and your relationship with work. And through this lens, I'll share my own story, the one memory that most encapsulates my burnout experience. More importantly, I see this as the genesis of *the Beyond Burnout Blueprint*. Within this moment of intense physical and emotional pain, the seeds were planted for my burnout liberation.

References

CNBC. (2022, July 12). *54% of people can't disconnect from work on vacation – Here's why*. CNBC. https://www.cnbc.com/2022/07/12/54percent-of-pe ople-cant-disconnect-from-work-on-vacation-heres-why.html

Dinesh, S., & Parker, K. (2023, August 10). *More than 4 in 10 U.S. workers don't take all their paid time off* [Short reads]. Pew Research Center. https://www.pe wresearch.org/short-reads/2023/08/10/more-than-4-in-10-u-s-workers-dont-t ake-all-their-paid-time-off/

Freudenberger, H. J. (1974). Staff burnout. *Journal of Social Issues, 30*(1), 159–165. https://doi.org/10.1111/j.1540-4560.1974.tb00706.x

Gilbert, P. (2010). *Compassion focused therapy: Distinctive features*. Routledge/ Taylor & Francis Group. https://doi.org/10.4324/9780203851197

Hayes, S. C., Strosahl, K. D., & Wilson, K. G. (2012). *Acceptance and commitment therapy: The process and practice of mindful change* (2nd ed.). Guilford Press.

John, A., Bouillon-Minois, J. B., Bagheri, R., Pélissier, C., Charbotel, B., Llorca, P. M., Zak, M., Ugbolue, U. C., Baker, J. S., & Dutheil, F. (2024). The influence of burnout on cardiovascular disease: A systematic review and meta-analysis. *Frontiers in Psychiatry, 15*, 1326745. https://doi.org/10.3389/fpsyt.2024.1326745

Koutsimani, P., Montgomery, A., & Georganta, K. (2019). The relationship between burnout, depression, and anxiety: A systematic review and meta-analysis. *Frontiers in Psychology, 10*, 284. https://doi.org/10.3389/fpsyg.2019.00284

Moodle. (2025, February 27). *AI for workplace training in America: Employees are ready, but are employers?* Moodle. https://moodle.com/us/news/ai-for-workplace-training-in-america

Pega, F., Náfrádi, B., Momen, N. C., Ujita, Y., Streicher, K. N., Prüss-Üstün, A. M., Technical Advisory Group, Descatha, A., Driscoll, T., Fischer, F. M., Godderis, L., Kiiver, H. M., Li, J., Magnusson Hanson, L. L., Rugulies, R., Sørensen, K., & Woodruff, T. J. (2021). Global, regional, and national burdens of ischemic heart disease and stroke attributable to exposure to long working hours for 194 countries, 2000–2016: A systematic analysis from the WHO/ILO Joint Estimates of the Work-related Burden of Disease and Injury. *Environment International, 154*, 106595. https://doi.org/10.1016/j.envint.2021.106595

Pryce-Jones, J. (2010). *Happiness at work: Maximizing your psychological capital for success*. Wiley-Blackwell. https://doi.org/10.1002/9780470666845

Saad, L. (2014, September 2). The "40-hour" workweek is actually longer – By seven hours [Gallup Work and Education Survey]. Gallup. https://news.gallup.com/poll/175286/hour-workweek-actually-longer-seven-hours.aspx

Salvagioni, D. A. J., Melanda, F. N., Mesas, A. E., González, A. D., Gabani, F. L., & Andrade, S. M. (2017). Physical, psychological and occupational consequences of job burnout: A systematic review of prospective studies. *PLOS ONE, 12*(10), e0185781. https://doi.org/10.1371/journal.pone.0185781

Schon, K. R., Parker, A. P. J., & Woods, C. G. (2020). Congenital insensitivity to pain overview. In M. P. Adam, G. M. Mirzaa, R. A. Pagon, S. E. Wallace, L. J. H. Bean, K. W. Gripp, & A. Amemiya (Eds.), *GeneReviews®*. University of Washington, Seattle. https://www.ncbi.nlm.nih.gov/books/NBK532922/

World Health Organization. (2019, May 28). *Burn-out an "occupational phenomenon": International Classification of Diseases (ICD-11)*. World Health Organization. https://www.who.int/news/item/28-05-2019-burn-out-an-occupational-phenomenon-international-classification-of-diseases

Chapter 1

The Beyond Burnout
Origin Story

It's December 2020. I'm at my kitchen table with an open laptop, a cup of coffee, and piles of scribbled notes. It's the weekend—though that concept has become laughable. Any imagined boundary between personal time and work dissolved the moment the pandemic arrived. The closest comparison is those first weeks with a newborn, when you're never sure if it's 5 a.m. or 5 p.m. Your life orbits the baby, not a neat 24-hour clock. It felt like that perpetual fog of exhaustion of those early days of motherhood, sans the bundle of joy. Nursing and diaper changes were replaced by emails and Zoom meetings. Everything was urgent; it was due yesterday. It was never-ending.

We were living in a two-bedroom house on a tree-lined street in the West Bronx. The Bronx, birthplace of hip-hop and home to the Yankees and Justice Sonia Sotomayor, was also a "hotspot within a hotspot" for COVID-19. The South Bronx, in particular, bore the brunt of historic neglect, and those inequities showed up everywhere. I worked at a nearby hospital that was devastated by COVID. I was a Division Director with clinical and administrative oversight of ambulatory and emergency psychiatry. The responsibility was massive; the role, poorly defined and ever expanding. At night, after an already-at-capacity day and between childcare and life admin, I saw therapy clients, mostly hospital employees, despite my already packed schedule that was busting at the seams.

The familiar sound of the Frozen track plays in the background, while my three-year-old daughter and seven-year-old son are glued to the screen. My husband is at work, serving as a doorman in Brooklyn. Elsa and Ana will need to be their surrogate parents for the next hour or two, while I barely make a dent in my to-do list. Stopping to eat lunch wasn't an option, so I grabbed a sleeve of saltine crackers from the pantry to provide sustenance while I expertly crafted yet another memo related to the ever-changing COVID-19 protocols.

Mid-sentence, I hear an audible crack accompanied by a shooting pain in my tooth. I knew immediately my tooth had broken on my sorry excuse

DOI: 10.4324/9781003640592-2

for a meal. I mentally scan in my mind *how many dentist appointments I've canceled since that toothache emerged two months ago. Was it two? No, it was definitely three.* The appointment times kept conflicting with time-sensitive meetings and looming deadlines. I can't quite remember why they were so important at this moment when it feels like I'm being bludgeoned in the face with a baseball bat. *I'm literally falling apart!* I thought to myself with my fractured tooth in hand to prove it.

It was at that moment I knew I was completely at the mercy of my burnout. I was already aware that I was experiencing symptoms of burnout. There had been signs of course; the dread of getting up for work in the morning, the quickening turnover of the pinot grigio on the wine rack, the unrelenting tension in my neck, the tightening pants, and the shortening temper. My curated self-care skills had fallen by the wayside months ago in favor of whatever kept my burnout symptoms tempered long enough to push through whatever task was in front of me.

As a social worker, in some ways, I'd seen burnout as an inevitable occupational hazard—maybe at moments even as a badge of honor for my sacrifice and commitment to my clients. I thought I had it under control. It also felt so normalized. Working in health care during COVID was not for the faint of heart. Most of my colleagues and work friends appeared to be at or approaching burnout. My comrades looked war-torn. The clients I saw at the time, primarily health-care workers, weren't just experiencing burnout; they were depressed, traumatized, and anxious, largely influenced by their acute work stress.

I felt the heat of the tears running down my face. Everything I had been pushing away felt like it was rushing to the surface, waiting to be exiled along with my chipped tooth. I blurted out to absolutely no one at all, "I can't do this anymore!" and dissolved into tears among the table full of dozens of half-completed tasks.

I heard footsteps approaching behind me. I turned to see the kind and consoling freckled face of my seven-year-old son, Levi. I was met with his grin, also missing a tooth for more developmentally appropriate reasons. He said, "You're okay, Mama. Whatever it is, it won't last forever." I felt his arms wrap around me, and he whispered in my ear, "I love you so much." In the midst of all that was going on, his warm hug enveloped me in pure compassion. His head nuzzled into mine, and the soft refrain of "Let it Go" played in the background. All there was, was that moment.

If my Frozen references are going over your head, the movie centers around a newly crowned Queen Elsa who's cursed with generating sometimes whimsical and frequently dangerous cold weather conditions when feeling intense emotions. In the finale of the movie, Elsa is on the precipice of accidentally freezing her sister to death and burying Arendale, the town she's responsible for governing, in an uninhabitable blizzard. It is at this moment she accepts that her efforts to control her powers are an exercise in futility. Only in her surrender of control does she realize "Love thaws"— revealing her powers weren't so much the problem as her unwillingness to have them. Spoiler alert: Elsa accesses this internal knowing, her sister is saved, and the town is restored to pre-climate change weather patterns. I had a similar lightbulb moment akin to "Love Thaws." What Levi had unveiled to me in that moment was the transformative power of compassion and being connected to the present moment.

My descent into burnout was inevitable once my self-compassion became a distant memory, and an inner voice, I used to know, became completely vacant from my day-to-day experience. I was so in my head, so dominated by my stress and overwhelm, that I felt disconnected from the life that was going on around me. My life had become an intricate dance with my burnout, which I was constantly fighting to lead. Instead, I was being dragged around the dance floor. My efforts to stay in control were keeping me stuck in a perpetual samba of suffering. I had completely forgotten that not dancing was an option (which is best metaphorically and literally, given my dance skills).

That was the start of developing my burnout resilience. Like Elsa, I had to access something I already knew but had been evading me in all my internal struggles. Five years later, with my full smile intact, I am proud to share with you *the Beyond Burnout Blueprint*, your road map for Burnout Resilience.

The Essence of the Blueprint

I'm an integrative therapist. In practice, that means I draw from multiple therapeutic frameworks based on a client's needs. I see the merit in many approaches, open to all with an allegiance to none. I'm trained in a host of evidence-based treatments that can read like alphabet soup: IPT, CBT, ACT, CPT, and more. Even at the height of my burnout, I loved being a therapist. If I hit the jackpot tomorrow, I'd still keep a caseload. (And for the record: You do not have to feel that way about your job to benefit from this book. At my peak burnout, therapy was only a small slice of my professional pie.)

Six years into my career, probably in part fleeing my own burnout, I left a high-volume clinic role to become a clinical manager. That led to broader leadership and administrative roles. Over the last decade, I've increasingly focused on burnout as a clinical target. Across hundreds of clients and many modalities, the approaches that have landed best for burnout are third-wave cognitive behavioral therapies (CBTs).

Third-wave CBT prioritizes how we relate to our internal, private experiences including thoughts, urges, sensations, memories, and feelings, over trying to change the content of those experiences (Hayes & Hofmann, 2017). Core elements include acceptance, mindfulness, personal values, and metacognition (thinking about thinking). These therapies help you clarify what truly matters and support meaningful behavioral change aligned with those values.

Counterintuitively, they don't aim to eliminate symptoms or "cure" diagnoses. They shift the frame from dysfunction to wellness: Learning to relate to life's inevitable pain with more skill and compassion while building a purposeful, connected life.

My own recovery grew from two of these evidence-based therapies *ACT and CFT* braided together with hard-earned life lessons.

How to Use This Book

This book is your companion for cultivating burnout resilience and systemic responsiveness. I'll share my experiences and composite vignettes (significantly altered to protect privacy) to illustrate how these concepts apply in real life.

You'll find two types of hands-on elements throughout:

- Beyond Burnout Exercises: Reflection prompts to help you pause, notice, and deepen insight as you move through the material.
- Beyond Burnout Practices: Repeatable skills and strategies to keep in your resilience toolbox. Tools you'll return to during flare-ups and as part of ongoing well-being.

How to get the most from each part is explained in the next subsections.

Part I: Burnout Recovery Foundations

We'll get into the who, what, why, and how of burnout and take an honest look at what's been tried and what actually helps. You'll learn why ACT and CFT are the right vehicles for your recovery journey and get the essential background to make Part II powerful.

Part II: The Beyond Burnout Blueprint

This is the heart of the book: A six-step journey to unlock your burnout resilience. These chapters weave evidence-based strategies from ACT and CFT (with a sprinkle of integrative techniques) into a practical framework for your burnout recovery. Set aside focused time. Keep a notebook nearby. Immerse yourself in the visualizations and complete the written and experiential practices. Then apply and practice them at work and at home.

Part III: Broader Applications for the Beyond Burnout Blueprint

We'll broaden the lens to examine structural forces and workplace culture, with a focus on systemic responsiveness. Leaders will learn how to apply these principles to hiring, feedback, and role design, while teams will practice compassionate leadership, authentic vulnerability, and values-driven culture shaping. Together, we'll explore organizational changes that truly aim to *prevent* burnout, shifting away from surface-level fixes toward humanity-centered ways of structuring work that authentically promote well-being.

While you may have come seeking a burnout survival guide, the truth is that you already know how to survive. That fateful winter day in my kitchen, I was stuck in survival mode. Your burnout is a testament to your functioning survival instincts. This book is about the expansion that happens when your life is not structured around the threat you are evading. This book is about what happens when you get out of survival mode. This book is about becoming the Beyond Burnout version of you.

Reference

Hayes, S. C., & Hofmann, S. G. (2017). The third wave of cognitive behavioral therapy and the rise of process-based care. *World Psychiatry*, *16*(3), 245–246. https://doi.org/10.1002/wps.20442

Part I

Burnout Recovery Foundations

Chapter 2

Burnout Basics

I'd like to think that I have a keen eye for spotting burnt-out employees in the wild. There's something unmistakable in their body language—the slumped shoulders, the weary gait, the way their once-bright enthusiasm has been dimmed to a flicker. Sometimes, it's in their eyes—that light that once reflected passion now dulled by exhaustion. Other times, it's an aura of heightened franticness, as if they are perpetually running on fumes.

Despite my knack for clocking burnout, researchers have done extensive work to quantify it in ways that go beyond instinctual observations. Various models attempt to categorize burnout, helping us make sense of the different ways it manifests. One of the most useful frameworks was a burnout typology originally proposed by Dr. B.A. Farber (1990) based on his clinical observations of adults in helping and teaching professions. This framework breaks burnout down into three subtypes: *Frenetic, Under-challenged,* and *Worn-out* (Montero-Marín & García-Campayo, 2010). Think of them as the Hogwarts Sorting Hat of burnout. We may resonate with traits, symptoms, or experiences from more than one house, like my sense that I'm a rare Ravenclaw-Hufflepuff hybrid, but when it comes to burnout, one usually feels most like home. For me, that's *Casa Frenetic*, where the lights are always on and the to-do list never ends.

Frenetic burnout: This subtype feels like sprinting on a treadmill that never stops. An unyielding cycle of overcommitment, relentless job demands, and a ceaseless chase for success at any cost. In a desperate bid for recognition or relief, individuals pour everything into work, only to find that the harder they push, the more elusive respite becomes. In the wild, you'll see desks littered with empty coffee cups and energy drink cans, to-do lists longer than a CVS receipt, emails sent at 3 a.m., and "just one more meeting" crammed in during vacation. Productivity becomes a stand-in for self-worth, and even the thought of rest feels like a guilty indulgence. This subtype is often rooted in anxiety about falling behind, an identity fused with achievement, or chaotic workloads designed for three people but handed to one. Saying "yes" to everything becomes a desperate

DOI: 10.4324/9781003640592-4

attempt to quiet the gnawing feeling of not being enough until the inevitable crash.

Under-challenged burnout: This burnout subtype lives at the other end of the spectrum. Picture *The Office*'s Stanley Hudson: Physically present but mentally gone, crossword puzzle in hand, perfecting the art of doing just enough to collect a paycheck. These folks were "quiet quitting" before it was a trend. The signs? Boredom, emotional detachment, TikTok breaks between tasks, and keeping their camera off in meetings. The driver is often a lack of meaning, untapped skills, or a stagnant work environment where curiosity and growth go to die. Without intellectual stimulation or purpose, motivation evaporates into ennui, the French word for the particular kind of soul-deep boredom that makes every hour feel twice as long.

Worn-out burnout: This subtype is what happens when exhaustion and cynicism take over completely. It's the slow erosion of drive into resignation. The deep fatigue of someone who's given everything and now has nothing left to give. They've stopped trying, not because they don't care, but because they've learned their efforts won't change anything. At first, you might just notice more sick days or closed office doors. But when you do spot them, it's hard to miss: They're navigating the workplace like a raw nerve, with the smallest inconvenience triggering an outsized reaction. Tears in the bathroom, unchecked rage in a meeting, sloppy or abandoned work. Worn-out burnout often evolves from years of Frenetic burnout, the "Pokémon evolution" of pushing through exhaustion, illness, and alarm bells until the mind or body finally collapses.

Beyond Burnout Exercise: The Burnout Sorting Hat

Step 1: Identify Your Primary Burnout Subtype

Once you've read through the descriptions of Frenetic, Under-Challenged, and Worn-Out burnouts, take a moment to reflect: Which of these descriptions resonates with you most right now? If it helps, visualize these burnout subtypes as "houses" you've lived in throughout your professional journey. Where have you spent the most time? Where do you find yourself now? Do you shift between them depending on workload, environment, or energy levels? Does one feel like your default state while the other emerges under specific conditions?

Step 2: Reflect on the Drivers Behind Your Burnout

Once you've identified your primary burnout subtype, consider the why.

What's fueling your burnout right now (e.g., unrealistic expectations, lack of challenge, overcommitment, workplace dysfunction)?

How is your work environment reinforcing your current burnout subtype?

What beliefs or narratives about success, work ethic, or identity might be keeping you in this cycle?

Step 3: Take a Micro-Action to Shift the Pattern

Small shifts can create meaningful change. Based on your subtype, try one of these:

Frenetic Burnout: Identify one task you can delegate, delay, or drop. Give yourself permission to take a break.

Under-Challenged Burnout: Find a small way to re-engage, whether it's pitching a new idea, signing up for a training, or setting a goal outside of work that sparks your curiosity.

Worn-Out Burnout: Reach out for support. Whether it's a trusted colleague, mentor, therapist, or friend, share what you're going through.

The Systemic Drivers of Burnout

Knowing your burnout subtype tells you *how* burnout shows up for you. But it doesn't fully explain *why*. Burnout doesn't live solely inside the individual. It's shaped, fueled, and often sustained by the systems we work within. Psychologist Dr. Christina Maslach and colleagues, whose work since the 1970s has been foundational in burnout research, identified six key drivers that make burnout almost inevitable when left unchecked: Work overload, lack of autonomy, lack of reward, lack of community, mismatch of values, and lack of fairness (Maslach & Leiter, 1997).

Work Overload

Work overload happens when the math never adds up: More tasks than hours, more complexity than resources, more expectations than energy. It can be quantitative (too much) or qualitative (too complex for the time and tools you have). It's the "quick meeting" that swallows half the day, the project that arrives on Friday at 4:55 p.m., the steady drip of after-hours emails.

From a clinical perspective, prolonged overload triggers the body's threat response, surging cortisol, one of the natural stress responses of the body. Chronic threat response erodes cognitive flexibility and drains the emotional bandwidth we need for empathy, creativity, and problem-solving.

Overload is one of the most consistent predictors of burnout across professions. Maslach and Leiter describe it as the first domain of mismatch between people and their work: When demands regularly outstrip resources, energy is spent faster than it can be replenished. Overload isn't just a bad week or a difficult project. It becomes cultural when leaders frame it as "part of the job."

The serious consequences of overwork are especially apparent in Japan, where *karōshi* (過労死), or "death by overwork," refers to fatalities from excessive working hours, often resulting from strokes, heart attacks, and other health complications (Ericksen, 2020). A related phenomenon, *karōjisatsu* (過労自殺), describes suicides linked explicitly to workplace stress, further illustrating the toll of long hours and chronic occupational pressure.

Karōshi first emerged as a social issue during Japan's post-World War II recovery, when the drive to rebuild the nation fueled an unprecedented economic boom from the 1950s through the 1980s. Cultural norms and government policies reinforced company loyalty, normalizing extreme work practices where employees often logged more than 60 hours a week. This relentless pace accelerated Japan's economic growth but at a profound human cost (Widarahhesty, 2020).

In response to rising concerns, the Japanese government introduced initiatives such as "Premium Friday," which encouraged workers to leave early on the last Friday of each month. Yet, despite these efforts, long working hours remain culturally embedded and economically reinforced. The persistence of *karōshi* serves as a sobering reminder of the dangers of normalizing overwork at a collective level and highlights how cultural and systemic factors intertwine to shape occupational health risks.

Lack of Autonomy

Autonomy is the ability to decide *how*, *when*, and sometimes *where* you do your work. It can be a protective factor against burnout and one of the easiest for organizations to erode. Micromanagement, rigid protocols, and constant check-ins send the not-so-subtle message: "We don't trust you." That mistrust wears people down as much as the work itself.

Autonomy supports intrinsic motivation. People feel more engaged and less depleted when they have a say in how their work gets done. Research in occupational health psychology consistently links autonomy to higher job satisfaction and lower burnout (e.g., Schaufeli et al., 2009; Hakanen et al., 2019).

The pandemic offered a natural experiment. Many people thrived with remote or hybrid work, proving that productivity doesn't require proximity to a cubicle. Flexibility has since shifted from perk to expectation. While not all jobs can be done remotely, offering autonomy where possible—through flexible hours and greater control over workflow—pays dividends in retention, engagement, and well-being.

Lack of Reward

Humans are wired for recognition. It's not vanity, it's biology. "Reward" includes pay, yes, but also acknowledgment, job security, benefits, and the sense that your work matters. When people give their best and receive little in return, motivation erodes, and cynicism grows.

Lack of reward undermines self-efficacy and can lead to depressive symptoms. Evolutionary psychology reminds us that belonging and contributing to the group are survival imperatives (Baumeister & Leary, 1995); when contributions go unseen, the brain's threat pathways may activate in a manner similar to physical danger (Eisenberger & Lieberman, 2004).

Inadequate compensation is especially demoralizing in today's economic landscape. As living costs soar and wages remain stagnant, working hard yet struggling to afford basic necessities breeds deep resentment, whether it's from paying bills, covering student loans, or affording groceries.

I know this firsthand. One of my biggest grievances was discovering that I was making tens of thousands less than my colleagues in similar roles. The biggest blow came when I was cc'd on an email reclassifying my position. I was reclassified to a director role while the assistant director role I held was eliminated. What should have been a celebratory promotion wound up being an unceremonious ultimatum. My heart sank when I saw the insulting proposed salary increase, particularly when my supervisor accidentally left the prior director's salary in the email chain. My new salary had been slashed nearly in half of what my predecessor was earning. I tried to advocate for myself, but my concerns fell on deaf ears. I had no one in my corner, and I couldn't afford to walk away. My boss, under pressure to cut costs, saw hiring me at a steep discount as a win for the bottom line.

At the time, my husband and I were living paycheck to paycheck with daycare costs that rivaled rent and crippling student loan debt. It's not just about money; it's about dignity, stability, and the ability to fully engage in both work and life. When organizations fail to recognize or fairly compensate their employees, they create a perfect storm for burnout, resentment, and disengagement.

And even when someone is financially secure, the sting of being overlooked persists. Whether it's being passed over for promotions, facing pay discrepancies, watching others receive credit for your work, or feeling invisible in meetings, these experiences erode motivation and self-worth, making you question your value not only at work but also in the world.

Lack of Community

Humans need connection the way plants need sunlight. Without it, workplaces become emotionally barren. Isolation can happen anywhere. Remote workers might feel disconnected, while in-office workers can still be outsiders if the culture lacks trust and inclusion.

Social support is one of the most powerful buffers against stress. Community isn't about proximity, it's about quality of connection. Pizza parties and "forced fun" don't create belonging; psychological safety, genuine appreciation, and collaborative problem-solving do.

When organizations invest in authentic community, the impact is measurable: Burnout rates drop, job satisfaction climbs, and people are more likely to innovate and stay. Research shows that organizational culture, inclusivity, and a sense of belonging significantly predict work satisfaction, which in turn reduces burnout (Trinkenreich et al., 2023).

Mismatch of Values

When work repeatedly forces people to act against their deeply held values, the progression toward burnout accelerates. This is often described as *moral injury*, a term first used in military contexts (Litz et al., 2009) but now widely recognized across professions, particularly in health care (Dean et al., 2019). Unlike typical job stress, moral injury cuts at the core of a person's identity. It's not just *I don't like my job* but *This job is making me into someone I don't want to be.*

Moral injury creates a deep, identity-level wound. Academic research links it to shame, depression, alienation, and even post-traumatic stress disorder (PTSD)-like symptoms (Litz et al., 2009; Williamson et al., 2018). What makes moral injury particularly insidious is that it undermines integrity and meaning, two of the most powerful buffers against burnout. A social worker pressured to meet productivity quotas that prevent them from providing adequate care, or a compliance officer directed to overlook unethical practices to protect the company's bottom line, both illustrate how professionals can feel complicit in harm and betrayed by the very systems they serve.

Related, though less severe, are value mismatches, when the stated values of an organization clash with an employee's personal or professional values. These mismatches may not always rise to the level of moral injury, but over time, they can still erode trust, breed cynicism, and fuel disengagement (Maslach & Leiter, 2016). A teacher who believes in creativity and exploration but works in a system that prizes standardized testing or an office employee who values work–life balance but works in a culture that glorifies constant availability may not feel morally wounded, but will likely experience disconnection and frustration that chip away at engagement.

Lack of Fairness

Burnout thrives in environments where favoritism, bias, secrecy, and discrimination go unchecked. Fairness is not just an ethical imperative, it is a biological one. Research shows that experiencing discrimination activates the body's threat response, including heightened cardiovascular reactivity and stress physiology (Mendes et al., 2008; Pascoe & Smart Richman, 2009). Over time, this chronic activation contributes to disengagement, rumination, and stress-related symptoms, laying a fertile ground for burnout.

Unfairness often surfaces as workplace discrimination and harassment. The U.S. Equal Employment Opportunity Commission (2023) reported more than 70,000 discrimination charges in a single year, with 30% related to race and 32% to sex-based discrimination. Yet, official numbers underestimate the problem. The Workplace Bullying Institute (2021) found that 19% of employees reported being bullied, and nearly 30% had witnessed bullying. Similarly, Pew Research Center surveys show that 42% of women (Parker & Funk, 2017) and 41% of Black workers in the United States (Pew Research Center, 2023b) have personally experienced workplace discrimination.

Decades of research confirm the consequences: Discrimination, whether based on race, gender, sexual orientation, size, ability, or other identity factors, is strongly linked to poorer mental health outcomes, including anxiety, depression, and increased burnout risk (Pascoe & Smart Richman, 2009; Meyer, 2003; Bondanini et al., 2024). And the harm is not limited to those directly targeted. Employees who witness harassment or hostility also report declines in well-being, job satisfaction, and organizational commitment (Miner-Rubino & Cortina, 2004).

Addressing fairness requires more than compliance checkboxes. It calls for leadership that listens, policies that actively challenge bias, and structures that ensure equal access to opportunity. When equity becomes a lived organizational value, not just a legal requirement, trust and belonging grow. These are the conditions that buffer against burnout and sustain authentic engagement.

These six drivers don't just create unpleasant workplaces. They systematically drain human energy, disrupt cognitive and emotional functioning, and make burnout the default outcome. The good news? Because they're systemic, they can also be systematically changed.

Beyond Burnout Exercise: Your Workplace Report Card

Purpose: To identify which systemic factors in your work environment may be fueling burnout and begin to reflect on what you need to feel more supported and aligned.

Step 1: Grade Your Workplace

Use the scale below for each domain:
A = Excellent | B = Solid | C = Some concerns | D = Major issues |
F = Unsustainable
Workload: ____
Job Autonomy: ____
Reward: ____
Values Alignment: ___
Community: ____
Fairness: ____

Step 2: Reflect

Choose one or two lowest-scoring domains and consider:
- What makes this domain hard to tolerate right now?
- What does it cost you mentally, emotionally, or physically?
- What kind of support or change would make a meaningful difference?

Tracking Your Burnout

Understanding the systems that contribute to burnout is essential but so is knowing how to measure where you are right now. Psychologists first developed the *Maslach Burnout Inventory (MBI),* which became the foundation for decades of research and introduced the three dimensions of exhaustion, depersonalization, and reduced accomplishment (Maslach et al., 1997).

Today, more comprehensive tools capture how burnout affects both body and mind. My preferred approach is the *Burnout Assessment Tool (BAT)* (Schaufeli, De Witte, et al., 2020), which broadens the scope by looking at four dimensions:

1. *Exhaustion*—depletion of mental and physical energy
2. *Mental Distance*—emotional withdrawal and detachment from work
3. *Emotional Impairment*—difficulty managing and regulating emotions
4. *Cognitive Impairment*—challenges with focus, memory, and decision-making

The BAT also accounts for secondary symptoms, the ways prolonged stress shows up in the body. Muscle tension, headaches, stomach upset, disrupted sleep, low mood, and reduced immune function reflect how burnout is not just a "work problem" but a whole-body stress response that reshapes how we think, feel, and relate to others.

Perhaps most importantly, the BAT recognizes burnout as an intrapersonal process, considering the impact on our inner experiences. It infiltrates self-talk, shapes beliefs about worth and competence, and colors how we engage with the world. This means external fixes (a lighter workload, a better boss) can help, but true recovery also requires tending to the inner world.

When used thoughtfully, the BAT does more than put a number to your stress. It highlights where attention is needed, so recovery can be targeted in a way that is both systemic and deeply personal.

How to Take the BAT

Instructions: The following statements describe different experiences related to burnout. For each statement, select the number (1–5) that best represents how often you experience it.

Scoring Guide is as follows:

1—Never (This statement does not apply to me at all)
2—Rarely (I experience this occasionally, but it is not a regular issue)
3—Sometimes (I experience this moderately, but not all the time)
4—Often (I experience this frequently, and it affects me regularly)
5—Always (This is a persistent issue for me)

Table 2.1 presents the BAT—General version (Schaufeli, De Witte, et al., 2020).

Scoring and interpretation are as follows:

- Low Scores (1–2 on most items)—likely no significant burnout; stress levels are manageable.
- Moderate Scores (3 on multiple items)—possible early signs of burnout. It may be beneficial to assess workload, self-care, and emotional well-being.
- High Scores (4–5 on multiple items)—burnout may be significantly affecting your well-being. Consider making changes to workload, seeking professional support, or implementing burnout recovery strategies.

Table 2.1 Burnout Assessment Tool (BAT)—General Version

Category	Statements	1 (Never)	2 (Rarely)	3 (Sometimes)	4 (Often)	5 (Always)
Exhaustion	I feel mentally exhausted	☐	☐	☐	☐	☐
	Everything I do requires a great deal of effort	☐	☐	☐	☐	☐
	At the end of the day, I find it hard to recover my energy	☐	☐	☐	☐	☐
	I feel physically exhausted	☐	☐	☐	☐	☐
	When I get up in the morning, I lack the energy to start a new day	☐	☐	☐	☐	☐
	I want to be active, but somehow I am unable to manage	☐	☐	☐	☐	☐
	When I exert myself, I quickly get tired	☐	☐	☐	☐	☐
	At the end of my day, I feel mentally exhausted and drained	☐	☐	☐	☐	☐
Mental Distance	I struggle to find any enthusiasm for my work	☐	☐	☐	☐	☐
	I feel a strong aversion toward my job	☐	☐	☐	☐	☐
	I feel indifferent about my job	☐	☐	☐	☐	☐
	I'm cynical about what my work means to others	☐	☐	☐	☐	☐
Cognitive Impairment	I have trouble staying focused	☐	☐	☐	☐	☐
	I struggle to think clearly	☐	☐	☐	☐	☐
	I'm forgetful and distracted	☐	☐	☐	☐	☐
	I have trouble concentrating	☐	☐	☐	☐	☐
	I make mistakes because I have my mind on other things	☐	☐	☐	☐	☐
Emotional Impairment	I feel unable to control my emotions	☐	☐	☐	☐	☐

(Continued)

Table 2.1 (Continued)

Category	Statements	1 (Never)	2 (Rarely)	3 (Sometimes)	4 (Often)	5 (Always)
	I do not recognize myself in the way I react emotionally	☐	☐	☐	☐	☐
	I become irritable when things don't go my way	☐	☐	☐	☐	☐
	I get upset or sad without knowing why	☐☐	☐☐	☐☐	☐☐	☐☐
	I may overreact unintentionally	☐	☐	☐	☐	☐
Psychological Complaints	I have trouble falling or staying asleep	☐	☐	☐	☐	☐
	I tend to worry	☐☐	☐☐	☐☐	☐☐	☐☐
	I feel tense and stressed	☐	☐	☐	☐	☐
	I feel anxious and/or suffer from panic attacks	☐	☐	☐	☐	☐
	Noise and crowds disturb me	☐☐	☐☐	☐☐	☐☐	☐☐
Psychosomatic Complaints	I suffer from palpitations or chest pain	☐	☐	☐	☐	☐
	I suffer from stomach and/or intestinal complaints	☐	☐	☐	☐	☐
	I suffer from headaches	☐☐	☐☐	☐☐	☐☐	☐☐
	I suffer from muscle pain, for example, in the neck, shoulder, or back	☐	☐	☐	☐	☐
	I often get sick	☐	☐	☐	☐	☐

Source: Schaufeli, De Witte, et al. (2020)

Beyond Burnout Practice: Being with Your Body

Purpose: Now that you've explored your burnout subtype and reflected on your BAT score, take a moment to step out of analysis mode and into direct experience. Burnout isn't just a concept, it's something that shows up in our bodies, minds, and emotions.

Step 1: Check in with Your Body

- Find a comfortable position. Take a slow, steady breath in. Exhale fully. Now, bring your attention inward.
- Where do you physically feel burnout? Tightness in your chest? A heaviness in your limbs? A dull headache that lingers?
- Notice the tension points. Are your shoulders up near your ears? Is your jaw clenched? Is your stomach tight?
- Without judgment, simply acknowledge what's there.

Step 2: Observe Your Thoughts and Emotions

- Now, shift your focus to what's coming up mentally and emotionally in response to your burnout score and subtype reflection.
- Are you feeling validated? Frustrated? Overwhelmed?
- What are you feeling? What thoughts come to mind?
- Are any thoughts looping in your mind—perhaps about work, responsibilities, or expectations?
- There is no need to change anything. Just notice.

Step 3: Practice "Being With"

- Instead of immediately trying to fix, solve, or push past these experiences, try sitting with them for a moment. Take another deep breath. Imagine making just a little more space for whatever you're feeling, without forcing it away.
- If it helps, silently acknowledge:
  "This is where I am right now. I don't have to fight it. I don't have to fix it at this moment. I can just notice."
- Let yourself pause here for a few breaths.
- Burnout often thrives in constant motion. This practice of pausing, of checking in without immediately reacting, is a small but powerful way to reclaim space for yourself.
- When you feel ready, gently bring your attention back to the present. No rush. No pressure. Just awareness.

Step 4: Reflect

What thoughts and feelings, thoughts or body sensations felt tricky? Take note as you move through the upcoming chapters.

Who Burns Out and Why?

Burnout doesn't spare anyone, but it isn't evenly distributed. Vulnerability is shaped by structural inequities, chronic emotional labor, and mismatches between what work demands and what it gives back in respect, resources, and rest.

Demographic Vulnerabilities

Young adults report the highest burnout symptoms, nearly 40% of those aged 18–29 (Marchand et al., 2018). Women, especially those balancing paid work with unpaid caregiving, also face elevated risk (Maslach & Leiter, 2016; WHO, 2019). And for people navigating racism, sexism, ableism, homophobia, or xenophobia, the constant vigilance required to endure invalidating environments compounds the toll (Pavalko et al., 2003; Roberts et al., 2004).

Occupational Risk

Some fields consistently report higher burnout:

- *Health Care and Mental Health:* Over half of physicians report burnout (Shanafelt et al., 2015), often tied to moral injury when systemic barriers prevent needed care.
- *Education:* One in four teachers report depressive symptoms, double the national rate (RAND, 2021), as resources dwindle and demands escalate.
- *Law, Finance, and Tech:* Competitive, high-stakes cultures reward overwork and constant availability; 71% of lawyers report burnout (ABA, 2022).
- *Service, Retail, and Manual Labor:* Low pay, unstable schedules, customer aggression, and physical strain erode health and resilience.
- *Entrepreneurs:* Autonomy and innovation come with financial risk, chronic uncertainty, and isolation, fueling sustained stress.
- *Nonprofit Workers:* Mission-driven roles often involve high emotional labor, secondary trauma, and under-resourced environments, creating unique burnout risks.

Burnout: What's Been Tried, What's Failed, and What Actually Works

Given burnout's pervasive reach draining individual well-being, eroding company culture, and driving costly turnover, countless solutions have been proposed. Some have merit. Others, despite good intentions, amount to little more than a Band-Aid on a bullet wound. Let's start with what hasn't worked.

Flop #1: Consumer-Driven Self-Care

Self-care didn't begin in a spa brochure or on an Instagram grid. Its roots are political and collective. The modern self-care movement grew out of Black activism in the 1960s and 1970s as a radical response to racial violence, systemic neglect, and exclusion from mainstream health care (Wyatt & Ampadu, 2022).

The Black Panther Party built community health clinics, free breakfast programs, and wellness initiatives not just to meet urgent needs but also to assert dignity, autonomy, and the right to thrive in a system designed to deplete Black communities (Heynen, 2009). Black feminist thinkers such as Audre Lorde emphasized self-care as an act of survival and resistance, inseparable from caring for one's community and challenging systemic oppression (Lorde, 1988). In that tradition, self-care was never about luxury, it was about preservation, resilience, and collective strength.

Over time, however, the concept was diluted. Like many practices rooted in Black culture, self-care was mainstreamed and commercialized, reframed through the lens of Western individualism and consumerism. This version often shifts the focus from collective resilience to individual consumption, managing exhaustion alone instead of drawing on the strength of community.

That doesn't mean that there's anything wrong with enjoying products, rituals, or aesthetics as part of self-care. For many, those practices genuinely bring comfort, beauty, and a sense of grounding. But true recovery from burnout can't be reduced to consumption alone. It requires reconnecting with the deeper foundations of care, rest, belonging, meaning, and reciprocity that make renewal possible.

Flop #2: Workplace Wellness Without Structural Change

When organizations finally began acknowledging burnout, many rushed to roll out wellness programs. In theory, these were a step forward. In practice, they often became yet another task for already overextended employees.

It's difficult to focus on breathing exercises when your inbox is stacked, your workload is unmanageable, and you're staying late to cover for vacancies. Without adjusted workloads, protected time, or a supportive culture, wellness initiatives tend to attract the already-engaged and healthiest workers (Mattke et al., 2013), while the most burned out remain alienated.

Data backs up this mismatch: Over 85% of large U.S. employers now offer wellness programs, and 97% provide Employee Assistance Programs (EAPs) (Business Group on Health, 2023). Yet, only 6.9% of eligible employees actually use EAP benefits (National Behavioral Consortium, 2023). A large randomized controlled trial (RCT), considered the gold standard for testing effectiveness, followed 30,000 employees and found minimal impact of wellness programs on absenteeism, performance, or health-care costs (Song & Baicker, 2019).

When an organization treats burnout as an individual lifestyle problem alone, rather than a systemic issue, wellness becomes more about optics than outcomes. True prevention requires redesigning work itself: Fair workloads, psychologically safe cultures, flexible arrangements, trained managers, and accessible mental health resources.

Flop #3: Resignation Nation

The early 2020s brought two major workforce trends into the spotlight: *Quiet quitting* and *The Great Resignation*. Both represented collective responses to burnout and disillusionment with modern work culture. *Quiet quitting*, a term popularized on TikTok, described employees doing only what their job required—no unpaid overtime, no emotional overextension as a quiet rebellion against hustle culture and unsustainable expectations (Mahand & Caldwell, 2023). While it may temporarily reduce pressure, quiet quitting does not address the root causes of burnout. Stepping back without intentionally setting boundaries, fostering resilience, or reconnecting with one's values can still leave individuals feeling depleted and disengaged.

Meanwhile, *The Great Resignation* marked a more definitive form of retreat. In 2021 and 2022, millions of workers voluntarily left their jobs in search of better pay, flexibility, and healthier work environments. However, many found that burnout followed them. A 2023 Paychex survey reported that 80% of employees who resigned during this period regretted the decision, with Gen Z workers expressing the highest levels of dissatisfaction. Of those who attempted to return to their former roles, only 27% were rehired (Paychex, 2023).

These trends underscore a key lesson: Burnout isn't just about *where* you work. It's about *how* you work, how you relate to stress, and whether you have the internal and external resources to break out of survival mode.

So, what actually works to address burnout? The truth is less glamorous than a social media "hack" but far more effective: Burnout is best addressed through a combination of meaningful individual strategies and sustained systemic change.

Success #1: Flexibility, Choice, and Empowerment

The pandemic revealed something profound: Productivity does not depend on being in the same building from 9 to 5. When organizations embraced remote work, flexible scheduling, and clearer boundaries, many employees experienced relief from burnout. Not because they suddenly worked less, but because they gained more agency over when and how they worked.

Healthy workplaces lean into this lesson. They design systems that give employees real choice in structuring their day, the chance to use their unique strengths and aptitudes, and opportunities to shape how their work is done. Autonomy fuels energy. Working in alignment with personal talents creates flow. Together, these factors foster motivation, protect against burnout, and increase innovation.

Flexibility also comes in many forms beyond remote work. Compressed workweeks, shift-swapping, flexible start and end times, or more generous paid time off, all create space for recovery. Importantly, when these practices are paired with clear cultural norms that respect off-the-clock time, employees return more engaged. Evidence supports this: In the UK's four-day workweek trial, employees reported lower burnout and absenteeism alongside stable or improved productivity (Shiri et al., 2022).

The takeaway is simple: When people are trusted to manage their time, empowered to work to their strengths, and supported with recovery space, the result isn't lost productivity. It's often sustainable performance and thriving employees.

Success #2: Workload Reduction as a Leadership Priority

Thriving workplaces recognize that sustainable performance depends on balance. Instead of pushing people to "do more with less," they align demands with resources, so employees have what they need to do their best work.

The most effective organizations redesign workflows to reduce redundancy, staff appropriately to meet actual needs, and invest in tools that make tasks more efficient. Demand–capacity matching has emerged as a practical strategy, helping leaders spot pressure points early and adjust staffing before stress spirals into burnout or turnover (Myrberg et al., 2024).

Equally important, progress happens where leaders cultivate psychological safety. When employees trust, they can voice concerns and propose changes without fear, and they become active partners in shaping smarter systems. In this environment, the workforce is not stretched thin but engaged as co-creators of solutions (Edmondson, 2023).

Success #3: Labor Protections That Anticipate the Future

Workplace protections in the United States such as the Fair Labor Standards Act, the Occupational Safety and Health Act (OSHA), and the Family and Medical Leave Act were hard-won victories born out of collective advocacy against unsafe and exploitative conditions. Each was transformative in its time. At the start of the 20th century, nearly 1 in 5 children between the ages of 10 and 15 were employed in industrial or hazardous jobs, often under grueling conditions (U.S. Census Bureau, 1900; National Archives, 2016). The Fair Labor Standards Act of 1938 banned oppressive child labor, established a federal minimum wage, and limited the workweek to 40 hours, reshaping the very concept of fair work in the United States (Grossman, 1978). The passage of the Occupational Safety and Health Act in 1970 created OSHA, granting the federal government authority to set and enforce workplace safety standards. Since its implementation, workplace fatalities have declined by more than 60%, and injury rates have fallen from 10.9 incidents per 100 workers in 1972 to just 2.7 per 100 in 2021 (OSHA, 2023). The Family and Medical Leave Act of 1993 added another layer of protection by guaranteeing qualified employees up to 12 weeks of unpaid, job-protected leave for serious health or caregiving needs, affirming that health and family responsibilities are legitimate priorities, not professional shortcomings (Klerman et al., 2012). Together, these reforms demonstrated that legislation can be one of the most powerful levers for advancing dignity, safety, and fairness at work.

The task now is to extend that legacy into the modern era. Workers face a new generation of challenges: Widening income inequality, the health and safety consequences of environmental degradation, digital surveillance, and the looming disruption of AI-driven automation. Each of these realities affects not only productivity but also the physical and mental health of workers, contributing to burnout and disengagement on a scale that can no longer be ignored.

Forward-looking protections could include a guaranteed living wage, universal paid family and medical leaves, stronger whistleblower safeguards, thoughtful AI regulation, universal access to health care, and legal standards for mental health and work–life integration. From a burnout prevention standpoint, legislative reform remains one of the most scalable tools we have. By raising the baseline for fairness, safety, and well-being, society ensures that resilience is not left to individuals alone but supported collectively through the very structure of work itself.

Success #4: Psychological Approaches That Build Resilience Now

Systemic change takes time. Burnout doesn't wait. That's why addressing the *individual's* internal capacity to cope, recover, and re-engage is essential. Especially in high-pressure systems that may remain flawed for years.

Two approaches stand out are ACT and Compassion-focused interventions. ACT is a behavioral therapy that cultivates *psychological flexibility*, the ability to stay present, open up to difficult experiences, and choose actions guided by one's deepest values, even when stress or pain is present. Compassion-focused interventions, while rooted in multiple traditions, use compassion as an active psychological intervention to regulate threat, reduce self-criticism, and promote a sense of safeness and connection. While the broader research base focuses on compassion rather than CFT specifically, CFT places compassion at the center of its model, making it a natural lens through which to understand these findings.

Evidence is robust: ACT has been shown to reduce burnout and distress in health-care, social care, and public service professionals (Towey-Swift et al., 2023; Prudenzi et al., 2022). Self-compassion, a core target of CFT, is repeatedly linked to lower emotional exhaustion and greater resilience (Inwood & Ferrari, 2018), and compassion for others can buffer against burnout in care professions (Babenko et al., 2021).

In my clinical experience, these approaches have been nothing short of transformational. The research is compelling, but what strikes me most are the daily realities I witness in therapy. I've seen ACT help people anchor back into their values when burnout has stripped life of meaning, and I've seen compassion practices soften relentless self-criticism that only deepened exhaustion. Through ACT and CFT, clients often rediscover a sense of agency, even when they're working in environments that feel unsupportive or overwhelming.

The Beyond Burnout Blueprint rests on the belief that prevention requires *both* scaffolding the individual *and* reshaping the system. The next chapters will dive deeper into how ACT and CFT can help you stop treading water and start swimming toward a life that feels worth living whether or not your workplace is ready to change.

References

American Bar Association. (2022). *Profile of the legal profession: Lawyer well-being and burnout.* https://www.americanbar.org/content/dam/aba/administrative/news/2022/potlp2022.pdf

Babenko, O., Mosewich, A., Lee, A., & Koppula, S. (2021). Compassion for others and self-compassion predict resilience in medical students. *Medical Education Online, 26*(1), 1836393. https://doi.org/10.1080/10872981.2020.1836393

Baumeister, R. F., & Leary, M. R. (1995). The need to belong: Desire for interpersonal attachments as a fundamental human motivation. *Psychological Bulletin, 117*(3), 497–529. https://doi.org/10.1037/0033-2909.117.3.497

Bondanini, G., Lo Presti, A., & Ingusci, E. (2024). The relationship between a discriminatory work environment and employee psychological distress: The mediating role of supervisor support and economic stress. *Journal of Health and Social Sciences, 9*(3), 312–333. https://doi.org/10.19204/2024/thrp5

Business Group on Health. (2023). *2023 large employers' health care strategy and plan design survey.* https://www.businessgrouphealth.org/resources/2023-large-e mployers-health-care-strategy-survey-intro

Dean, W., Talbot, S., & Dean, A. (2019). Reframing clinician distress: Moral injury not burnout. *Federal Practitioner, 36*(9), 400–402. https://www.ncbi.nlm.nih. gov/pmc/articles/PMC6752815/

Edmondson, A. C. (2023). *Right kind of wrong: The science of failing well.* Atria Books/Simon & Schuster.

Eisenberger, N. I., & Lieberman, M. D. (2004). Why rejection hurts: A common neural alarm system for physical and social pain. *Trends in Cognitive Sciences, 8*(7), 294–300. https://doi.org/10.1016/j.tics.2004.05.010

Ericksen, L. (2020). 過労死 (Karōshi)'s phenomenon and its collective existential damage. *Civitas – Revista de Ciências Sociais, 20*(2), 476–487. https://doi.org/1 0.15448/1984-7289.2020.2.34255

Farber, B. A. (1990). Burnout in psychotherapists: Incidence, types, and trends. *Psychotherapy in Private Practice, 8*(1), 35–44. https://doi.org/10.1300/ J294v08n01_05

Grossman, J. B. (1978). Fair Labor Standards Act of 1938: Maximum struggle for a minimum wage. *Monthly Labor Review, 101*(6), 22–30. https://www.jstor.org/ stable/41840910

Hakanen, J. J., Bakker, A. B., & Schaufeli, W. B. (2019). Burnout and work engagement among teachers. *Journal of School Psychology, 77*, 12–27. https://doi. org/10.1016/j.jsp.2019.10.001

Heynen, N. (2009). Bending the bars of empire from every ghetto for survival: The Black Panther Party's radical antihunger politics of social reproduction and scale. *Annals of the Association of American Geographers, 99*(2), 406–422. https://doi. org/10.1080/00045600802683767

Inwood, E., & Ferrari, M. (2018). Mechanisms of change in the relationship between self-compassion and psychological distress in clinical and non-clinical populations: A systematic review. *Mindfulness, 9*(3), 737–750. https://doi. org/10.1007/s12671-017-0818-2

Klerman, J. A., Daley, K., & Pozniak, A. (2012). *Family and Medical Leave in 2012: Technical report.* U.S. Department of Labor. https://www.dol.gov/sites/ dolgov/files/OASP/legacy/files/FMLA-2012-Technical-Report.pdf

Litz, B. T., Stein, N., Delaney, E., Lebowitz, L., Nash, W. P., Silva, C., & Maguen, S. (2009). Moral injury and moral repair in war veterans: A preliminary model and intervention strategy. *Clinical Psychology Review, 29*(8), 695–706. https:// doi.org/10.1016/j.cpr.2009.07.003

Lorde, A. (1988). *A burst of light.* Firebrand Books.

Mahand, T., & Caldwell, C. (2023). Quiet quitting – Causes and opportunities. *Business and Management Research, 12*(1), 9–19. https://doi.org/10.5430/bmr. v12n1p9

Marchand, A., Blanc, M.-E., & Beauregard, N. (2018). Do age and gender contribute to workers' burnout symptoms? *Occupational Medicine, 68*(6), 405–411. https://doi.org/10.1093/occmed/kqy088

Maslach, C., Jackson, S. E., & Leiter, M. P. (1997). Maslach burnout inventory: Third edition. In C. P. Zalaquett & R. J. Wood (Eds.), *Evaluating stress: A book of resources* (pp. 191–218). Scarecrow Education.

Maslach, C., & Leiter, M. P. (1997). *The truth about burnout: How organizations cause personal stress and what to do about it.* Jossey-Bass.

Maslach, C., & Leiter, M. P. (2016). Understanding the burnout experience: Recent research and its implications for psychiatry. *World Psychiatry, 15*(2), 103–111. https://doi.org/10.1002/wps.20311

Mattke, S., Liu, H., Caloyeras, J. P., Huang, C. Y., Van Busum, K. R., Khodyakov, D., & Shier, V. (2013). *Workplace wellness programs study: Final report.* RAND Corporation. https://www.rand.org/pubs/research_reports/RR254.html

Mendes, W. B., Major, B., McCoy, S., & Blascovich, J. (2008). How attributional ambiguity shapes physiological and emotional responses to social rejection and acceptance. *Journal of Personality and Social Psychology, 94*(2), 278–291. https://doi.org/10.1037/0022-3514.94.2.278

Meyer, I. H. (2003). Prejudice, social stress, and mental health in lesbian, gay, and bisexual populations: Conceptual issues and research evidence. *Psychological Bulletin, 129*(5), 674–697. https://doi.org/10.1037/0033-2909.129.5.674

Miner-Rubino, K., & Cortina, L. M. (2004). Working in a context of hostility toward women: Implications for employees' well-being. *Journal of Occupational Health Psychology, 9*(2), 107–122. https://doi.org/10.1037/1076-8998.9.2.107

Montero-Marín, J., & García-Campayo, J. (2010). A newer and broader definition of burnout: Validation of the "Burnout Clinical Subtype Questionnaire (BCSQ-36)." *BMC Public Health, 10*, 302. https://doi.org/10.1186/1471-2458-10-302

Myrberg, K., Wiger, M., & Björkman, A. (2024). Development of a maturity model for demand and capacity management in healthcare. *BMC Health Services Research, 24*, Article 1109. https://doi.org/10.1186/s12913-024-11456-4

National Archives. (2016). *Teaching with documents: Photographs of Lewis Hine – Documentation of child labor.* https://www.archives.gov/education/lessons/hine-photos

National Behavioral Consortium. (2023). *EAP industry trends report.* https://www.nationalbehavioralconsortium.org/docs/NBC_EAP_Trends_Report_2023.pdf

Occupational Safety and Health Administration. (2023). *OSHA at 50: Protecting workers then and now.* https://www.osha.gov/sites/default/files/publications/OSHA3302.pdf

Parker, K., & Funk, C. (2017, December 14). Gender discrimination comes in many forms for today's working women. *Pew Research Center.* https://www.pewresearch.org/short-reads/2017/12/14/gender-discrimination-comes-in-many-forms-for-todays-working-women/

Pascoe, E. A., & Smart Richman, L. (2009). Perceived discrimination and health: A meta-analytic review. *Psychological Bulletin, 135*(4), 531–554. https://doi.org/10.1037/a0016059

Pavalko, E. K., Mossakowski, K. N., & Hamilton, V. J. (2003). Does perceived discrimination affect health? Longitudinal relationships between work discrimination and women's physical and emotional health. *Journal of Health and Social Behavior, 44*(1), 18–33. https://doi.org/10.2307/1519813

Paychex. (2023). *Employee regret after the great resignation.* https://www.paychex.com/articles/human-resources/exploring-the-great-regret

Pew Research Center. (2023b, April 27). *Black Americans' experiences with discrimination.* https://www.pewresearch.org/short-reads/2023/04/27/black-americans-experiences-with-discrimination/

Prudenzi, A., Graham, C. D., Heron, J., Dawson, D. L., & Chalder, T. (2022). The effectiveness of a brief ACT intervention for NHS healthcare workers: A randomized controlled trial. *Mindfulness, 13*, 2783–2793. https://doi.org/10.1007/s12671-021-01648-2

RAND Corporation. (2021). *Stress topped the reasons teachers quit, even before COVID–19*. https://www.rand.org/pubs/research_reports/RRA1121–1.html

Roberts, R. K., Swanson, N. G., & Murphy, L. R. (2004). Discrimination and occupational mental health. *Journal of Mental Health, 13*(2), 129–142. https://doi.org/10.1080/09638230410001669395

Schaufeli, W. B., De Witte, H., & Desart, S. (2020). *Manual Burnout Assessment Tool (BAT)*. KU Leuven, Belgium.

Schaufeli, W. B., Leiter, M. P., & Maslach, C. (2009). Burnout: 35 years of research and practice. *Career Development International, 14*(3), 204–220. https://doi.org/10.1108/13620430910966406

Shanafelt, T. D., Hasan, O., Dyrbye, L. N., Sinsky, C., Satele, D., Sloan, J., & West, C. P. (2015). Changes in burnout and satisfaction with work-life balance in physicians and the general US working population between 2011 and 2014. *Mayo Clinic Proceedings, 90*(12), 1600–1613. https://doi.org/10.1016/j.mayocp.2015.08.023

Shiri, R., Turunen, J., Kausto, J., Leino-Arjas, P., Varje, P., Väänänen, A., & Ervasti, J. (2022). The effect of employee-oriented flexible work on mental health: A systematic review. *Healthcare, 10*(5), 883. https://doi.org/10.3390/healthcare10050883

Song, Z., & Baicker, K. (2019). Effect of a workplace wellness program on employee health and economic outcomes: A randomized clinical trial. *JAMA, 321*(15), 1491–1501. https://doi.org/10.1001/jama.2019.3307

Towey-Swift, K. D., Lauvrud, C., & Whittington, R. (2023). Acceptance and commitment therapy (ACT) for professional staff burnout: A systematic review and narrative synthesis of controlled trials. *Journal of Mental Health, 32*(2), 452–464. https://doi.org/10.1080/09638237.2021.2022628

Trinkenreich, B., Stol, K.-J., Steinmacher, I., Gerosa, M., Sarma, A., Lara, M., Feathers, M., & Ross, N. (2023). A model for understanding and reducing developer burnout. *arXiv*. https://arxiv.org/abs/2301.09103

U.S. Census Bureau. (1900). *Twelfth census of the United States, 1900: Population, part 2*. Government Printing Office.

U.S. Equal Employment Opportunity Commission. (2023). *Charge statistics (charges filed with EEOC)*. https://www.eeoc.gov/statistics/charge-statistics-charges-filed-eeoc

Widarahhesty, Y. (2020). Otsukaresamadeshita!: A critical analysis of Japan's toxic work culture. *International Journal of East Asian Studies, 9*(1), 32–47. https://doi.org/10.22452/IJEAS.vol9no1.3

Williamson, V., Stevelink, S. A. M., & Greenberg, N. (2018). Occupational moral injury and mental health: Systematic review and meta-analysis. *The British Journal of Psychiatry, 212*(6), 339–346. https://doi.org/10.1192/bjp.2018.55

World Health Organization. (2019, May 28). *Burn-out an "occupational phenomenon": International Classification of Diseases*. https://www.who.int/mental_health/evidence/burn-out/en/

Workplace Bullying Institute. (2021). *2021 WBI U.S. workplace bullying survey*. https://workplacebullying.org

Wyatt, J. P., & Ampadu, G. G. (2022). Reclaiming self-care: Self-care as a social justice tool for Black wellness. *Community Mental Health Journal, 58*(2), 213–221. https://doi.org/10.1007/s10597-021-00884-9

Chapter 3

ACT for Burnout Recovery

Our modern relationship with work and happiness cannot be understood without acknowledging the influence of capitalism. Capitalism is an economic system in which private individuals or corporations own the means of production and operate for profit, thriving on competition, innovation, and growth. At its best, capitalism rewards creativity, drives innovation, and has advanced medicine, technology, and quality of life. It can provide upward mobility and the freedom to build one's path in a way many other economic systems have failed to achieve. At its worst, it concentrates wealth, restricts mobility, and perpetuates systemic inequality, with corporate interests prioritizing profit over public welfare.

Scholars often use the term *late capitalism* to describe the advanced stage of capitalist development in the 20th century, characterized by globalization, corporate consolidation, consumer credit, and the spread of multinational markets (Mandel, 1975). The phrase first appeared in the early 20th century with German economist Werner Sombart, who used *Spätkapitalismus* to describe the final stages of capitalist expansion. Decades later, Marxist theorist Ernest Mandel reintroduced and popularized the term in his book *Late Capitalism* (1975), situating it in the post-World War II era of rapid technological growth, global finance, and mass consumption. In popular culture, the phrase has evolved into *late-stage capitalism,* a colloquial term often used in journalism and online discourse to highlight the absurdities, contradictions, and inequities of modern economies, pointing out, for example, how billionaires take expeditions to space for fun, while essential workers struggle to afford health care (Hedges, 2019). It is the societal critique of the lived experience of inequality, exploitation, and exhaustion under contemporary capitalism.

Consumerism, which emerged alongside capitalism, extends beyond economics into culture. It is the belief that economic prosperity and individual happiness are closely linked to the acquisition and consumption of goods and services beyond our basic needs. In this way, consumerism translates capitalism's drive for profit into a personal narrative about what

DOI: 10.4324/9781003640592-5

makes a "good life." Through consumerism, we are sold the idea that happiness must be earned through productivity and consumption. It does not just shape what we buy, it shapes who we think we should be. The same system that drives innovation and opportunity also manufactures cycles of discontent, leaving us exhausted while selling costly solutions for the very burnout it creates (Bauman, 2007).

Consumerism also lays the groundwork for one of our culture's most persistent myths that happiness is our natural baseline, a permanent state we should achieve and hold onto. Pop psychology, music, art, literature, social media, and broader societal narratives equate happiness with success, telling us that once we land the perfect job, relationship, or work–life balance, happiness will finally arrive—and stay. In this view, difficult emotions like worry, boredom, sadness, or fatigue are framed as problems to eliminate rather than experiences to understand. The result is a culture that pressures us to suppress or override distressing or painful emotions instead of learning from them (Cabanas & Illouz, 2019).

This is not an argument for rejecting capitalism. I benefit from the system by selling this book, running a business, and hosting a podcast. My social location as a white, cisgender woman in a U.S. suburb affords me access to its advantages. Acknowledging this is not anti-capitalist, it is about being honest about the structures shaping burnout. Addressing these forces requires both systemic and personal work: Advocating for fair wages and labor protections, while also developing personal practices that prevent us from being consumed by these pressures.

This is where ACT offers a radically different lens. ACT does not view pain as a problem to be eliminated but as an inevitable part of human life. Rather than promising happiness once discomfort disappears, it teaches us to live meaningfully alongside it, building growth, purpose, and psychological flexibility along the way (Hayes et al., 2012).

What Is ACT?

ACT, pronounced like "act," was developed in the early 1980s by psychologist Steven C. Hayes, who, influenced by his own struggles with panic disorder, sought an approach that emphasized living meaningfully rather than symptom elimination (Hayes et al., 2012). ACT integrates behavioral principles with mindfulness-based strategies to cultivate *psychological flexibility*: The ability to engage with life's challenges while staying aligned with one's values.

ACT encourages present-moment awareness and responsiveness, rather than defensive reactivity. Rather than getting entangled in judgments, people learn to observe experiences as they are and take action guided by long-term well-being, even in the context of burnout or broader structural forces such as our current economic system or dominant cultural narratives. Central to ACT is its view of being human: None of us escapes mortality, uncertainty, stress, or loss. ACT rejects the idea that difficult emotions are pathological. Guilt, anxiety, or fatigue do not mean a person is "broken." Intrusive thoughts, self-doubt, and despair are not malfunctions but inevitable aspects of life. ACT invites us to make space for discomfort, learn from it, and allow it to inform purposeful action. The therapeutic question shifts from "How do I get rid of this?" to "How can I build a meaningful life alongside this?"

ACT is grounded in three interrelated theoretical frameworks:

1. *Relational Frame Theory (RFT):* RFT explains how we create meaning through language. Our minds don't just store isolated facts; they weave intricate connections between thoughts, symbols, words, and experiences, shaping how we perceive the world. These automatic mental associations influence our emotions and behaviors, often without us realizing it. By understanding how these relational frames shape our responses, ACT helps us create new, healthier associations that align with our values rather than automatic, unexamined beliefs (Hayes et al., 2001; Dymond et al., 2010).
2. *Applied Behavior Analysis (ABA):* The science of behavior that examines how actions are shaped and maintained by reinforcement and environmental contingencies (Baer et al., 1968; Cooper et al., 2020). ABA illustrates, for example, how overworking may be reinforced by social praise or financial incentives, even as it contributes to burnout. Understanding these reinforcement loops enables us to disrupt them and cultivate more sustainable patterns.
3. *Functional Contextualism:* The philosophical foundation of ACT and contextual behavioral science. Context refers to the circumstances, such as time, place, culture, and societal influences that shape how situations, events, and behaviors are understood. Rather than judging actions as inherently good or bad, functional contextualism evaluates behavior in terms of its effectiveness within a given context, asking: *Is this working in the service of my values?* (Hayes et al., 2011; Biglan & Hayes, 2015).

Together, these frameworks provide the backbone of ACT's clinical model. Through reflection, metaphor, and experiential exercises, individuals learn to notice unhelpful mental patterns, loosen rigid rules, and experiment with new, values-driven ways of responding.

The Six Core Processes of Psychological Flexibility in ACT

ACT is supported by a strong empirical base, with more than 1,000 randomized controlled trials and numerous meta-analyses demonstrating its effectiveness across a wide range of psychological difficulties, including anxiety, depression, chronic pain, and burnout (Hayes et al., 2011; Gloster et al., 2020). At the center of these outcomes is *psychological flexibility* which is the capacity to stay present, openly experience thoughts and feelings, and persist or change behavior when doing so serves personally chosen values (Hayes et al., 2012). Psychological flexibility is consistently identified as the primary mechanism of change, making ACT uniquely suited to addressing the exhaustion and disconnection at the heart of burnout (Kashdan & Rottenberg, 2010). ACT cultivates psychological flexibility through six interrelated processes that work together, rather than in isolation. They form a flexible toolkit for navigating life's difficulties while moving toward meaning and vitality. These six processes are visually represented in the ACT Hexaflex model (see Figure 3.1), which is commonly attributed to the work of Hayes and colleagues (2006).

1. **Attention to the Present Moment.** Instead of being pulled into regrets about the past or worries about the future, mindfulness practices help anchor awareness in the here and now, creating space for more adaptive responses (Hayes et al., 2011, 2012).
2. **Acceptance.** Acceptance involves making room for unpleasant emotions and experiences rather than expending energy on resistance. Crucially,

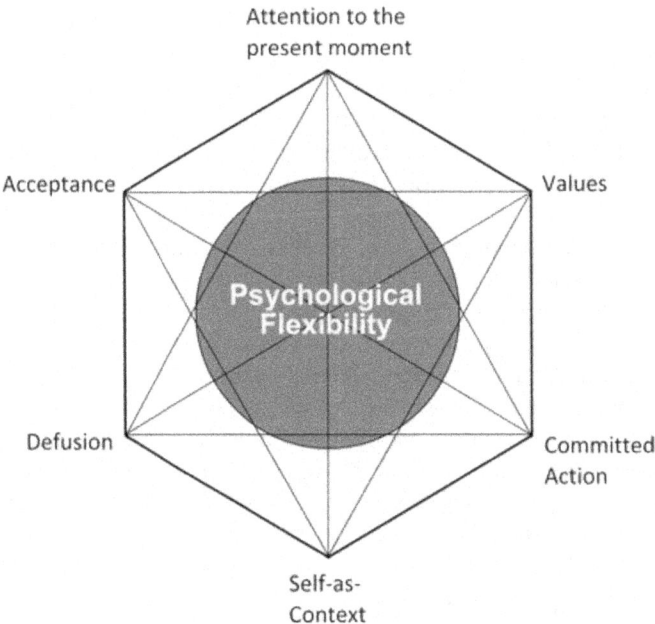

Figure 3.1 The ACT Hexaflex. Copyright Steven C. Hayes et al. (2006) (used by permission).

acceptance is not about liking, condoning, or resigning ourselves to suffering, nor does it mean tolerating unworkable systems such as racism, sexism, or economic exploitation. Instead, it means dropping the futile struggle against internal experiences so that energy can be redirected toward meaningful, values-based action (Hayes et al., 2011, 2012).

3. **Defusion.** Defusion means stepping back from thoughts and feelings so they are seen as passing mental events rather than literal truths. For example, shifting from "I'm a failure" to "I'm noticing the thought that I'm a failure" allows greater behavioral flexibility (Hayes et al., 2012).

4. **Self-as-Context.** This process highlights the stable, observing self, the perspective from which experiences are noticed without being reduced to them. It provides distance from rigid self-stories that can keep people stuck (Hayes et al., 2012).

5. **Values.** Clarifying deeply held, freely chosen values provides an internal compass for life direction, helping distinguish meaningful pursuits from avoidance or external approval (Hayes et al., 2011, 2012).

6. **Committed Action.** Taking purposeful, values-based steps, even when uncomfortable, transforms values into lived reality through consistent choices and habits (Hayes et al., 2012).

How Psychological Inflexibility Traps You in Burnout

Burnout feeds on psychological inflexibility. These rigid response patterns keep us stuck in avoidance, overidentifying with thoughts, and drifting away from what matters. Research consistently shows that psychological inflexibility, characterized by experiential avoidance, fusion, and loss of values-based direction, is a key risk factor for emotional exhaustion and disengagement (Bond et al., 2011; Ruiz, 2010). Each flexibility process has an opposite that fuels exhaustion:

1. **Past-Future Focus (Opposite of Present-Moment Attention).** Becoming absorbed in regret about the past or worrying about the future pulls us out of the only place change can occur: The present. Rumination and anxiety drain energy and perpetuate stress (Bakker et al., 2014).

2. **Experiential Avoidance (Opposite of Acceptance).** Attempts to suppress or numb feelings, whether through overwork, avoidance of conflict, or distraction with social media, food, or substances offer short-term relief but worsen long-term distress. Experiential avoidance has been shown to predict higher burnout and lower well-being (Bond et al., 2011; Hayes et al., 2012).

3. **Fusion (Opposite of Defusion).** Fusion is treating thoughts as literal truth and feeling as permanent states and reinforces rigid rules and self-criticism. Fusion narrows our perspective and limits behavioral flexibility, leaving us vulnerable to burnout (Hayes et al., 2012; Ruiz, 2010).

4. **Self-as-Content (Opposite of Self-as-Context).** Defining ourselves through rigid, self-critical labels ("I'm pathetic," "I'm a failure," "I'll never measure up") fosters hopelessness. These burnout-laden narratives, often reinforced by chronic exhaustion, convince us that change is impossible (Lloyd et al., 2013).
5. **Lack of Direction (Opposite of Values).** Without clarity about what matters most, we drift, chasing external validation, staying in unfulfilling roles, or prioritizing comfort or familiarity over meaning. Value-incongruence is strongly linked to disengagement and burnout (Van Den Broeck et al., 2008).
6. **Inaction/Stuck (Opposite of Committed Action).** Fear, doubt, or overwhelm can lead to paralysis and procrastination. Waiting for the "perfect" moment to act prolongs stagnation, while growth arises from small, imperfect steps taken in the present (Hayes et al., 2012).

Together, these inflexibility patterns create a cycle where avoidance and rigidity deepen exhaustion, amplify self-criticism, and erode connection to meaning, which are the hallmarks of burnout.

Beyond Burnout Exercise: Spotting Inflexibility

Purpose: This exercise helps you recognize where psychological inflexibility is fueling burnout. The goal isn't to change your behavior yet. It's to notice patterns and shift how you relate to them. By developing awareness now, you'll be better equipped to work with these patterns when we dive into skills later in the book.

Step 1: Identifying Your "Stuck" Patterns

Think back to a recent moment when you felt burned out, overwhelmed, or emotionally drained.

- What was happening? (Briefly describe the situation)
- What thoughts and emotions were present?
- How did you respond?

Now, review the six inflexibility processes below. Notice which ones showed up for you (likely more than one will resonate).

Past-Future Focus (Opposite of Present-Moment Attention)

Was I stuck in regret about the past or anxiety about the future instead of being present?
Rethinking Presence
If I had been fully present, what might I have noticed or done differently?

Experiential Avoidance (Opposite of Acceptance)

Did I try to numb, suppress, or escape discomfort instead of facing it?
Rethinking Discomfort

- What was I trying to avoid at that moment?
- What might have happened if I had acknowledged and allowed it, instead of pushing it away?

Fusion (Opposite of Defusion)

Did I get "hooked" by unhelpful thoughts or emotions and treat them as absolute truths?
Rethinking Thoughts and Feelings

- What thoughts felt like absolute truths in this moment?
- What feelings felt overwhelming or intolerable?
- If I treated my thoughts as just thoughts rather than facts, how might that have changed my perspective?
- If I saw emotions as passing experiences rather than permanent states or problems to eliminate, how might that have shifted how I felt?

Self-as-Content (Opposite of Self-as-Context)

Did I define myself rigidly (e.g., "I'm pathetic," "I'm a failure," "I'm lazy," "I'll never measure up")?
Rethinking Identity
If I viewed myself as someone having these experiences rather than being defined by them, how would that change my perspective?

Lack of Direction (Opposite of Values)

Did I feel disconnected from what truly matters to me?
Rethinking Meaning

- In that moment, what truly mattered to me?
- Was I acting out of external pressure or avoidance, instead of in alignment with my values?

Inaction/Stuck (Opposite of Committed Action)

- Did fear, doubt, or overwhelm keep me from taking action?
- Did I wait for the "perfect" moment instead of moving forward?
Rethinking Avoidance
- What small step could I have taken, even if imperfect?
- How might any action, however small, have shifted my experience?

Step 2: Bringing It All Together

Take a few minutes to reflect on your responses. This isn't about forcing positivity or immediate change. It's about curiosity. Seeing your burnout patterns clearly, without judgment. Simply recognizing and rethinking them are already a powerful first step toward change.

The Role of Compassion in Burnout Recovery

Psychological flexibility is essential to your burnout recovery, but true burnout resilience also requires something more: Deep, intentional compassion (Arch et al., 2022; Kirby et al., 2017). Compassion is not formally one of ACT's six core processes, yet it is deeply woven throughout the model. It emerges in acceptance, where distress is met with kindness rather than resistance; in self-as-context and defusion, where it softens the hold of harsh self-narratives; and in values and mindfulness, where it fosters awareness that is grounded in curiosity rather than judgment (Hayes et al., 2012; Arch et al., 2022).

Many clinicians strengthen this implicit thread by integrating ACT with CFT, especially when working with shame, self-criticism, or trauma-related burnout. A formal blend has been described in practitioner literature as CF-ACT (Tirch et al., 2014). While *the Beyond Burnout Blueprint* isn't CF-ACT per se, it draws from both approaches: Grounding recovery in psychological flexibility while explicitly integrating compassion skills and other evidence-based methods to address burnout's unique challenges (Gilbert, 2014; Kirby et al., 2017; Leaviss & Uttley, 2015).

CFT strengthens ACT by addressing how compassion regulates the nervous system. Burnout often arises from chronic stress and systemic pressures, but compassion activates affiliative "tend-and-befriend" pathways that downshift threat arousal and promote safeness, warmth, and connection (Gilbert, 2014; Taylor et al., 2000). This physiological shift reduces shame, supports recovery, and creates the conditions for values-based action. In short, compassion makes the flexibility ACT cultivates more accessible and sustainable.

References

Arch, J. J., Eifert, G. H., & Davies, C. D. (2022). Acceptance and Commitment Therapy processes and mediation. *Journal of Contextual Behavioral Science, 26,* 1–16. https://doi.org/10.1016/j.jcbs.2022.08.001

Baer, D. M., Wolf, M. M., & Risley, T. R. (1968). Some current dimensions of applied behavior analysis. *Journal of Applied Behavior Analysis, 1*(1), 91–97. https://doi.org/10.1901/jaba.1968.1-91

Bakker, A. B., Demerouti, E., & Sanz-Vergel, A. I. (2014). Burnout and work engagement: The JD–R approach. *Annual Review of Organizational Psychology and Organizational Behavior, 1*(1), 389–411. https://doi.org/10.1146/annurev-orgpsych-031413-091235

Bauman, Z. (2007). *Consuming life*. Polity Press.

Biglan, A., & Hayes, S. C. (2015). Functional contextualism and contextual behavioral science. In R. D. Zettle, S. C. Hayes, D. Barnes-Holmes, & A. Biglan (Eds.), *The Wiley handbook of contextual behavioral science* (pp. 37–61). Wiley-Blackwell. https://doi.org/10.1002/9781118489857

Bond, F. W., Hayes, S. C., Baer, R. A., Carpenter, K. M., Guenole, N., Orcutt, H. K., Waltz, T., & Zettle, R. D. (2011). Preliminary psychometric properties of the Acceptance and Action Questionnaire–II: A revised measure of psychological inflexibility and experiential avoidance. *Behavior Therapy, 42*(4), 676–688. https://doi.org/10.1016/j.beth.2011.03.007

Cabanas, E., & Illouz, E. (2019). *Manufacturing happy citizens: How the science and industry of happiness control our lives*. Polity Press.

Cooper, J. O., Heron, T. E., & Heward, W. L. (2020). *Applied behavior analysis* (3rd ed.). Pearson.

Dymond, S., May, R. J., Munnelly, A. M., & Hoon, A. E. (2010). Evaluating the evidence base for relational frame theory: A citation analysis. *The Psychological Record, 60*(1), 97–116. https://doi.org/10.1007/BF03395689

Gilbert, P. (2014). The origins and nature of compassion focused therapy. *British Journal of Clinical Psychology, 53*(1), 6–41. https://doi.org/10.1111/bjc.12043

Gloster, A. T., Walder, N., Levin, M. E., Twohig, M. P., & Karekla, M. (2020). The empirical status of Acceptance and Commitment Therapy: A review of meta-analyses. *Journal of Contextual Behavioral Science, 18*, 181–192. https://doi.org/10.1016/j.jcbs.2020.09.009

Hayes, S. C., Barnes-Holmes, D., & Roche, B. (2001). *Relational frame theory: A post-Skinnerian account of human language and cognition*. Springer. https://doi.org/10.1007/b108413

Hayes, S. C., Luoma, J. B., Bond, F. W., Masuda, A., & Lillis, J. (2006). Acceptance and commitment therapy: Model, processes and outcomes. *Behaviour Research and Therapy, 44*(1), 1–25. https://doi.org/10.1016/j.brat.2005.06.006

Hayes, S. C., Strosahl, K. D., & Wilson, K. G. (2012). *Acceptance and commitment therapy: The process and practice of mindful change* (2nd ed.). Guilford Press.

Hayes, S. C., Villatte, M., Levin, M. E., & Hildebrandt, M. (2011). Open, aware, and active: Contextual approaches as an emerging trend in the behavioral and cognitive therapies. *Annual Review of Clinical Psychology, 7*, 141–168. https://doi.org/10.1146/annurev-clinpsy-032210-104449

Hedges, C. (2019). *America: The farewell tour*. Simon & Schuster.

Kashdan, T. B., & Rottenberg, J. (2010). Psychological flexibility as a fundamental aspect of health. *Clinical Psychology Review, 30*(7), 865–878. https://doi.org/10.1016/j.cpr.2010.03.001

Kirby, J. N., Tellegen, C. L., & Steindl, S. R. (2017). A meta-analysis of compassion-based interventions. *Clinical Psychology Review, 49*, 40–58. https://doi.org/10.1016/j.cpr.2016.09.001

Leaviss, J., & Uttley, J. (2015). Psychotherapeutic benefits of compassion-focused therapy: An early systematic review. *Psychological Medicine, 45*(5), 927–945. https://doi.org/10.1017/S0033291714002141

Lloyd, J., Bond, F. W., & Flaxman, P. E. (2013). Work-related self-efficacy as a moderator of the impact of a worksite stress management training intervention: Intrinsic work motivation as a mediator. *Journal of Occupational Health Psychology, 18*(3), 255–265. https://doi.org/10.1037/a0031800

Mandel, E. (1975). *Late capitalism*. New Left Books.

Ruiz, F. J. (2010). A review of Acceptance and Commitment Therapy (ACT) empirical evidence: Correlational, experimental psychopathology, component and outcome studies. *International Journal of Psychology and Psychological Therapy*, *10*(1), 125–162.

Taylor, S. E., Klein, L. C., Lewis, B. P., Gruenewald, T. L., Gurung, R. A. R., & Updegraff, J. A. (2000). Biobehavioral responses to stress in females: Tend-and-befriend, not fight-or-flight. *Psychological Review*, *107*(3), 411–429. https://doi.org/10.1037/0033-295X.107.3.411

Tirch, D., Schoendorff, B., & Silberstein, L. R. (2014). *The ACT practitioner's guide to the science of compassion: Tools for fostering psychological flexibility*. New Harbinger.

Van den Broeck, A., Vansteenkiste, M., De Witte, H., & Lens, W. (2008). Explaining the relationships between job characteristics, burnout, and engagement: The role of basic psychological need satisfaction. *Work & Stress*, *22*(3), 277–294. https://doi.org/10.1080/02678370802393672

Chapter 4

CFT for Burnout Recovery

Whatever chaos existed in my home as a child, I still lived a deeply privileged life. My basic needs were met and then some. I attended one of the country's top public schools, spent summers at camp, took art classes, and even enjoyed childhood outings like seeing a real Broadway show in New York City. It was on one such trip, when I was about five or six years old, that I experienced what I now think of as my first compassion crisis. My mom took me to see a show in Manhattan, a short 45-minute train ride from our upper-middle-class suburban bubble. I don't remember the play, but I remember the sidewalks close to the venue: Lined with cardboard boxes, sleeping bags, and, to my horror, people sleeping on the street with no better alternative than to endure the freezing winter elements. I tugged at my mother's hand in panic. *Why was no one helping these people?* I locked eyes with a man whose bare feet were in direct contact with the piss and cigarette-butt-laden concrete. I asked my mom what we could do, desperate for an answer. She shushed me, ushering me quickly toward the theater lights. I continued to plead that maybe they could stay with us, at least the man with no shoes. My mom praised me for being kind and caring, yet, in the same breath, discouraged me from acting on that care. The contradiction left me confused and led to several sleepless nights, haunted by images of the man's cold, calloused feet.

That early memory marks where I now see the differences between sensitivity, empathy, and compassion beginning to take shape. Sensitivity is the capacity to notice and register suffering or need, both in others and in yourself. It is a perceptual skill, involving attunement to tone, temperament, and body language, as well as awareness of your own physical and emotional signals. Empathy is relational. It involves feeling with someone, imagining their experience so deeply that their distress echoes inside you. Compassion, however, takes sensitivity and empathy further: It introduces intention, the courage to move toward suffering with care, to relieve or prevent it (Gilbert, 2014; Singer & Klimecki, 2014). On that icy Manhattan sidewalk, I had sensitivity and empathy in abundance. What I was quickly

DOI: 10.4324/9781003640592-6

taught to quiet was my compassion. Before long, I learned to do what everyone else seemed to do in these situations: Keep walking.

Our society often teaches us to turn away from the suffering of marginalized people like those who are unhoused or anyone who seems "too different" from us. This cultural conditioning is powerful and pervasive. The burden feels too big, the pain too vast. Guilt rises when we confront the contrast with our own resources, and to avoid the harder questions of why that disparity exists, we cope by distancing, otherizing, or even dehumanizing, keeping our compassionate impulse at bay (Nussbaum, 2013).

The same cultural lessons that taught me to turn away from others' suffering also trained me to turn away from my own as I grew up. I cut myself no slack. I neglected my needs. I spoke to myself in ways that, if directed at another person, could easily be recognized as abusive. Many of us grow up in environments that prize toughness, perfectionism, competition, self-reliance, or productivity over gentleness and care. We learn to silence our pain, dismiss our exhaustion, and treat our own struggles as weaknesses to be conquered rather than signals to be met with compassion.

CFT speaks directly to this dilemma, offering an antidote to the social conditioning that distances us from our compassionate nature. It reminds us that compassion is both innate and essential, not simply a feeling, but a skill and practice that can be strengthened even when cultural forces or inner habits push us to turn away. Like physical training, cultivating compassion is a twofold process. First, we develop habits that uncover and reinforce our natural capacity for compassion, much as exercise and nutrition fortify the body. Second, we recognize that context matters: External conditions can either support or make compassion harder to access. Just as food security, medical care, and access to safe green spaces promote physical well-being, compassion may be harder to cultivate in environments marked by trauma, poverty, or constant criticism. The goal is to understand how your current conditions and lived experience are impacting your relationship with compassion.

This book draws from the work of Dr. Paul Gilbert, clinical psychologist and founder of CFT, who integrates CBT, evolutionary psychology, neuroscience, and mindfulness to foster a compassionate mind. He observed that logic alone doesn't soothe our inner self-critical voices. What's needed is felt warmth and acceptance to shift from "I'm broken" to a clearer understanding: *I'm human, and my brain is responding exactly as it was designed to.*

Gilbert explains this design through what he calls our "old brain" and "new brain" systems. The old brain is ancient, hundreds of millions of years old, and it houses survival functions we share with other animals. It is fast; automatic; and geared toward threat detection, fight-flight-freeze responses, and basic drives like food, sex, and safety. Its evolutionary purpose was simple: Keep us alive in a dangerous world.

By contrast, the new brain is relatively young, emerging only in the last two million years with the evolution of early humans. This newer system gave us language, imagination, abstract thought, planning, and self-awareness. Its evolutionary purpose was to help us cooperate, innovate, modify our environment, and build complex social worlds.

On their own, both systems are adaptive and necessary. But the interaction between them is what makes things tricky. The old brain can't distinguish between a real, immediate danger and a threat imagined by the new brain. So, when the new brain spins out scenarios such as *what if I get fired? and what if I'm not enough?*, the old brain reacts as if those dangers are happening right now. It floods the body with anxiety, shame, or anger, even in the absence of actual threat.

This is the essence of what Gilbert calls the "tricky brain": Ancient survival circuits colliding with modern human abilities. That collision leaves us vulnerable to rumination, relentless comparison, and harsh self-criticism (Gilbert, 2014; Gilbert & Simos, 2022). CFT frames this not as a personal defect but as a universal human predicament. Recognizing this universality can be profoundly freeing: We all have tricky brains, wired by evolution in ways we did not choose.

Building on the "old brain/new brain" framework, Paul Gilbert's CFT identifies three core emotional regulation systems: *Threat, drive,* and *soothing.* In balance, these systems help us stay safe, pursue goals, and feel connected to others. In burnout, however, they often fall out of sync, leaving us stuck in cycles of hypervigilance, overdrive, or emotional depletion

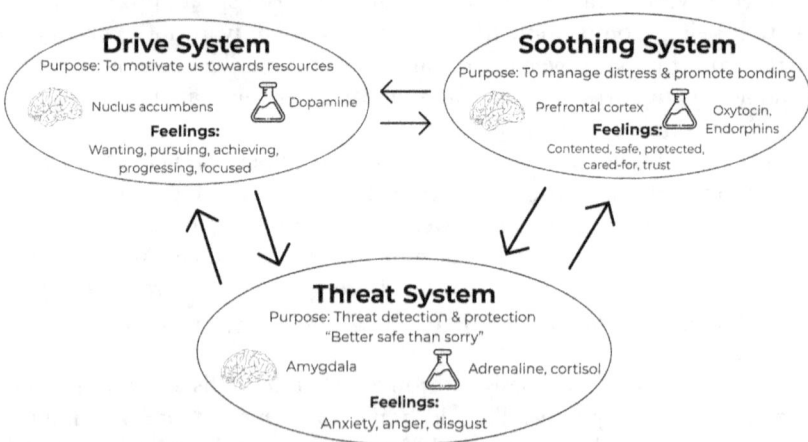

Figure 4.1 The Three Emotional Regulation Systems. Adapted from Gilbert, P. (2009). *The compassionate mind.* London: Constable & Robinson and Oaklands, CA: New Harbinger (reproduced with permission).

(Gilbert, 2009, 2014). These three systems are often illustrated using the CFT three-circle model (see Figure 4.1).

The Threat System

The threat system is our brain's alarm system. It evolved to detect danger, mobilize an immediate response, and commonly fight, flight, or freeze. In early human life, this kept us alive in the face of predators, resource loss, and hostile rivals. It's important to acknowledge that for many people across the world today, this system is still responding to the kinds of imminent dangers our ancestors faced: War, famine, political violence, limited access to clean water, or the daily threat of starvation. Even the most privileged among us are not immune to collective stressors such as political unrest, climate disasters, and interpersonal trauma. In these contexts, the threat system continues to serve an essential protective role. But for most of us, our everyday lives don't involve outrunning predators or surviving enemy raids. Instead, the alarm system is activated by modern stressors—missed deadlines, critical emails, tense conversations as though they were life-or-death events. While these challenges matter, reacting with the same survival responses often keeps us locked in hypervigilance, reactivity, and exhaustion rather than helping us adapt wisely.

This dynamic is amplified by *Social Rank Theory*, which suggests that humans evolved to be acutely sensitive to hierarchical positions because social rank determined access to food, protection, mates, and resources. In ancestral groups, falling in rank could mean fewer chances of survival and reproduction (Gilbert, 2000; Price & Sloman, 1987). That wiring has not disappeared. Today, financial stability and social status still shape opportunities, health care, safety, romantic partners, and even how others treat us. Awareness of rank can still serve adaptive purposes. But the problem comes when our brains treat every dip in status as a survival crisis. An important presentation, a missed promotion, or even a colleague's success can trigger the same ancient alarm system. Instead of motivating thoughtful adjustments, the rank system can trap us in shame, self-criticism, overwork, or withdrawal (Gilbert, 2000; Wetherall et al., 2019). This mismatch between ancient survival wiring and modern stressors is one of the ways the "tricky brain" fuels burnout. Under sustained threat, our behavioral repertoire is largely limited to our basic survival modes: Fight (conflict, pushback), flight (avoidance, quitting), freeze (paralysis, indecision), fawn (appeasement, overcommitment), or flop (shutdown, disengagement).

The threat system is centered in the amygdala, an almond-shaped structure deep in the brain that rapidly evaluates stimuli and triggers survival responses (LeDoux, 2000). When activated, it releases stress hormones like adrenaline (epinephrine), which increases heart rate and energy for immediate action, and cortisol, which sustains the body's alertness and mobilization over longer periods (McEwen, 2007). Its evolutionary purpose is clear: Detect danger quickly and mobilize survival responses. It is also the dominant system, meaning that when danger is perceived, it overrides the drive and soothing systems to prioritize survival above all else (Gilbert, 2009, 2014).

In the body, this shows up as a racing pulse, shallow or rapid breathing, blood pumping into the large muscles, tense jaws and shoulders, clenched stomach, sweaty palms, and narrowed attention. Psychologically, it often feels like worry, irritability, fear, or shame. In contexts where there is somewhere to run or fight, these changes are incredibly adaptive: Adrenaline sharpens thinking, fuels reflexes, and helps you sprint or defend yourself, while cortisol provides stamina if the threat is prolonged. But in modern life, where the "predator" is a missed deadline, a critical email, or a colleague's glare, the same physical mobilization has nowhere to go. Muscles remain tight, headaches and digestive issues build, sleep becomes disrupted, and exhaustion sets in. Instead of keeping us alive, the threat system, when chronically activated, wears us down and contributes directly to burnout.

The Drive System

The drive system motivates us to pursue rewards and achieve goals. It is anchored in the nucleus accumbens, a hub of the brain's reward pathway, and powered by dopamine, which fuels wanting, pursuit, and reinforcement learning (Haber & Knutson, 2010; Berridge & Robinson, 2016). In the body, dopamine release feels like alertness and motivation. Heart rate and circulation increase, attention narrows, and energy surges to support pursuit behaviors. In adaptive contexts like studying for an exam, training for a sport, working toward a long-term project, this system is invaluable. Dopamine rewards persistence and helps us push through challenges, creating a sense of satisfaction once goals are achieved.

Historically, this system supported persistence in survival tasks like tracking game, foraging for food, building shelter, and maintaining social alliances. Dopamine was hard-earned, released after sustained efforts reinforcing the behaviors that kept us alive (Salamone & Correa, 2012). In contrast, modern life overwhelms us with opportunities for instant dopamine hits: Social media notifications, online shopping, swiping on dating apps, processed foods, binge-worthy shows, drugs, and alcohol (Volkow et al., 2011). These stimuli are designed to deliver rapid spikes of dopamine without the effort or context that historically made the system adaptive. Over time, this can create what researchers describe as dopamine addiction—not addiction to dopamine itself, but to the repeated behaviors that overstimulate the reward system (Robinson & Berridge, 2003; Volkow & Morales, 2015).

This hijacking fuels compulsive consumption pathways: Excessive shopping, binge eating, pornography addiction, compulsive gaming, endless scrolling, and overwork. The brain learns to keep chasing the "wanting" signal even when the reward itself provides little or no real satisfaction. We become hooked not on the outcome but on the *pursuit*, returning again and again for the next hit. These quick spikes rarely bring restoration. In balance, the drive system creates focus, determination, and satisfaction. But under burnout conditions, it becomes overactivated, often as an attempt to outrun threat. Chronic overdrive can manifest physically as teeth grinding, restless legs, insomnia, digestive strain, high blood pressure, and fatigue. Psychologically, it shows up as compulsive striving, irritability, and restlessness.

The bidirectional relationship between our threat and drive systems can keep us stuck in loop that looks like this:

1. *Threat system activates* → fear of falling behind, losing status, or failing.
2. *Drive system kicks in* → work harder, achieve more, chase rewards.
3. *Dopamine spikes* → temporary relief.
4. *Drop-off reactivates threat* → cycle repeats.

Over time, this cycle leaves little space for genuine rest, keeping the body and mind locked in survival mode.

The Soothing System

The soothing system counterbalances threat and drive by helping us rest, connect, and recover. It is supported by the prefrontal cortex, the brain's executive center that regulates emotional responses and perspective-taking (Miller & Cohen, 2001). It is also fueled by oxytocin (which promotes trust and connection), endorphins (the body's natural painkillers and mood enhancers), and parasympathetic activation, the "rest and digest" branch of the nervous system (Heinrichs et al., 2009; Boecker et al., 2008).

When active, the soothing system slows heart rate, deepens breathing, relaxes muscles, warms facial expression, and restores digestion. It is associated with feelings of calm, safety, compassion, and connection. This is profoundly adaptive: In ancestral times, soothing promoted bonding between caregivers and children, trust within groups, and emotional recovery after stress.

But in burnout, soothing is often the most neglected system. High achievers may resist rest, avoid intimacy, or replace true recovery with numbing habits like alcohol, scrolling, or binge-watching. Without soothing, the body never fully resets. Physically, this absence shows up as shallow sleep, immune suppression, fatigue, muscle tightness that never resolves,

and difficulty feeling safe or relaxed. Psychologically, it feels like disconnection, numbness, or an inability to "switch off." Over time, this deficit
erodes resilience and compassion both toward others and ourselves.

Finding Balance

The goal is not to eliminate any of these systems but to cultivate balance
among them. Ideally, the threat system activates only when necessary, the
drive system fuels sustainable motivation, and the soothing system provides recovery and connection. When the three work in concert, we are
adaptable, emotionally grounded, and better equipped to thrive.

I often ask clients to sketch these three systems as circles, labeling them
T (Threat), D (Drive), and S (Soothing). Almost every time, the T or D
circles take up most of the page, while the S circle is drawn small and over-
shadowed. This simple exercise makes visible what burnout so often con-
ceals: A life dominated by stress and striving, with little space left for rest,
compassion, or recovery. Figure 4.2 is an example of this exercise based on
Gilbert's (2009) emotional regulation model.

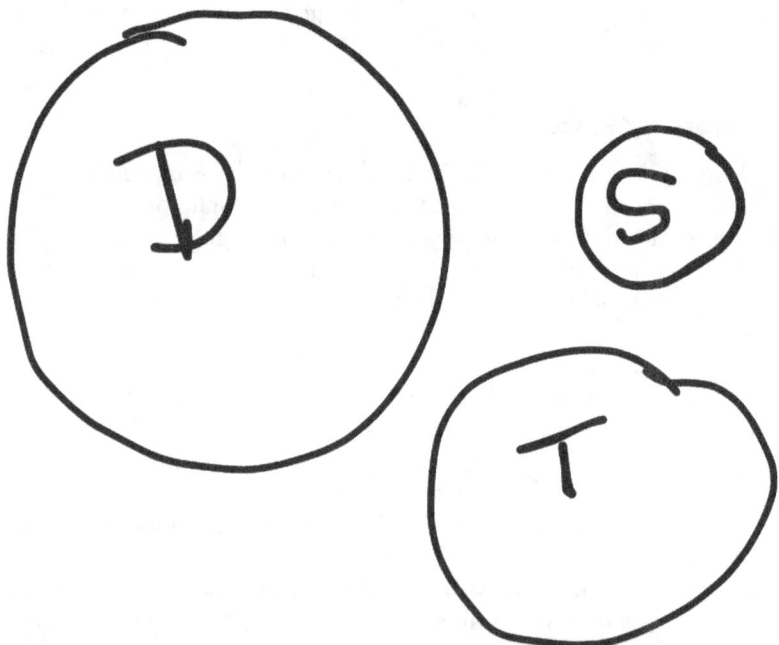

Figure 4.2 Sample Three Circles. Adapted from Gilbert, P. (2009). *The compassionate mind*. London: Constable & Robinson and Oaklands, CA:
New Harbinger (reproduced with permission).

Beyond Burnout Practice: Check in on Your Systems

Purpose: To better understand the current state of your three emotional regulation systems.

Instructions

Take a blank page and draw three circles. Label them *T (Threat), D (Drive), and S (Soothing)*. Adjust the size of each circle based on how active each system feels in your life right now. If you'd prefer you can also use colors, *red for T, green for D, and blue for S,* to make the differences stand out visually.

If you prefer a digital option, visit threecirclesapp/demo.com for a guided check-in. Resize the red, green, and blue circles to reflect your current balance.

This quick reflection helps you visualize your emotional state, notice patterns, and track changes over time.

Reflection Questions

• Is my D (Drive) system running on overdrive? If so, what feels urgent?
• Am I operating mostly from T (Threat) mode? If so, what feels threatening?
• Is my S (Soothing) system active, or is it neglected? If so, what might feel soothing?

Why Compassion? The Neuroscience Behind It

One of the most effective ways to activate the soothing system is through compassion for both yourself and others. Compassion is not simply a moral virtue or lofty philosophy; it is a biologically grounded process that calms the nervous system, builds resilience, and strengthens our capacity for connection (Gilbert, 2014).

Neuroscience shows that compassion practice reshapes the brain. The anterior insula is a part of the brain that supports empathy and emotional attunement and becomes more active when practicing compassion (Klimecki et al., 2013). Compassion also triggers the release of oxytocin, a bonding hormone that quiets the amygdala, reduces fear and hypervigilance, and helps the body recover more quickly from stress (Heinrichs et al., 2009; Kirsch et al., 2005). The anterior cingulate cortex (ACC), critical for managing emotions and resolving internal conflict, is also strengthened through compassion practice. A well-developed ACC makes it easier to respond thoughtfully instead of reacting impulsively, reducing the overactivation of the threat system (Lutz et al., 2008).

Over time, compassion practice can even increase gray matter in the prefrontal cortex. Gray matter houses the nerve cell bodies that support decision-making, memory, self-awareness, and emotional regulation. More gray matter means denser processing power, stronger regulation, and greater adaptability (Hölzel et al., 2011). Put simply: Compassion physically strengthens the parts of the brain that help us stay balanced, focused, and resilient under stress. By intentionally cultivating compassion, we quite literally rewire the brain. Emotional balance and self-regulation become more accessible, stress becomes easier to manage, and our motivation and relationships grow stronger (Singer & Klimecki, 2014).

The Skills That Strengthen Your Core

Compassion isn't just something you either have or don't have. It's a trainable capacity. Like a muscle, it grows stronger with consistent, intentional practice. In *the Beyond Burnout Blueprint*, the goal is to get your "compassionate core" metaphorically ripped by developing skills across five domains:

1. **Compassionate Imagery:** Visualizing warmth, care, or safety to activate the soothing system and make self-compassion feel more natural.
2. **Compassionate Attention:** Training your focus toward what supports well-being instead of remaining stuck in threat-based thinking.
3. **Compassionate Reasoning:** Reframing harsh inner dialogue into wise, supportive perspectives, especially in moments of struggle or failure.
4. **Compassionate Emotion:** Meeting your feelings with kindness rather than avoidance or judgment, which allows you to stay present through discomfort.
5. **Compassionate Behavior:** Putting compassion into action by setting boundaries, practicing rest, or offering genuine encouragement to yourself and others.

Together, these domains form the building blocks of emotional fitness. The more you practice them, the more you train your brain to meet stress with clarity, regulation, and compassion, transforming how you respond not just to burnout but also to life.

Moving from Insight to Action

With this foundation in place, you've completed Part I, *Burnout Recovery Foundations*, exploring the roots of burnout and the clinical framework behind this model. Now it's time to turn knowledge into practice.

Part II, *The Beyond Burnout Blueprint*, will guide you through six essential steps for building a life that is sustainable, fulfilling, and aligned with your values:

1. **Create a Compelling Vision:** Shift from survival mode to imagining a meaningful future.
2. **Welcome the Unwanted:** Make space for discomfort so it no longer dictates your choices.
3. **Watch Your Words:** Use compassionate, flexible language and defusion practices to change how you relate to yourself and others.
4. **Understand Your Unique Gifts:** Reconnect with strengths and skills that go deeper than productivity.
5. **Be Kind to Yourself and Others:** Protect your well-being while fostering strong, authentic relationships.
6. **Let Your Values Take the Wheel:** Make decisions guided by who you truly are, not burnout-driven habits.

This blueprint isn't about working harder to "fix" yourself. It's about reclaiming your energy, your purpose, and your sense of self, using evidence-based strategies that cultivate resilience, compassion, and sustainable well-being. So, let's get started!

References

Berridge, K. C., & Robinson, T. E. (2016). Liking, wanting, and the incentive-sensitization theory of addiction. *American Psychologist*, 71(8), 670–679. https://doi.org/10.1037/amp0000059

Boecker, H., Sprenger, T., Spilker, M. E., Henriksen, G., Koppenhoefer, M., Wagner, K. J., & Tölle, T. R. (2008). The runner's high: Opioidergic mechanisms in the human brain. *Cerebral Cortex*, 18(11), 2523–2531. https://doi.org/10.1093/cercor/bhn013

Gilbert, P. (2000). The relationship of shame, social anxiety and depression: The role of the evaluation of social rank. *Clinical Psychology & Psychotherapy*, 7(3), 174–189. https://doi.org/10.1002/1099-0879(200007)7:3<174::AID-CPP236>3.0.CO;2-U

Gilbert, P. (2009). *The compassionate mind: A new approach to life's challenges*. Constable & Robinson.

Gilbert, P. (2014). The origins and nature of compassion focused therapy. *British Journal of Clinical Psychology*, 53(1), 6–41. https://doi.org/10.1111/bjc.12043

Gilbert, P., & Simos, G. (2022). *Compassion focused therapy: Clinical practice and applications*. Routledge.

Haber, S. N., & Knutson, B. (2010). The reward circuit: Linking primate anatomy and human imaging. *Neuropsychopharmacology*, 35(1), 4–26. https://doi.org/10.1038/npp.2009.129

Heinrichs, M., von Dawans, B., & Domes, G. (2009). Oxytocin, vasopressin, and human social behavior. *Frontiers in Neuroendocrinology*, 30(4), 548–557. https://doi.org/10.1016/j.yfrne.2009.05.005

Hölzel, B. K., Carmody, J., Vangel, M., Congleton, C., Yerramsetti, S. M., Gard, T., & Lazar, S. W. (2011). Mindfulness practice leads to increases in regional brain gray matter density. *Psychiatry Research: Neuroimaging, 191*(1), 36–43. https://doi.org/10.1016/j.pscychresns.2010.08.006

Kirsch, P., Esslinger, C., Chen, Q., Mier, D., Lis, S., Siddhanti, S., . . . Meyer-Lindenberg, A. (2005). Oxytocin modulates neural circuitry for social cognition and fear in humans. *Journal of Neuroscience, 25*(49), 11489–11493. https://doi.org/10.1523/JNEUROSCI.3984-05.2005

Klimecki, O. M., Leiberg, S., Lamm, C., & Singer, T. (2013). Functional neural plasticity and associated changes in positive affect after compassion training. *Cerebral Cortex, 23*(7), 1552–1561. https://doi.org/10.1093/cercor/bhs142

LeDoux, J. E. (2000). Emotion circuits in the brain. *Annual Review of Neuroscience, 23,* 155–184. https://doi.org/10.1146/annurev.neuro.23.1.155

Lutz, A., Brefczynski-Lewis, J., Johnstone, T., & Davidson, R. J. (2008). Regulation of the neural circuitry of emotion by compassion meditation: Effects of meditative expertise. *PLoS ONE, 3*(3), e1897. https://doi.org/10.1371/journal.pone.0001897

McEwen, B. S. (2007). Physiology and neurobiology of stress and adaptation: Central role of the brain. *Physiological Reviews, 87*(3), 873–904. https://doi.org/10.1152/physrev.00041.2006

Miller, E. K., & Cohen, J. D. (2001). An integrative theory of prefrontal cortex function. *Annual Review of Neuroscience, 24,* 167–202. https://doi.org/10.1146/annurev.neuro.24.1.167

Nussbaum, M. C. (2013). *Political emotions: Why love matters for justice.* Harvard University Press.

Price, J. S., & Sloman, L. (1987). Depression as an adaptation. *Ethology and Sociobiology, 8*(1), 47–61.

Robinson, T. E., & Berridge, K. C. (2003). Addiction. *Annual Review of Psychology, 54,* 25–53. https://doi.org/10.1146/annurev.psych.54.101601.145237

Salamone, J. D., & Correa, M. (2012). The mysterious motivational functions of mesolimbic dopamine. *Neuron, 76*(3), 470–485. https://doi.org/10.1016/j.neuron.2012.10.021

Singer, T., & Klimecki, O. M. (2014). Empathy and compassion. *Current Biology, 24*(18), R875–R878. https://doi.org/10.1016/j.cub.2014.06.054

Volkow, N. D., & Morales, M. (2015). The brain on drugs: From reward to addiction. *Cell, 162*(4), 712–725. https://doi.org/10.1016/j.cell.2015.07.046

Volkow, N. D., Wang, G. J., Fowler, J. S., Tomasi, D., & Baler, R. (2011). Food and drug reward: Overlapping circuits in human obesity and addiction. *Brain Imaging and Behavior, 5*(1), 24–35. https://doi.org/10.1007/s11682-011-9176-5

Wetherall, K., Robb, K. A., & O'Connor, R. C. (2019). Social rank theory of depression: A systematic review of self-perceptions of social rank and their relation with depressive symptoms and suicide risk. *Journal of Affective Disorders, 246,* 300–319. https://doi.org/10.1016/j.jad.2018.12.045

Part II

The Beyond Burnout Blueprint

Chapter 5

Step 1

Create a Compelling Vision

When we're burned out, it's easy to lose sight of where we're headed. Tasks pile up, the work feels endless, and purpose gets buried under survival mode. Yet, having a clear, values-based vision can change the way we relate to the grind. Vision gives us direction when motivation wanes and helps us frame even tedious or difficult work within a larger story of meaning. As Steve Jobs once put it, "If you are working on something that you really care about, you don't have to be pushed. The vision pulls you" (Isaacson, 2011). This not only captures the power of vision but also invites us to examine its shadow. Jobs transformed technology, but he also left behind stories of alleged narcissism, employee mistreatment, and cruelty toward family (Isaacson, 2011). His brilliance was real, but so was the harm.

That tension matters for how we hold vision. In this Blueprint, vision isn't about sacrificing your well-being or exploiting others for the sake of achievement. Instead, it's about cultivating a vision grounded in compassion—for yourself, your work, and those you serve. A vision that honors your values, not just your goals. One that aligns with your humanity, not just your productivity. This chapter will help you craft a vision that compels rather than coerces, with compassion at its center. Start by defining your Beyond Burnout life, then plan backward. If your burnout struggles disappeared tomorrow, what would you be doing differently?

Build Your Cathedral

After the Great Fire of London in 1666, architect Christopher Wren was tasked with rebuilding St. Paul's Cathedral. The story goes that when he asked two laborers what they were doing, one replied, "I'm laying bricks," while the other said, "I'm building a cathedral." The first saw drudgery; the second, meaning. Burnout makes every task feel like another brick. A compelling vision transforms those same tasks into steps toward something purposeful.

DOI: 10.4324/9781003640592-8

This doesn't mean your vision will erase tedious or difficult work. When I was deep in burnout, writing clinical notes felt very much like lugging a bag of bricks. In a burnout-resilient state, I see the same task as connected to my mission: Providing ethical, compassionate care and remaining accessible to clients by accepting insurance. It's still not my favorite task, but now I accept it as part of a meaningful whole.

Some parts of your work may genuinely be unnecessary or harmful, that's valid to question. But for now, embracing the unavoidable as part of your vision can foster motivation rather than resentment.

You probably already apply this thinking elsewhere. Dog lovers accept vet bills, chewed-up shoes, and the occasional accident on the carpet for the joy of companionship. Parents endure sleepless nights and endless laundry for the love of their children. Athletes push through sore muscles and early mornings for the thrill of the game. Anything truly meaningful comes with its share of metaphorical bricks.

In Buddhist teachings, there's a saying: *No mud, no lotus* (Nhat Hanh, 1998). The lotus flower, known for its beauty and purity, only grows in thick, muddy water. Without the mud, there would be no lotus. In the same way, the difficulties we face—frustrations, tedious tasks, discomfort are often the very conditions that make growth, beauty, and meaning possible. In my house, we say it a little differently: You can't go swimming without getting wet.

One summer, my daughter Lily, aged five at the time, announced she wanted to swim on the condition she wouldn't get wet. She worried about her hair getting ruined, the cold water shocking her system, and the extra shower I would insist on afterward. All reasonable concerns. But as she talked about playing Marco Polo with her brother, pretending to be a mermaid with a pink tail, and showing off her new swim strokes, her energy shifted. As she focused on the fun, imagination, and growth she was about to experience, she easily stirred up a compelling vision convincing enough to cannonball into the pool with glee. Her hair was ruined, she shrieked from the frigid water, and yes, I had her shower afterward. But it was totally worth it. The discomforts she had anticipated were still there, but they no longer outweighed the pull of the experience.

That's the power of a compelling vision: It reframes the obstacles as part of the journey, not reasons to abandon it.

Clinical Vignette: Jackie

Jackie, a 38-year-old mother of a toddler, came to me with depression, anxiety, and clear signs of burnout. She worked in the male-dominated field of finance, underpaid, overlooked, and unsupported by leadership. She constantly strove to prove her worth, was highly self-critical, and struggled to set boundaries.

Through our work, Jackie clarified her priorities: More time with her daughter, financial empowerment, creative and collaborative work, reasonable expectations from her employer, and opportunities for professional growth. Over the course of a year, she negotiated a better title and a $15,000 raise, secured an assistant for high-level projects, and established a hybrid schedule that allowed more time at home. She still experienced burnout symptoms, but she was no longer organizing her life around them. Instead, she was taking committed action based on her highest values.

So, I was surprised when she announced one day, "I'm going back to school for my master's degree." Tuition would be nearly $30,000 annually, the classes would take place in the evenings and weekends, and her current job didn't require an advanced degree. On the surface, it seemed like an admirable goal. After all, higher education is widely reinforced as a "good thing to do." But for Jackie, it was misaligned with the life she had worked so hard to create. It would drain her time, put her back into debt, and reduce her time with her daughter.

As we explored her decision, it became clear: Jackie wasn't being pulled toward a vision that inspired her. She was running from feelings of inadequacy and imposter syndrome. The degree was a sophisticated, expensive way to avoid her discomfort, not a move toward something truly aligned with her values. This is why it's important to ensure that you're not confusing your compelling vision with a sophisticated escape route.

Being the Architect of Your Blueprint

Jackie's story highlights an important truth: A compelling vision must be rooted in what excites and matters to you. That doesn't mean it has to be your "passion" in the romanticized sense. In fact, pursuing your passion is often a privilege. Many people can't afford to center their vision entirely on a dream career. They must first be passionate about keeping the lights on and meeting their basic needs.

That's why the compelling vision framework works for everyone. It's not about finding the perfect job right now; it's about threading meaning through your current reality and connecting it to the life you are building toward. Even if your work is pragmatic, your vision can link today's tasks to future goals, values, and higher pursuits.

External influences like family expectations, cultural norms, and societal messages can easily cloud this process. Motives like keeping your job to pay rent or retaining health insurance are valid, but they can keep you in a constant threat state. In CFT, this threat system contrasts with the soothing and drive systems, which foster connection, support, and sustainable motivation (Gilbert, 2014). Shifting your vision into these systems helps you frame your professional and personal life around contentment, fulfillment, and harmony rather than fear.

For example, Helen, a social worker I supervised, took a pragmatic approach to her compelling vision. Being a mom was her highest priority. She valued her union protection, benefits package, and clear boundaries that allowed time with her son. She did her job well but didn't overextend herself to meet traditional "team player" standards. Her vision was not about climbing the career ladder. It was about protecting her capacity to nurture the relationship that mattered most. Because she was so clear on that, she remained virtually untouched by burnout despite carrying a heavy caseload.

Building with Intention

I often work with physicians who, after years of training, begin to question why they entered medicine at all. In some families, becoming a doctor is an expectation tied to status, security, or tradition. These external pressures can push people into decades-long commitments that may not match their interests or aptitudes. Finding their "why," whether tied to patient care, advocacy, or stability, becomes essential for long-term fulfillment.

As you reflect on your own path, consider both the internal and external influences that have shaped it. Which align with your deepest values? Which are about avoiding rejection, fear, or disapproval? Are you building a cathedral, or are you sprinting away from a threat?

Your compelling vision doesn't have to be altruistic or righteous. It's not about posturing for approval or living up to some moralistic ideal. While naming what's broken is essential, tearing systems down without imagining what you'll build in their place is only demolition. Being *for* something is always more powerful than being *against* something. This exercise is about creation, not performance. It's about shaping a vision that resonates with your values and sustains you over time. A true vision positions you to build with purpose, exchanging perfectionism for refinement and fear-driven urgency for sustainable progress.

Your vision might include financial abundance, beauty, or luxury or it might not. What matters is that it's intentional, values-aligned, and yours (not borrowed from someone else's metrics). Liking nice things isn't shallow; chasing them to numb distressing feelings or win approval is what hollows a vision out. If your *why* is clear and compassionate, abundance can live inside a healthy, meaningful plan.

For some, the pull is deeply collective: Making your family proud, creating stability across generations, uplifting your community, or honoring cultural and spiritual commitments. These are not second-tier motives. If they're authentic to you and actually energize you, they belong at the center of your vision.

A quick gut-check as we move through this chapter: *Is this vision mine? Does it pull me, even when it's inconvenient? Am I willing to carry the real costs it entails?* If yes, you're pointed in the right direction.

Beyond Burnout Exercise: Reclaiming and Refining Your Professional Vision

Purpose: To deepen awareness of the forces that have shaped your professional path, both internal and external, and clarify whether your current trajectory aligns with your authentic values

Step 1: Grounding in the Present Moment

Begin by taking a few deep breaths. Let your attention settle into your body and the space around you. Notice the weight of your body in your seat, the sensations of breathing, and the sounds in the room. There is nothing to fix or solve right now. Just an opportunity to notice.

Step 2: Reflective Writing Prompt

Without judgment, reflect on the following:

- When you imagine your professional identity—your title, the work you do, how others see you, what comes up?
- Who or what helped shape this path? Consider family messages, cultural expectations, community norms, religious teachings, mentors, or media influences.
- Which of these influences feel like "gifts" you want to carry forward and which feel more like obligations or protective armor?
- Are there moments when you made a choice to be accepted, to be safe, or to avoid disapproval? How did that shape your direction?
- Do these influences still align with what feels deeply important to you now?

Step 3: Values Reconnection

Now bring to mind the metaphor of a cathedral, a structure built slowly and intentionally, brick by brick, with a larger vision in mind.
Ask yourself:

- If I were no longer afraid of judgment, rejection, or imperfection, what kind of work would I be doing? How would I be doing it?

- If I could lay one meaningful brick today toward a professional life that feels energizing, honest, and deeply mine, what would that brick represent?
- Are there things I've been tearing down (internally or externally) without a clear vision of what I want to build in their place?

Creating and Relating to Your Compelling Vision

This chapter offers two key invitations:

1. To create a compelling professional vision.
2. To build a compassionate relationship with that vision.

A compelling vision isn't about rigid goal-setting, unrelenting achievement, or chasing someone else's definition of success. It's a dynamic, values-driven path that grows with you. How you hold your vision matters just as much as what it contains. Does it inspire you, or has it become another source of pressure, comparison, or perfectionism?

Your vision will and should evolve. You are constantly shaped by new experiences, challenges, and insights, and your vision should reflect that. In ACT, this flexibility is supported by the concept of self-as-context, the understanding that you are more than your thoughts, emotions, or roles (Hayes et al., 2012). Viewing yourself from this broader perspective frees you from past narratives and self-imposed limits. You don't have to be "ready" or "qualified" to dream boldly.

One of my most formative career moments happened during my internship at a day treatment program for adults with severe and persistent mental illness. I was assigned to lead a men's group, most of whom were in recovery from substance use and navigating sobriety, stigma, and life stressors. One day, a new participant named Gary spoke about the exhaustion of his "transition." I assumed he meant the life transition of early sobriety and facilitated the discussion accordingly.

After group, Gary gently pulled me aside to clarify he was talking about his gender transition. He was a Black trans man taking hormone replacement therapy. Though gracious, I could see the weariness in his face. He had come seeking support, only to find himself educating me, a young, white, straight, cis woman on how to meet his needs as a client.

I didn't have the language or training at the time, but I felt an internal shift. I realized how much I didn't know, and how unfair it was for someone seeking care to also shoulder the burden of my ignorance. That moment crystallized a new thread in my vision: To become a gender-affirming clinician.

At that point, I didn't personally know any transgender people. The media I'd absorbed was rife with harmful, dehumanizing portrayals. I doubted whether I belonged in this work. I lacked mentors, training, and community support. But the vision took root anyway. Ready or not, it called me forward. I read everything I could find, attended every training available, and sought out trans voices both online and in person.

Working in a Bronx community clinic, I began asking all clients about their pronouns and gender identity, regardless of appearance. As I created space for gender-diverse clients to show up authentically, more came. Some wanted to medically transition, and I learned to conduct readiness assessments and write letters of support for affirming care, something few providers in the area were doing. Word spread, and I began supervising and training other clinicians.

Over time, my work expanded: Co-developing a psychiatry residency elective, launching an ambulatory consult service for surgical readiness, collaborating across departments like endocrinology and urology, and adapting evidence-based psychotherapy protocols for gender-diverse clients. And through it all, my vision continued to evolve, just as I did.

That brief hallway conversation with Gary charged with guilt, discomfort, and humility became a turning point. It taught me that a compelling vision isn't something you wait to be "qualified" for. It's born from reflection, genuine desire, and the willingness to grow.

My work with gender-diverse clients has been a master class in vision, courage, and authenticity. Many transgender folks have faced violence, rejection, homelessness, discrimination, and medical gatekeeping, and yet they persist. They haven't waited for the world to evolve before they begin evolving themselves. Neither should you.

Clarifying Your Compelling Vision

Mark Twain is often credited with saying, "I've suffered a great many catastrophes in my life. Most of them never happened." While attribution is debated, the sentiment captures how our tricky brains operate. The human mind is extraordinary. It can anticipate, plan ahead, imagine, and innovate. But the same capacity that allows us to invent tools, write novels, and dream up futures also allows us to create elaborate stories of our own demise.

Psychologists call this *catastrophic thinking*: The tendency to envision worst-case scenarios and respond as if they were inevitable. It happens where two forces intersect. First, there's the *negativity bias*, our brain's tendency to notice, prioritize, and remember threats; mistakes; and failures more than neutral or positive experiences (Rozin & Royzman, 2001).

Evolutionarily, overlooking danger is far more costly than overlooking opportunity.

Then our tricky brain adds its unique capacity: To simulate, to rehearse, to run mental time travel. This is usually an advantage. It helps us solve problems and prepare for challenges. But combined with the negativity bias, it pulls us into catastrophic thinking. We don't just anticipate danger, we live it, over and over again, in detail so sharp that our bodies react as though it were real.

I see this all the time in burnout stories. In their minds, clients have been fired a hundred times over. They've killed a patient on the surgical table. They've humiliated themselves in front of an audience. They've already been rejected from the job they haven't even applied for. None of these events actually occurred, yet the brain and body respond as though they did. Neuroimaging research shows why this feels so real: The same brain regions activate whether we are imagining an event or actually experiencing it (Kosslyn et al., 2001). To your brain, an imagined threat when conjured with enough detail and emotional intensity can be indistinguishable from reality.

This is why intentionally shaping your inner imagery matters. If left unchecked, the tricky brain will return to its negativity-biased default. But by deliberately crafting a compelling vision, you shift from survival mode to design mode, using imagination not just to anticipate problems but to vividly rehearse possibilities, values, and desired outcomes.

If your negativity bias feels like it's taking up all of your mental space right now, sometimes it's easier to begin imagining your vision, starting with what you don't want. In the next exercise, we will explore what that may be revealing about your desires, values, and aspirations.

- "I don't want to feel incompetent" might point to "I want to feel capable and confident."
- "I never want to be like my terrible boss" might point to "I want to emulate someone who is present, fair, and empowering."

In the exercise that follows, you'll have the chance to identify your own "don'ts" and begin flipping them into the "do's" that point toward your vision.

Beyond Burnout Practice: What You Don't Want →
To What You Do Want

Purpose: In moments of burnout, stuckness, or uncertainty, it is often easier to identify what you do not want than to articulate what you do want. This exercise uses contrast as a source of clarity.

Examples: Turning Avoidance into Alignment

- I don't want to feel invisible at work → I want to feel seen, respected, and included.
- I'm tired of overcommitting and burning out → I value balance, boundaries, and sustainability.
- I want to stop hiding how overwhelmed I feel → I long for honesty, support, and space to be human.
- I wish I didn't have to prove my worth every day → I want to feel secure in my role and appreciated for who I am.
- I don't want to keep pretending I'm passionate about this → I want to reconnect with work that feels purposeful to me.

Now You Try: Your Reflection

I don't want to feel _____ → I want to feel more _____.

I'm tired of _____ → I value

_____.

I want to stop _____ → I long for

_____.

I wish I didn't have to _____ → I'd prefer to

_____.

I don't want to keep pretending _____ → I want to show up with _____.

Now that you've explored what you *don't* want and uncovered the values and desires hidden within those frustrations, you've begun to map the contours of your future. This contrast work is more than just venting about what's wrong; it's the first step in shifting your focus from avoidance to intentional creation.

From here, the task is to imagine how those elements could take shape in your professional life. This is where your compelling vision begins to take form. Think of it as zooming out from individual brushstrokes to see the larger canvas—the life you're building toward, not just the challenges you're trying to escape.

The next exercise invites you to dream a little. Consider it your "Magic Wand Moment" (de Shazer et al., 2007): If nothing stood in your way, no financial constraints, no self-doubt, no competing obligations, what kind of life would you build? Who would you be in it? What would your days look and feel like? Visioning techniques like this draw on the power of mental imagery, which research shows can shape motivation, emotion, and behavior (Kosslyn et al., 2001).

Let this be playful, bold, and unapologetically yours. At the same time, ground it in your values so that it doesn't become a fantasy that floats away the moment life gets hard. In ACT, values are often described as a compass or "north star," a steady guide even when the terrain is rough (Hayes et al., 2012). Your vision will serve this role: Something to return to when burnout clouds your perspective or fear pulls you off course.

Beyond Burnout Practice: The Compelling Vision Brainstorm

Purpose: Distill a clear, values-aligned picture of your Beyond Burnout life, one that pulls you forward. Use this as a compact compass for choices and a touchstone when burnout flares.

Step 1: Reflect and Respond to the Prompts Below. You Can Write, Type, or Voice Note Your Answers, Whatever Makes It Feel Most Alive For You.
When I am living my compelling vision . . .

- What qualities or ways of showing up will I embody more often?
  (e.g., calm, creative, focused, authentic)

- What emotions might show up along the way and how do I want to relate to them?
  (e.g., I expect fear and doubt might visit me, but I'll meet them with compassion and courage.)

- Who will I be interacting with?
  (e.g., clients I care about, colleagues who inspire me, a community I trust)

- Where will I be?
  (e.g., working from home in the mornings, then walking to a cozy co-working space or leading retreats in the mountains)

- What kind of habits and activities will shape my days?
  (e.g., deep work, long walks, meaningful conversations, laughter, rest)

- What kind of impact will I be making?
  (e.g., helping people feel seen and safe, advocating for systems change, mentoring others)

- What role models or careers will I be emulating?

(e.g., people who lead with integrity, balance creativity with boundaries, and care deeply without burning out)

- What accomplishments will I be achieving?
  (e.g., publishing work I'm proud of, building a sustainable business, creating change in my field)

- What principles will guide my daily choices?
  (e.g., compassion over perfection, progress over pressure, authenticity over performance)

- How will I treat myself and others?
  (e.g., with respect, kindness, clarity, and care)

Step 2: Finish These Sentences

Use these to distill your vision into something you can revisit often. Try saving it to your Notes app, writing it on an index card for your wallet, or posting it somewhere visible.
I am creating a future where _____
My work is meaningful because _____
I am committed to _____
The impact I want to make is _____
My guiding values are _____

If you've just finished this exercise and still feel unsure what your vision looks like, you're not alone. For many people, clarity doesn't arrive in a single lightning-bolt moment. It emerges gradually, like a picture coming into focus.

You don't have to be a natural daydreamer to engage in this process. Just like any skill, the ability to envision a vivid future can be strengthened with practice, and it doesn't rely on visual imagery alone. In the coming exercises, we'll tap into other senses, emotional cues, and grounding techniques to make your vision feel real, motivating, and emotionally resonant even if it starts out a bit fuzzy.

We'll begin with one of the most tangible tools: A vision board. You might think vision boards are best left to the TikTok manifestation crowd, but they can actually be a grounded, visual representation of your compelling vision, especially useful when visualization feels elusive. By assembling images, words, and symbols that resonate with your aspirations, you create a concrete reminder of the life you're working toward.

Research supports this practice. In counseling and therapeutic contexts, vision boards have been shown to help people clarify and visualize their goals, providing a creative pathway to translate aspirations into action

(Burton & Lent, 2016). In educational settings, vision boards have also been used as a culturally responsive tool for identity exploration and career development, particularly among adolescents from underrepresented backgrounds (Waalkes et al., 2019). More recently, studies of digital vision boards have demonstrated their potential to strengthen reflection, motivation, and autonomy over time (Jerrems, 2025).

Taken together, these findings show that vision boards are more than an aesthetic exercise. They are psychologically grounded tools that bridge values-based imagination with intentional action, giving you something tangible to return to when your vision feels distant or blocked by burnout.

Beyond Burnout Exercise: Create a Vision Board

Purpose: This vision board exercise helps translate your compelling future into something you can see and touch. By engaging both visual and tactile elements, it transforms abstract goals into a sensory experience, one that strengthens emotional connection, motivation, and clarity around your values-based direction.

Step 1: Gather Materials

- Use a physical poster board or a digital tool (e.g., Canva, Pinterest, a collage app).
- Collect magazine clippings, printed photos, or digital images that represent your goals.

Step 2: Include Images Aligned with Your Vision

- Include colors, textures, symbols, and images connected to your vision.
- Include affirmations, quotes, or words that best reflect your vision.
- Choose images that reflect your first-person perspective (i.e., what you see, rather than an outside view of you). Example: Instead of a picture of someone giving a keynote speech, use an image that resembles the view from the podium.
- Integrate images or words that reflect milestones you've already reached to reinforce your progress and integrate these aspirational images with things you already see as achievable.

Step 3: Place It Where You'll See It Daily

- Set it as your phone or computer background if you have a digital version.

- Display it in a prominent place in your office or home if you have a physical version.

After exploring your vision through sight and touch with the vision board, it's time to add another dimension: Sound. Music has a remarkable ability to bypass logic and speak directly to emotion.

Research consistently shows that music engages deep emotional and neurological processes. It activates brain regions tied to reward and emotion, such as the limbic system, and can reliably shift mood, enhance motivation, and even support well-being (Koelsch, 2014; Saarikallio & Erkkilä, 2007). Because of this, music has been widely used in therapeutic contexts to reduce anxiety, foster resilience, and enhance self-expression.

By pairing music with your compelling vision, you create more than just a playlist. You build a personal soundtrack. Each song becomes a sensory anchor, a reminder of the version of yourself you're growing into. When burnout creates those mental bricks, pressing play allows you to reconnect quickly to the energy, hope, and emotion tied to your vision.

Beyond Burnout Practice: Create Your Beyond Burnout Playlist

Purpose: Music can bypass logic and speak directly to emotion, shifting mood, increasing motivation, and strengthening your emotional connection to your vision. By intentionally curating music that reflects the mindset and energy you want to embody, you create a portable, on-demand tool to reconnect with your compelling vision.

Instructions

Curate Your Playlist: Choose songs that evoke the qualities you want to bring into your life: Motivation, calm, confidence, hope, joy, or focus. Let the melodies, rhythms, or lyrics reflect the version of yourself you are building toward.

Select Your Anthem: Identify one song that resonates so strongly with your vision that it becomes your personal theme. This is the track you play when you need to align with your purpose before big decisions, presentations, or challenging days.

Use Music as a Trigger: Play your anthem or parts of your playlist during moments when you want to shift your mindset before starting work, heading into a meeting, or beginning a creative project.

Integrate It into Your Day: Fold your playlist into natural routines: On your commute, while cooking, during a walk, or as part of your morning ritual. Over time, these songs will become sensory anchors, instantly reconnecting you with your vision.

When you listen, let yourself fully feel what the music evokes, whether it's energy, peace, determination, or joy. Those feelings are part of the future you're creating.

Now that you've connected with your vision through sound, it's time to add another layer: Movement and physical presence. Burnout often leaves us feeling small, hunched, and disconnected from our own sense of agency. But the body can be a powerful entry point back into confidence and momentum. Research shows that posture and movement don't just reflect our inner state; they also can actively shape it. Even subtle shifts, like standing tall or opening the chest, can influence mood, stress levels, and perceived confidence (Nair et al., 2015).

This is because the body and mind are deeply interconnected. Adopting expansive, grounded postures can send signals to the nervous system, which promote regulation and resilience, counteracting the contracted, protective stances that so often accompany exhaustion and overwhelm (Peper et al., 2017). In other words, how you hold yourself physically can become a rehearsal for how you want to hold yourself psychologically.

The next exercise draws on this wisdom of the body, inviting you to literally stand in the confidence, strength, and clarity of your future self. Through movement, posture, and embodied presence, you'll begin to anchor your vision not only in thought and imagination but also in lived, physical experience.

Beyond Burnout Practice: Take a Stance

Purpose: Using your body can create a physical connection to your compelling vision. These techniques align bodily sensations with mental imagery, reinforcing confidence and motivation.

Step 1: Stand Tall

Place your feet shoulder-width apart, with shoulders back and chin lifted. If standing does not feel available to you, choose a comfortable place to sit with a long spine.

Step 2: Expand Your Posture

Take up more space—arms on hips, arms up, or standing firm.

Step 3: Breathe Deeply

Take slow, steady breaths to ground yourself.

Step 4: Hold the Position

Maintain this stance for two minutes, while visualizing your future self, achieving a meaningful goal.

Reflection Prompts

- How does changing your posture affect your internal confidence?
- Do you notice a shift in motivation or sense of authority?
- Could this technique be used before important meetings, presentations, or decisions?

Your Relationship with Your Compelling Vision

Creating a compelling vision is only part of the journey. How you relate to that vision matters just as much. When we're burned out, it's easy to turn our vision into a weapon of self-criticism, a yardstick of how far we've fallen short. But your vision is meant to inspire you, not shame you. The mindset you bring to your vision can either reinforce the burnout cycle or help you move beyond it with compassion and clarity.

Consider two very different ways of holding your future self in mind. When the relationship with your vision is burnout-driven, you may:

- Speak to yourself in a shaming, attacking, or overly critical way
- Feel driven by a desire to punish yourself for "not being there yet"
- Focus almost exclusively on deficits, mistakes, and shortcomings
- Rehash the past, replaying failures and regrets
- Experience an emotional tone dominated by anxiety, frustration, or contempt

When the relationship with your vision reflects the Beyond Burnout approach, you are more likely to:

- Offer compassionate self-correction rather than harsh criticism
- Feel motivated by a desire to learn and improve
- Focus on strengths, progress, and growth opportunities
- Keep attention on a forward-looking vision
- Experience emotions like hope, compassion, and enthusiasm

In the first mindset, your vision becomes a moving target, always out of reach, a reminder of inadequacy. In the second, it becomes a steady lantern, lighting the path ahead and making the journey itself more sustainable.

To strengthen this second kind of relationship, we'll draw on CFT practices such as compassionate imagery and compassionate attention. These skills are designed to activate affiliative emotions, warmth, safeness, encouragement, and connection so that your vision becomes something that uplifts you rather than something that pressures or criticizes you (Gilbert, 2014; Kolts, 2016).

And if imagery doesn't come naturally, that's okay. As CFT expert Dr. Russell Kolts emphasizes, one of the most powerful tools isn't visual at all, it's breath. *Soothing Rhythm Breathing* is a simple but profound way to stimulate the parasympathetic nervous system, shifting you out of threat mode into a calmer, more regulated state (Gilbert, 2009; Kolts, 2016). It's a foundational CFT skill that I invite you to return to often, either before or after any of the other practices in this Blueprint.

Beyond Burnout Practice: Soothing Rhythm Breathing

Purpose: Soothing rhythm breathing is a foundational CFT Therapy practice that helps calm the body and mind, regulate emotion, and create the internal safety needed to connect with your compassionate self or compelling vision. It's a powerful tool you can return to anytime you feel overwhelmed, self-critical, or stuck.

Step 1: Find a Comfortable Posture

Sit upright but relaxed. Rest your hands on your lap or at your sides. You may close your eyes or soften your gaze. Whatever helps you feel grounded.

Step 2: Bring Awareness to Your Breath

Begin by simply noticing your breath. Where do you feel it most—your chest, your belly, your nose?

Step 3: Slow Down and Soften the Rhythm

Gently slow your breathing. Aim for a rhythm that feels steady and soothing, not forced. Try inhaling for a count of 5, pausing briefly, and exhaling for a count of 5. Adjust the count to whatever feels most natural and calming to your body.

Step 4: Focus on the Feeling of Soothing

As you breathe, imagine your breath flowing in and out like waves—steady, rhythmic, calming. You might silently say to yourself with each exhale: "Safe." or "Soothe."

Step 5: Practice for 2–5 Minutes

Continue this rhythm for several minutes. If your mind wanders, that's okay, gently return your focus to the breath.

Reflection Prompts

- How did your body feel before versus after this practice?
- Could you imagine using this before work, therapy, or sleep?
- How might this shift your internal state when you feel overwhelmed?

Compassionate Rhythm Breathing is a simple yet powerful practice that helps settle the body, activate the soothing system, and create the inner conditions for compassion to emerge. It's something you can return to anytime: Before starting work, in moments of overwhelm, or as a daily centering ritual. Even a few minutes a day can gradually shift your emotional baseline toward greater calm, steadiness, and connection (Gilbert, 2009; Kolts, 2016).

Once you've anchored yourself in this calmer state, you are better able to engage in the next set of CFT skills: *Compassionate imagery.* These practices begin with *compassionate memory*, recalling a time you felt safe, cared for, or deeply supported. From there, we move into *compassionate imagination*, where you intentionally envision either an ideal compassionate figure or a wise, supportive future version of yourself (Gilbert, 2014).

Paired with *compassionate attention*, directing your focus toward soothing, encouraging experiences or inner states, these exercises train the mind to generate warmth, safeness, and caring emotions toward yourself and your vision (Rockliff et al., 2011).

In doing so, you're not just *thinking* about compassion as an abstract idea, you're *feeling* it, practicing it, and making it increasingly accessible in the moments you need it most.

Beyond Burnout Practice: Compassionate Memory Activation

Purpose: To intentionally generate warm, supportive emotions by recalling meaningful moments of care, growth, or connection, activating the soothing system and cultivating an internal sense of safety and compassion.

This practice draws on two core CFT skills:

- *Compassionate Memory* (recalling a time you felt safe, supported, cared for, or proud)
- *Compassionate Attention* (gently focusing on that memory and the soothing feelings it evokes)

We begin and end this exercise with Soothing Rhythmic Breathing, a foundational CFT practice that helps regulate the nervous system and create the inner space to receive and expand compassion. If accessing a positive memory from the past year feels difficult, that's okay. You can use any memory or even a comforting image that brings a sense of warmth or ease.

Step 1: Begin with Soothing Rhythmic Breathing

Sit comfortably in a quiet space. Let your hands rest gently on your lap or over your heart. Close your eyes or soften your gaze. Begin breathing in a slow, steady rhythm—in for a count of five . . . out for a count of five. Imagine your breath is warm and steady, like a soft wave or breeze. Let this breath ground you. Stay with it for 1–2 minutes to settle your body and prepare your mind for the memory.

Step 2: Recall a Compassionate Memory

Bring to mind a memory that evokes calm, connection, or care. If helpful, reflect on one of the following:

- A moment when you felt safe, supported, or accepted.
- A time you felt proud of your growth or contribution.
- A meaningful interaction with a client, colleague, or loved one.
- An experience where you felt seen, appreciated, or deeply connected.
- If nothing specific comes to mind, visualize a peaceful image (waves, sunlight, a favorite place) that brings comfort.

Step 3: Deepen the Experience with Compassionate Attention

As the memory or image comes into focus, notice what emotions arise. Gently scan your body. Do you feel warmth, softening, lightness, or peace? Let your soothing breath "hold and expand" these sensations. Breathe into the warmth, as if you're nourishing it with each inhale. If your attention wanders, kindly guide it back to your breath or the comforting feeling in your body. Stay here for a minute or two, allowing the experience to settle in.

Step 4: Return to Soothing Rhythmic Breathing

Come back to your slow, steady breath, in for five, out for four counts. Let your breath soothe and regulate your system as you gently transition out of the practice.

When you're ready, open your eyes or lift your gaze. See if you can carry even a small thread of this warmth with you into the rest of your day.

After grounding yourself in a memory that evokes care, safety, or connection, your body and mind are better prepared to hold your vision not with pressure or perfectionism, but with warmth, encouragement, and flexibility.

If this first exercise feels difficult, especially if you struggle with shame or self-criticism, you're not alone. Research shows that many people find it challenging to access feelings of compassion at first, particularly those who are highly self-critical (Gilbert, 2014; Kelly et al., 2010). It often takes several tries before the experience of truly receiving compassion begins to feel real. There's no rush. You might pause here, repeating the same practice over multiple sessions, allowing the sense of care and connection to gradually deepen. The more familiar this state becomes, the more internal safety and openness you'll bring to the next step.

That next practice builds on the emotional tone you've cultivated through compassionate memory. Here, you'll engage your imagination and attention to envision a future that aligns with your values. We are often experts at vividly picturing worst-case scenarios, rehearsing disasters that never come to pass. This exercise invites you to redirect that same mental power toward imagining what it looks and feels like when you are thriving (Kosslyn et al., 2001).

Beyond Burnout Practice: Compassionate Imagination Activation

Purpose: To activate a warm, supportive emotional state and use it to imagine your compelling vision from a compassionate, values-aligned perspective.

Step 1: Soothing Rhythm Breathing

Before we dive into imagery, let's prepare the body and mind by practicing a few minutes of soothing rhythm breathing. This helps regulate the nervous system and opens the door to compassion. Begin by gently closing your eyes or softening your gaze. Breathe in slowly for a count of five . . . Exhale slowly for a count of five . . . Repeat this soothing rhythm for 2–3 minutes. As you continue, imagine your breath as a gentle wave—steady, calming, supportive.

Step 2: Reconnect with Your Compassionate Memory

Now that you've grounded yourself, gently bring to mind the compassionate memory you explored in the previous exercise. Let yourself reconnect with the warmth, care, or safety that arose. Notice where you feel that warmth in your body. Imagine this compassion as a light, color, or presence that stays with you. Stay with the feeling for a few breaths, allowing it to infuse your body and mind.

Step 3: Revisit Your Compelling Vision

Before moving into this next visualization, pause to recall the vision you previously created for your professional or personal future. You may wish to revisit what you wrote in the Beyond Burnout Practice, "The Compelling Vision Brainstorm." If it feels helpful, take a moment to read through your notes or visualize that version of yourself again. Once you feel connected to that vision, bring the compassionate memory you just recalled into focus. Let it become the emotional lens through which you view that future.

Step 4: Envision Your Future Through a Compassionate Lens

With your compassionate memory holding you, imagine yourself living aligned with your vision. Let compassion infuse every part of this imagined future. Use the prompts below to guide your visualization:

- Where are you? Notice the environment. Is it indoors or outdoors, quiet or vibrant? What's the light like? What do you see around you?
- Who is with you? Picture the people who support and energize you. Can you hear their voices? Feel their presence?
- What are you doing? Imagine a moment where you feel focused, connected, or joyful. What habits or actions fill your time?
- How do you feel? Tune into your emotions and physical sensations. Do you feel calm, confident, playful, purposeful?
- What energy do you bring? How do others respond to you? What qualities are you embodying?
- What are you no longer carrying? What burdens, fears, or pressures have softened, loosened, or been left behind?
- Let the imagery unfold naturally. If your mind wanders, return gently to the warmth you cultivated earlier. This is not about getting it "right." It's about giving yourself the experience of possibility, from a place of kindness.

Step 5: Anchoring Your Compelling Vision

Take a few moments to reflect and bring your imagined future into clearer focus. Use the prompts below to help solidify and integrate what arose. If it would be helpful, jot down what comes up.

- One image, moment, or detail from the visualization that felt especially vivid or meaningful:
- One quality or emotion you noticed in your future self that you'd like to cultivate more often:
- A small step I can take this week that moves me even 1% closer to that future is:
- When doubt or self-criticism arises, I can return to this visualization by remembering:

You began this chapter by reconnecting with something deeper than symptom relief: A vision of life beyond burnout. Not just a life you can tolerate, but one that energizes you to live fully. In the thick of burnout, the world can shrink down to survival mode. This chapter has been an invitation to remember not only what you want to move away from but also what you want to move toward. You've explored the power of a clear, emotionally resonant vision, not as a rigid plan to execute, but as a compass to guide you. A touchstone you can return to whenever exhaustion, doubt, or disconnection threatens to pull you under.

And before your drive system pushes you into overdrive, let this be your reminder to slow down. This isn't a sprint, and it isn't a checklist to power through. Let each practice settle into you. Take one exercise a week if that feels right. Stay with what resonates. Leave what doesn't. You set the pace.

References

Burton, L., & Lent, J. (2016). The use of vision boards as a therapeutic intervention. *Journal of Creativity in Mental Health, 11*(1), 52–65. https://doi.org/10.1080/15401383.2015.1092901

de Shazer, S., Dolan, Y., Korman, H., Trepper, T. S., McCollum, E. E., & Berg, I. K. (2007). *More than miracles: The state of the art of solution-focused brief therapy*. Haworth Press.

Gilbert, P. (2009). *The compassionate mind: A new approach to life's challenges*. Constable & Robinson.

Gilbert, P. (2014). The origins and nature of compassion focused therapy. *British Journal of Clinical Psychology, 53*(1), 6–41. https://doi.org/10.1111/bjc.12043

Hayes, S. C., Strosahl, K. D., & Wilson, K. G. (2012). *Acceptance and commitment therapy: The process and practice of mindful change* (2nd ed.). Guilford Press.

Isaacson, W. (2011). *Steve Jobs*. Simon & Schuster.

Jerrems, M. (2025). Utilizing digital vision boards in goal-setting and reflection. *The Journal of Kanda University of International Studies, 37*, 491–503. https://doi.org/10.69236/0002000248

Kelly, A. C., Zuroff, D. C., Foa, C. L., & Gilbert, P. (2010). Who benefits from training in self-compassionate self-regulation? A study of self-criticism, self-compassion, and depressive symptoms. *Personality and Individual Differences, 49*(7), 749–754. https://doi.org/10.1016/j.paid.2010.06.014

Koelsch, S. (2014). Brain correlates of music-evoked emotions. *Nature Reviews Neuroscience, 15*(3), 170–180. https://doi.org/10.1038/nrn3666

Kolts, R. (2016). *CFT made simple: A clinician's guide to practicing compassion-focused therapy.* New Harbinger.

Kosslyn, S. M., Ganis, W. L., & Thompson, W. L. (2001). Neural foundations of imagery. *Nature Reviews Neuroscience, 2*(9), 635–642. https://doi.org/10.1038/35090055

Nair, S., Sagar, M., Sollers, J., Consedine, N., & Broadbent, E. (2015). Do slumped and upright postures affect stress responses? A randomized trial. *Health Psychology, 34*(6), 632–641. https://doi.org/10.1037/hea0000146

Nhat Hanh, T. (1998). *No mud, no lotus: The art of transforming suffering.* Parallax Press.

Peper, E., Lin, I. M., Harvey, R., & Perez, J. (2017). How posture affects memory recall and mood. *Biofeedback, 45*(2), 36–41. https://doi.org/10.5298/1081-5937-45.2.01

Rockliff, H., Gilbert, P., McEwan, K., Lightman, S., & Glover, D. (2011). A pilot exploration of heart rate variability and salivary cortisol responses to compassion-focused imagery. *Clinical Neuropsychiatry, 8*(6), 325–332.

Rozin, P., & Royzman, E. B. (2001). Negativity bias, negativity dominance, and contagion. *Personality and Social Psychology Review, 5*(4), 296–320. https://doi.org/10.1207/S15327957PSPR0504_2

Saarikallio, S., & Erkkilä, J. (2007). The role of music in adolescents' mood regulation. *Psychology of Music, 35*(1), 88–109. https://doi.org/10.1177/0305735607068889

Waalkes, P. L., Gonzalez, L. M., & Brunson, C. N. (2019). Vision boards and adolescent career counseling: A culturally responsive approach. *Journal of Creativity in Mental Health, 14*(2), 205–216. https://doi.org/10.1080/15401383.2019.1602092

Chapter 6

Step 2

Welcome the Unwanted

Most people come to therapy with one main goal: To feel in control. When I ask what they hope will change, their answers usually boil down to wanting control or to get rid of a persistent feeling, thought, or belief that is unwanted and painful:

- "If I could just get my stress under control, I'd be fine."
- "I don't want to be anxious anymore. It has to stop."
- "I just want to be happy. I'm tired of being angry all the time."
- "If I could stop second-guessing myself, maybe I could finally move forward."

On the surface, these seem like reasonable goals. But when I suggest that control itself might be the problem, I'm often met with puzzled stares. I get it. At the height of my own burnout, I was a chaotic mess, grasping at anything that might provide even a momentary sense of stability. Surely, I needed more control. How could less control possibly be the answer?

The Control Agenda

ACT teaches that when we try to control our private experiences like our thoughts, emotions, memories, and bodily sensations, we often end up amplifying them instead (Hayes et al., 2012). This relentless effort to eliminate or avoid discomfort is called *the control agenda*—the belief that if we could just get rid of anxiety, grief, self-doubt, or burnout, then we'd finally be okay.

The problem is that trying to suppress or outrun pain often makes it stronger. Imagine holding a beach ball underwater. It takes constant effort, and when you let go, it shoots to the surface with more force. The same thing happens when we push down feelings, numb sensations, or try not to think certain thoughts (Wegner, 1994). The harder we push, the more energy they demand.

DOI: 10.4324/9781003640592-9

This doesn't mean control is always bad. In the external world, control strategies are essential for survival and comfort. We flip a light switch to control darkness, open an umbrella to control getting wet in the rain, avoid a hot stove to control the risk of burns, or organize collectively to control unsafe working conditions. These strategies work because they target the outside world, where cause-and-effect is more predictable. But the inner world doesn't always work that way.

Thoughts arrive automatically and often loop louder the more we resist them, like trying not to hear a song that's already stuck in your head. Emotions are biochemical responses shaped by hormones and nervous system activation; they can't simply be shut down, and attempts to push them away usually make them rebound more fiercely. Body sensations, tight shoulders, a racing heart, a sinking stomach, and exhaustion are vital signals meant to guide us. The task isn't to override or suppress them but to notice and respond wisely. When we treat these inner experiences as problems to be eliminated, we lose access to their information and often magnify the suffering we're trying to escape.

This is exactly where many people in burnout get stuck. Burnout sufferers pour enormous energy into battling their own inner life or, even more futile, try to control the inner worlds of others—trying to manage other people's emotions and perceptions of them. In ACT, pain is inevitable, but suffering can be amplified. Clean pain is the immediate, unavoidable distress of being human like grief after a loss, anxiety before change, the discomfort of illness or injury, and sadness when life disappoints us. Amplified pain is the added layer created when we resist, judge, or fight that natural pain: Criticizing ourselves for being anxious, numbing out to avoid grief, or spiraling into shame after a mistake (Hayes et al., 2012). Clean pain is part of life. Amplified pain is optional, and it's here that we have the most leverage to intervene. By shifting our relationship to thoughts, emotions, and sensations, we can reclaim energy for what matters most.

Before going further, it's crucial to separate control from personal agency. I've worked with people who have endured trauma, systemic oppression, and profound injustice. To suggest they were "in control" of those circumstances is not only inaccurate, it's unfair as well. Oppression constrains choice, shrinking access to safety, dignity, and opportunity. In these contexts, "control" is often an illusion.

To be clear, this is not about suggesting we are powerless or absolved of responsibility for our lives—quite the opposite. Agency means recognizing the choices we *do* have, however small, and taking radical responsibility for aligning those choices with our values. The paradox is that empowerment often begins with acknowledging what cannot be controlled and then redirecting our efforts toward where influence is possible.

This distinction between control and agency is not just theoretical. ACT has been applied in some of the most constrained circumstances imaginable, including refugee camps and post-conflict zones, where external control is nearly nonexistent. Even there, people can cultivate meaning, flexibility, and dignity by exercising agency in the smallest of choices: Where to place attention, how to make sense of experience, and what values to enact in behavior (Hayes et al., 2012; Tol et al., 2018).

Personal agency, then, is not about controlling everything around you. It is the flexible, expansive awareness of the choices available to you in any given moment and the willingness to act intentionally based on that awareness. With rare exceptions, choice, not control, shows up in three domains: Where we place our focus, how we assign meaning, and the behaviors we take in service of our values. By leaning into these domains, we loosen the grip of the control agenda and cultivate a form of resilience that can carry us even through the hardest seasons of burnout. Figure 6.1 is reproduced from original work by the author.

- **Focus:** The way we direct our attention—internally (toward our thoughts, feelings, or sensations) or externally (toward people, tasks, or surroundings). Focus is where we place our energy and deliberate awareness. Left on autopilot, it clings to problems or threats; used intentionally, it highlights what matters most.
- **Meaning:** The interpretation we *choose* to give an experience. Automatic thoughts happen quickly and without effort, but meaning is slower and deliberate—it's the perspective we decide to hold onto, shaping how events influence us going forward.
- **Behavior:** The actions we take, both in the moment and through habits and routines. Automatic behavior often aims to avoid discomfort or

Personal Agency

What are the current choices available to me?

Figure 6.1 The Three Levers of Personal Agency.

pain; intentional behavior is guided by values, creating momentum toward the life we want.

Together, focus, meaning, and behavior form the levers of agency. By working with them, we can shift from organizing life around avoiding pain to organizing it around what matters most. Before we strengthen these domains, pause to identify the experiences you spend the most energy trying to control. Naming them helps reveal where you might choose a different approach.

Beyond Burnout Exercise: Your Unwanted Experiences

Purpose: This exercise is designed to help you build awareness of the internal experiences you tend to avoid, suppress, or try to control. They may show up in your thoughts, emotions, or body. These experiences often drive burnout cycles when our energy gets spent avoiding them instead of moving toward what we care about.

Instructions: Read through each category and check off anything that resonates. Use the blank spaces to name your own experiences. There's no need to fix or change anything. Just notice what tends to show up and where you feel the urge to push it away.

Thoughts and Beliefs

Recurring or unwanted thoughts, judgments, or mental stories
☐ Self-criticism or harsh self-talk: _____
☐ Worry about the future: _____
☐ Regret or rumination about the past: _____
☐ Fear of failure or rejection: _____
☐ Doubts about your worth or competence: _____
☐ Intrusive or distressing mental images: _____
☐ Beliefs about not being "good enough" or needing to prove yourself: _____
☐ Feeling like an imposter or fraud: _____
☐ Negative comparisons or jealousy: _____
☐ Judgmental thoughts about others: _____
☐ Trying to control how others think or behave: _____
☐ Other: _____
☐ Other: _____

Emotions and Feelings

Difficult or vulnerable emotional states you tend to push away:
☐ Sadness or grief: _____
☐ Anxiety or fear: _____
☐ Anger, frustration, or resentment: _____
☐ Guilt or shame: _____
☐ Loneliness or disconnection: _____
☐ Hopelessness or despair: _____
☐ Envy or embarrassment: _____
☐ Emotional numbness or flatness: _____
☐ Other: _____
☐ Other: _____

Body Sensations

Physical symptoms, tension, cravings, and nervous system signals
☐ Muscle tension or tightness (e.g., shoulders, jaw, chest): _____

☐ Racing heart, shallow breathing, or shortness of breath: _____

☐ Fatigue or exhaustion: _____
☐ Nausea, stomach discomfort, or appetite changes: _____

☐ Shakiness, dizziness, or feeling lightheaded: _____

☐ Restlessness or urge to move, escape, or "do something": _____

☐ Cravings for food, substances, or compulsive behaviors: _____

☐ Numbness, dissociation, or feeling "checked out": _____

☐ Pain or chronic illness symptoms: _____
☐ Other: _____
☐ Other: _____

The exercise you just completed, identifying the thoughts, emotions, and sensations you tend to push away isn't about fixing them or eliminating them. It's about noticing what you've been trying to control or get rid of. This is the first step toward reclaiming your energy: Recognizing where it's been tied up in an unwinnable battle.

In ACT, the term *willingness* is often used interchangeably with *acceptance* (Hayes et al., 2012). Many people hear "acceptance" and assume that it means resignation—giving up or tolerating pain or mistreatment forever.

That's not what we mean here. In this context, acceptance and willingness both describe the active choice to allow an experience to be present, as it is, without needless defense. It means allowing those experiences to exist without letting them dictate your choices. Sometimes, you'll take action; sometimes, you'll decide that no action is needed. This is where agency begins: When you stop struggling against what's inside and free up the energy that was locked in a tug-of-war with your own mind (Hayes et al., 2012).

Unwillingness, on the other hand, is when we refuse to remain in contact with uncomfortable private events of the present moment (thoughts, urges, feelings, sensations) and instead fight to escape or avoid them. Ironically, the more we resist, the more power we give them. It's like getting caught in a riptide: Your instinct says to thrash your way back to shore, but that only exhausts you and pulls you further out. The way through is to stop fighting the current, float, regain strength, then swim parallel to the shore. Resisting discomfort only makes it stronger, while turning toward our unwanted experience with willingness creates the space to respond (Hayes et al., 2012).

Moving into Mindfulness

So, how do you actually make space for your unwanted internal experiences?

One powerful strategy is *mindfulness*. Mindfulness is the practice of paying attention to the present moment nonjudgmentally (Kabat-Zinn, 1990). This awareness can be directed toward your internal world or to your experience with the external world like mindfully eating, sipping tea, or walking.

If you just groaned, *not mindfulness!*, you're not alone. Many people (myself included) have had less-than-stellar experiences with mindfulness practices in the past. But when we strip away clichés and one-size-fits-all approaches, mindfulness becomes something far more practical and liberating.

Mindfulness also strengthens the three domains of personal agency:

- **Focus:** It helps you place your attention where it matters most, even when distractions internally or externally try to pull you away.
- **Meaning:** It creates the mental space to consciously observe and interpret events, rather than automatically reacting from old stories or assumptions.
- **Behavior:** It increases the likelihood that your actions reflect your values by reducing reactivity, rather than being led by whatever emotion or thought happens to be loudest in the moment (Shapiro et al., 2006).

When we bring mindfulness into burnout recovery, we're not trying to "clear the mind" or "think calm thoughts." We're practicing a more radical skill: Staying with what's here, without needless defense, so that we can act with intention.

Your Window of Tolerance

Before we jump into the "how" of mindfulness, it's worth understanding why it can be so powerful and why it sometimes backfires.

Research shows that consistent mindfulness practice is linked to:

- Lower stress hormones and reduced inflammation (Black & Slavich, 2016)
- Improved immune function (Black & Slavich, 2016)
- Increased resilience under stress and burnout (Good et al., 2016)
- Measurable brain changes in regions tied to emotion regulation, attention, and empathy (Hölzel et al., 2011)
- Reduced symptoms of anxiety, depression, and chronic pain (Khoury et al., 2013)
- Better focus and less rumination (Gu et al., 2015)

It's free, portable, and available at any moment. So why isn't everyone doing it?

Here's the catch: Mindfulness often asks you to turn toward your inner world. That includes sensations, emotions, and thoughts you might normally avoid. For many people, especially with trauma histories, chronic stress, or heightened sensitivity to internal cues, that inward shift can feel like being dropped into shark-infested waters. Instead of settling the nervous system, a sudden flood of awareness can overload it and kick you out of your optimal zone of functioning (Treleaven, 2018).

That optimal zone is the *window of tolerance*, a term coined by Dr. Dan Siegel (Siegel, 1999). This is the range in which we can think, feel, and relate effectively. Inside the window, we tend to stay grounded, regulated, and connected, even under stress. Outside it, we tip into:

- *Hyperarousal* (fight/flight: Anxiety, overwhelm, racing thoughts)
- *Hypoarousal* (freeze/shutdown: Numbness, exhaustion, disconnection)

Windows differ in size. Factors like trauma, burnout, and lack of support can narrow them, making it easier to be pushed out. Traditional practices like breath-tracking or long body scans, taught as one-size-fits-all, can act like opening a floodgate, especially if what's inside feels like dread, pain, or chaos.

My Mindful Meltdown

If you've tried mindfulness before and thought, *Nope, this is not for me,* you're not alone. In my late twenties, I signed up for a Mindfulness-Based Stress Reduction (MBSR) course, an eight-week, evidence-based program combining meditation, gentle movement, and body awareness to help manage stress and improve well-being (Kabat-Zinn, 1990). I was expecting zen, serenity, and a magical set of skills to make me blissed out. What I got instead was a harsh reality check.

The class was at night, which already made it difficult given my depleted energy levels. I'd finish a full day of work, race to pick up my son from day-care, then spend nearly two hours crawling through traffic from the Bronx to Long Island to drop him off with my grandmother. No quick hand-off, either, just the usual chaos of getting a small child settled, fed, and hugged goodbye. Then I'd get back in the car and drive another hour deeper into Long Island for a two-hour session. By the time I arrived, I'd been in motion for hours—working, parenting, commuting, and now I was supposed to sit still and "find my center."

What came up? Physical discomfort. Restlessness. Irritability. Dread. Regret. Guilt. And looping thoughts like, *Why did I do this to myself?*

Neutral wasn't my starting point. My nervous system was imprinted with childhood trauma, which made being present with my body difficult. On top of that, I hadn't yet come to understand my neurodivergent mind, which made stillness feel like friction. In hindsight, the clues were obvious: Chronic forgetfulness, disorganization, the compulsion to fidget, thoughts that outran my filter in meetings. Even with what felt like my body and mind working against me, I could stay within my window. Uncomfortably, yes, but in it. As the weeks went on, the mindfulness practices actually helped with the discomfort. After just a few weeks, I noticed my focus sharpening, my impulse control improving, and moments of unexpected gratitude and appreciation slipping into my daily life.

Just when I thought I was getting the hang of it, the full day of silence came. At first, I tried to settle in, shifting my seat, counting breaths, tracing the sounds in the room. But the stillness started pressing in, like the air itself was too thick. My focus narrowed to the smallest irritations: The ache in my back, the itch on my cheek, the heaviness in my legs. Soon my body started to feel like it was on fire from the effort of staying still, every muscle coiled like a spring. I noticed the thoughts and sensations of wanting to jump out of my skin, feeling overcome with fear and spikes of urges to scream. My window of tolerance had slammed shut.

I was in this class with other therapists, and I convinced myself that stopping wasn't an option. I'd feel like too much of a failure, a fraud, or an imposter compared to my much more regulated peers. But it absolutely would have been okay to stop. I understand that now. While mindfulness is not always comfortable or associated with positive feelings like calm, peace, or serenity, noticing when you are out of your window of tolerance and compassionately giving yourself permission to stop are absolutely okay (Treleaven, 2018).

There's a difference between being uncomfortable and being outside your window. Uncomfortable can mean sitting with unpleasant emotions or thoughts but still feeling relatively safe and able to stay connected. Being outside your window often comes with cues like feeling unsafe, flooded with intense physical and emotional sensations, or feeling trapped.

This is why dose, pacing, and anchoring matter:

- **Dose**—How much mindfulness you do in one sitting. Longer isn't always better.
- **Pacing**—The speed with which you increase intensity or duration. Go slow, not all at once.
- **Anchoring**—What you focus on to stay grounded. Breath, sound, touch, or movement can all work.

Mindfulness is most effective when it's trauma-informed, titrated, adapted, and infused with self-compassion (Neff & Germer, 2013; Treleaven, 2018).

Mindfulness doesn't have to mean sitting still with your eyes closed. It can happen while walking, eating, moving, listening to music. The options are endless. It's worth finding a version that works for you because research shows that consistent mindfulness practice can literally change your brain. It strengthens the prefrontal cortex (focus, decision-making, emotional regulation) and reduces activity in the amygdala (threat detection, fear responses), making it easier to stay in your window over time (Hölzel et al., 2011).

Let me share a mindfulness exercise that works for me. If you have a mind like mine that just will not *STFU*, always looping, commenting, narrating, rehearsing, replaying, this exercise may be for you. It involves simply saying "yes" to the thoughts, feelings, and body sensations you notice. It doesn't require you to be still or serene. It doesn't require a quiet mind. It only requires your consent. This is different from getting entangled in the content of a thought or swept away by a feeling.

For example, if you notice the thought, *Everyone is mad at me,* you respond internally with, *Yes, I am having the thought that everyone is mad at me.* Not, *Yes, everyone is mad at me.* That subtle shift creates just enough space to moderate your inner dialogue instead of being ruled by it. Especially for those of us with running minds (and sometimes running mouths).

Beyond Burnout Practice: The YES and NO Exercise

Purpose: This practice is designed to help you feel the difference between unwillingness and willingness in your body and mind.

Step 1: Find a Comfortable Position

Sit comfortably with your feet grounded, your spine upright but not rigid. Let your body feel supported. You can close your eyes or soften your gaze. Take a few slow breaths. Let your shoulders drop.

Step 2: Tune In

Bring your attention inward. Without trying to fix anything, just notice what's already here—any thoughts, emotions, sensations. Observe with curiosity.

Step 3: Experience Unwillingness (NO)

For the next minute or so, begin silently (or softly aloud) saying NO to whatever arises. A thought appears: NO (sharp, impatient, or even dismissive). A discomfort in your body: NO (tight, critical, "This shouldn't be happening"). A memory surfaces: NO (pushing it away, shutting the door). An urge or craving shows up: NO (clamping down, holding back). An emotion starts to rise: NO (tense, bracing against it). Let your tone be cynical, resistant, or critical. Pair it with a more closed or rigid posture: Cross your arms; Clench your fists slightly; Furrow your brow; Tighten your jaw; Lean back as if distancing yourself; Notice what happens in your breath, your muscles, your thoughts. Does your chest feel tighter?Does your breathing get shallower? Do your thoughts get louder or more agitated?

Step 4: Experience Willingness (YES)

Now gently shift. For the next minute or so, begin saying YES to whatever shows up. A thought arises: YES (warm, open, like welcoming someone in without needing to entertain them). An emotion bubbles up: YES (grounded, steady, compassionate). A physical sensation presents: YES (soft, allowing). A random, irrelevant mental image: YES (light, curious). Let your YES be warm, open, and receptive. Pair it with a long exhale and open posture: Hands resting gently, palms up (willing hands); A gentle, relaxed half smile; Unclenched jaw; Shoulders soft, chest open; Lean in slightly, as if turning toward what's here; You're not agreeing with the content of your thoughts or hoping discomfort will stay forever. You're simply saying: This is here right now, and I can allow it to be here without a fight.

Step 5: Reflect

Take a few slow breaths. Return to a neutral posture.
Ask yourself:

- How did the NO posture and tone feel in your body? In your mind?
- What changed when you said YES with your body and breath?
- Did your thoughts or sensations shift or did your relationship to them shift?

This exercise helps you feel the difference between unwillingness, rejecting or resisting unwanted internal experiences and willingness approaching hard moments with openness so that you can respond more flexibly to your pain and move toward what matters, rather than getting caught in the struggle (Hayes et al., 2012).

The next time you feel stuck, clenched, or reactive, try starting with your body. Shift into an open, *YES* posture and notice what changes.

Of course, most of us aren't walking around shouting *NO! NO! NO!* in our heads. Unwillingness usually shows up in subtler ways through action urges and thinking strategies that fall under what ACT calls experiential avoidance.

Experiential avoidance refers to the actions or inactions we use to suppress, escape, or avoid unwanted internal experiences such as difficult emotions, distressing thoughts, uncomfortable memories, or physical sensations. Within ACT, experiential avoidance is considered a core process that contributes to anxiety, depression, and maladaptive coping (Hayes et al., 1996; Chawla & Ostafin, 2007).

Russ Harris, a leading ACT clinician, uses the acronym *DOTS* to describe common experiential avoidance strategies (Harris, 2019):

1. **Distraction:** Keeping busy or overstimulated to avoid discomfort (e.g., endless scrolling, overworking, compulsive organizing).
2. **Opting Out:** Skipping situations that might trigger distress, such as social events, work meetings, difficult conversations, or new responsibilities. It can also look like absenteeism or procrastination.
3. **Thinking:** Getting stuck in rumination, worry, self-criticism, or over-analyzing, instead of feeling what's present.
4. **Substances, Self-Harm, and Other Strategies:** Using alcohol, drugs, self-injury, binge eating, or other numbing behaviors to avoid emotions.

Beyond Burnout Exercise: Connect the DOTS

Purpose: Build awareness of your experiential avoidance strategies, the ways you may be resisting or pushing away difficult internal experiences, and notice the patterns that show up for you.

Step 1: Identify Your DOTS

Think of a recent time when you felt overwhelmed, exhausted, or emotionally drained.

When you experienced burnout-related distress, which of these DOTS strategies did you use?

Check all that apply:

D—Distraction Activities (Avoiding the Feeling by Doing Something Else)

☐ Scrolling on social media mindlessly
☐ Binge-watching TV/YouTube/streaming
☐ Online shopping or browsing
☐ Overworking to avoid emotions
☐ Playing video games for hours
☐ Emotional eating/snacking
☐ Cleaning or organizing excessively
☐ Other: _____
☐ Other: _____

O—Opting Out (Avoiding Situations That Trigger Discomfort)

☐ Canceling plans with friends/family
☐ Avoiding opening/responding to emails, messages, or mail
☐ Skipping meetings or procrastinating work
☐ Not addressing a conflict or uncomfortable conversation
☐ Withdrawing from hobbies or activities once enjoyed
☐ Not pursuing opportunities that interest you at work
☐ Other: _____
☐ Other: _____

T—Thinking Strategies (Avoiding Emotions Through Overthinking)

☐ Blaming others ("If my boss wasn't so demanding . . .")
☐ Rehashing the past ("I should have said/done that differently . . .")
☐ Fantasizing ("If only I could quit and move somewhere peaceful . . .")
☐ Self-criticism ("I'm such a failure for feeling this way . . .")
☐ Overplanning ("I just need a perfect plan to fix this . . .")
☐ "What if" spirals ("What if I can't keep up? What if I let everyone down?")
☐ "Why me?" or "Not fair" thoughts ("Why do I have to deal with this?")
☐ Debating or denial ("I don't have burnout; I just need to push harder . . .")
☐ Beating yourself up ("I should be stronger than this . . .")
☐ Other: _____
☐ Other: _____

S—Substances, Self-Harm, and Other Strategies (Avoiding Emotions Through External Means)

☐ Drinking alcohol to unwind or cope
☐ Using caffeine excessively to push through exhaustion
☐ Taking unprescribed medications to suppress feelings rather than manage health
☐ Overeating or undereating due to stress
☐ Smoking, vaping, or using other substances
☐ Self-harm behaviors
☐ Engaging in reckless or numbing behaviors
☐ Other: _____
☐ Other: _____

Workability: Is Your Coping Strategy Helping or Hurting?

In ACT, coping strategies are evaluated through the lens of *workability*. Behavior isn't inherently good or bad, its value depends on whether it moves you toward or away from the kind of life you want (Hayes et al., 2012).

Workable strategies help you move in the direction of your values and support a fulfilling life over time. Unworkable strategies are often driven by the urge to avoid or control difficult feelings. While they may provide short-term relief, they can create new problems, pull you out of alignment with your values, or keep you stuck in the long run (Hayes et al., 2012; Twohig & Levin, 2017).

Many common strategies like distraction, opting out, overthinking, or even using substances can be workable in certain contexts:

- *Distraction* can provide short-term relief when you're overwhelmed (e.g., watching a funny show after a stressful day).
- *Opting out* can be a form of self-care (e.g., turning down an extra project to protect your well-being).
- *Thinking strategies* like planning can be helpful when used flexibly (e.g., making a schedule to manage stress).
- *Substances* such as a morning coffee for focus or a glass of wine with friends aren't inherently harmful unless they become your primary way of avoiding fatigue or discomfort.

There's no one-size-fits-all answer. What matters most is whether a coping choice is workable for you in the long term. When it isn't workable, that's when learning to welcome unwanted experiences, rather than push them away, can be a game changer (Hayes et al., 2012; Harris, 2019).

Beyond Burnout Exercise: Is Your DOTS Strategy Workable?

Purpose: This exercise is designed to help you build awareness of your control agenda—the things you've tried to make hard experiences go away. The goal isn't to judge or shame your coping strategies, but to honestly assess whether they serve you in the long run.

Step 1: Identify Your Strategies

Refer back to the DOTS exercise you just completed and identify your *Distraction, Opting Out, Thinking, Substances/Other Strategies,* and any other patterns you've noticed in yourself. Bring a few of these strategies to mind or jot them down so that you can work with them in the next steps.

Step 2: Ask Yourself the Big Questions

For each strategy, consider:

- Does this help me engage in what truly matters to me?
- Does it move me toward or away from the kind of person I want to be?
- Does it provide relief in a way that supports my well-being, or does it create more problems over time?
- If I continue using it, will it support the life I want in the long run?

Step 3: Explore Short-Term Relief Versus Long-Term Impact

- Does the strategy bring immediate relief?
- How long does that relief last before the distress returns?
- Over time, have you needed to use it more often or more intensely to get the same effect?

Step 4: Weigh the Long-Term Consequences

- Has this strategy led to unintended consequences?
- Has it interfered with my work, relationships, health, or sense of purpose?
- Has it prevented me from taking action toward something meaningful?

Step 5: What Happened to the Unwanted Experience?

- Did the uncomfortable thoughts, emotions, or sensations go away or did they return?
- When they came back, were they weaker, stronger, or about the same?

Final Reflection: Is This Strategy Workable?

Return to the guiding questions in Step 2. Consider whether this strategy is moving you toward a life that feels rich, full, and meaningful or keeping you stuck in the same loops.
You don't have to decide everything today. Awareness is the first step. From here, you can begin to choose more workable, values-aligned strategies. Ones that might not offer instant escape but instead move you closer to the life you actually want.

Most of the time, we're not consciously thinking: *Time to start avoiding, self-medicating, distracting, or talking myself out of this.* These responses are automatic. They are quick, reactive patterns we fall into without even realizing it. In psychology, this tendency to act from habit without awareness is often described as automaticity (Bargh & Chartrand, 1999).

What we need is a way to interrupt autopilot mode: To pause, to notice, and to create just a bit of space between the uncomfortable experience we're trying to avoid and the habitual reaction that follows. Research on mindfulness shows that practices which increase moment-to-moment awareness can reduce stress reactivity and promote more flexible responses to emotional triggers (Brown et al., 2013).

One effective approach is learning to take a *BEAT*, a brief, intentional self check-in developed by Dr. Ryan DeLapp (2025), author of *Empower Yourself Against Racial and Cultural Stress*. BEAT stands for:

- *Body sensations*
- *Emotions*
- *Action urges*
- *Thoughts*

This practice is simple but powerful. In just a few moments, you can shift from reacting on instinct to responding with intention. Instead of automatically pushing discomfort away, you slow down enough to notice what's happening in your inner world. That pause creates the opening to choose a response that is more workable and aligned with your values, one that moves you toward the life you want, rather than deeper into old patterns.

Importantly, research shows that coping strategies are more likely to be implemented when they are simple, memorable, and easy to practice, especially under stress (Kazantzis et al., 2010). Implementation science highlights that streamlined interventions are more sustainable and more likely to be used consistently in real-world settings (Stirman et al., 2013). The *BEAT* provides a cognitive shortcut that makes recall easier in high-stress moments, increasing the likelihood that the strategy will actually be applied.

Beyond Burnout Practice: Take a BEAT

Purpose: This exercise helps you practice pausing in the moment and checking in with yourself using the BEAT framework. It's especially helpful when you're feeling overwhelmed, disconnected, or tempted to fall into an old pattern of avoidance or reactivity.
You can do this seated, standing, or lying down—whatever feels most supportive.

Step 1: Ground Yourself in the Present

Take a few slow, intentional breaths. Feel your feet on the ground or your body supported by the chair. Let your shoulders drop away from your ears. Notice that you are here, now. When you're ready, move through each part of the BEAT check in slowly and mindfully.

B—Body Sensations

- What physical sensations are you noticing in your body right now?
- Are you holding tension anywhere—jaw, shoulders, chest, stomach?
- Is your breath shallow or deep?
- Is your heart racing or steady?
  Just observe. Notice what's present.

E—Emotions

- What emotions are coming up in this moment?
- Can you name the feeling(s)—anger, sadness, fear, guilt, shame, joy, boredom, etc.?
- How intense is the emotion on a scale from 1 to 10?
  If nothing comes up right away, that's okay. Stay curious. See if anything begins to surface.

A—Action Urges

- What are you feeling pulled to do right now?
- Is there an urge to escape, shut down, lash out, numb out, or avoid?

- Is there an urge to fix, overexplain, apologize, or withdraw? Name the urge without acting on it. You're just noticing.

T—Thoughts

- What thoughts are running through your mind right now?
- Are there any "should" or "always/never" statements?
- Any assumptions, judgments, worries, or beliefs about yourself or others?
- You don't need to change them. Just observe your thoughts like clouds passing through the sky.

Step 2: Gentle Reflection

Now that you've named your BEAT, take a moment to reflect:

- What was it like to slow down and check in?
- Did anything surprise you?
- Was there a pattern or theme in your internal experience?
- Do you notice more space between your experience and your response?

Practice taking a BEAT during everyday moments, not just during distress. The more you practice, the easier it becomes to access this tool when you really need it.

Clinical Vignette: Maria

Maria is a 42-year-old elementary school teacher who had been in the profession for nearly two decades. Teaching had once been her passion. She loved shaping young minds, building connections with her students, and fostering a sense of curiosity and joy in learning. But in recent years, her job has shifted from being fulfilling to fear-laden.

Like many public-school teachers, Maria had long been overworked and underpaid. She had navigated large class sizes, shifting curriculum demands, and the constant expectation to do more with fewer resources. While these challenges were exhausting, they had never shaken her deep commitment to her students. What had changed in recent years was the relentless fear that her school could become the next site of a mass shooting.

The rise in school violence not only accelerated her burnout but also took a heavy toll on her mental health. She experienced intrusive thoughts and vivid mental images of a school shooting in her classroom—children screaming, chaos everywhere, bodies injured, or worse. The more she tried to push these thoughts away, the more often they came back.

Where she had once felt deeply connected to her students, Maria now feared getting too close. Forming bonds with them only to lose them in a violent act felt unbearable. During active shooter drills, her heart pounded, her hands trembled, and dread overtook her. She began calling out sick on drill days, unable to endure the reenactment of a nightmare that already played on repeat in her mind.

To cope, Maria began drinking nightly. What started as a glass of wine to take the edge off turned into multiple drinks, numbing her fear for a few hours but leaving her with headaches and heavier dread the next morning. She also compulsively checked the news for reports of school shootings and other violent events. Her social media algorithm began feeding her a steady stream of tragedies. She told herself she was "staying informed," but deep down, she knew that it only reinforced her sense of helplessness. These strategies, alcohol use, doomscrolling, and emotional distance are examples of *experiential avoidance*, a process strongly linked with anxiety, depression, and substance misuse (Hayes et al., 1996; Chawla & Ostafin, 2007).

Maria's experience revealed how easily a control agenda can take over. Her energy went into avoiding fear rather than living in alignment with her values. The alcohol, doomscrolling, and withdrawal from students were all unworkable strategies: They offered short-term relief but deepened her distress over time. Avoidance made sense, no one should have to live with the threat of mass shootings, especially in schools, but it kept her outside her window of tolerance (Siegel, 1999). She swung between hyperarousal and collapse.

Jumping straight into mindfulness often overwhelmed her system, so we began with grounding. Grounding, unlike mindfulness, isn't about opening fully to thoughts and emotions. It's about anchoring to the here-and-now through sensory cues so the nervous system can shift out of threat mode and reestablish a sense of safety in the body. Research has found that grounding techniques can reduce acute distress, improve emotional regulation, and interrupt dissociative spirals by reorienting attention to immediate sensory input (Najmi et al., 2015; Schauer & Elbert, 2010). For Maria, this meant starting with simple anchors like noticing her feet pressing onto the floor before inviting in more awareness of her internal world.

This stepwise approach allowed her to gradually move from unwillingness to tentative willingness. By staying within her window of tolerance, she was able to practice noticing rather than reacting, making space for more workable strategies. Ones that didn't promise instant escape but did move her toward the life she wanted. Over time, she began to understand that her avoidance was not a personal failure but a creative survival strategy that had simply stopped serving her.

Beyond Burnout Practice: Soles of the Feet Meditation

Purpose: The Soles of the Feet Meditation is a grounding technique that uses physical sensations to steady your nervous system and bring you back into your *window of tolerance*—the zone where you can think, feel, and respond effectively. Unlike mindfulness, which invites full openness to your inner experience, grounding first focuses on stability and safety, making it especially useful when distress feels overwhelming or intrusive thoughts are too intense to face directly.

Step 1: Set Your Intention

Find a comfortable position sitting, standing, or lying down. If you're sitting, place your feet flat on the floor. If you're standing, let your weight settle evenly between both feet. If you're lying down or unable to place feet on the floor, you can adapt by focusing on other points of grounding (e.g., your back against the chair, hands resting in your lap, or the feel of a weighted blanket).
Remind yourself:

- This practice is not about getting rid of feelings but about finding an anchor to steady yourself.
- You are not trying to change your thoughts, only shifting your focus to a different point of awareness.

Step 2: Shift Attention to Your Feet (or Another Grounding Point)

Gently bring your awareness to your feet or the part of your body you've chosen as your anchor. Notice where they make contact with the ground, floor, or support surface. Sense pressure, warmth, coolness, or other sensations. Explore sensations in more detail. Wiggle your toes (or fingers if using hands as your anchor). Feel texture, weight, and contact points. Notice any subtle changes as you shift position.

Step 3: Engage Your Breath

Breathe naturally while maintaining focus on your anchor point. With each inhale, imagine the breath traveling to that point. With each exhale, imagine releasing tension into the support beneath you.

Step 4: Return to Your Anchor

Keep focusing on your anchor as thoughts and emotions come and go. When an intrusive or judgmental thought arises, acknowledge it gently: "I see you, thought."
Each time you feel pulled away, return to the anchor point, noticing the sensation in your feet or your contact point.

Step 5: Bringing It into Your Life

This practice is portable and adaptable:

- During a difficult meeting (look down at your feet or focus on your hands on your lap).
- While navigating a tense conversation with someone you find triggering.
- When overwhelmed in public spaces.
- While lying in bed with racing thoughts.

Reflection Questions

- What did you notice?
- How did your thoughts or emotions shift during the practice?
- What was it like to use this technique in a challenging situation or with a modified anchor?
- How might you know when you're out of your window of tolerance and ready to use this?

Supporting Maria begins with clarifying that acceptance does not mean condoning or resigning to tragedy. Her thoughts and fears are understandable responses to very real dangers, but struggling against them has only deepened her suffering (Hayes et al., 2012). In CFT, compassion involves validating the protective role of the threat system while cultivating a kinder, more balanced relationship with the mind (Gilbert, 2009).

Rather than continuing the exhausting battle to suppress or control her thoughts, Maria practiced shifting her relationship with them. One simple exercise we used was *Thank You, Mind* (Harris, 2019), which invites noticing thoughts as mental events rather than facts, with a touch of kindness for the mind's efforts to protect. Over time, this created space for Maria to act from her values rather than her fear.

Beyond Burnout Practice: Thank You, Mind

Purpose: This practice helps you step out of the exhausting struggle with your thoughts. Instead of trying to suppress, argue with, or believe every thought, you'll learn to acknowledge them with kindness and distance. In ACT, this is called defusion, a core skill for building psychological flexibility.

Step 1: Get Grounded

Sit or stand in a comfortable position. Take a slow breath. Feel the weight of your body on the chair or floor. If it helps, close your eyes.

Step 2: Bring to Mind a Difficult Thought, Feeling, or Situation

Choose something that's been showing up lately maybe a fear, judgment, or intrusive image. Pick something real, but not so intense that it overwhelms you.
Examples:

- "Something terrible is going to happen at work."
- "I'm not strong enough to handle this."
- "I'm so embarrassed about my presentation last week."
- "What's wrong with me?"

Step 3: Notice It as a Thought or Emotion

See it for what it is: A sentence, an image, a mental event, a memory, or a fleeting feeling. You don't have to believe it or push it away. Just notice it.

Step 4: Say Gently

"Thank you, mind."
Or, if it feels right:

- "Thank you, mind, for trying to protect me."
- "Thank you, mind, for working so hard."
- "Thank you, mind, I see you."

This isn't agreement or approval. It's simply acknowledging your mind's attempt to help you survive.

Step 5: Return to the Present

Bring your attention back to your body, your breath, your feet on the ground, or sounds around you. Let the thought stay or go. There's nothing to fix. Then, turn to the next small, workable action in front of you.
If "thank you" feels sarcastic or forced, try a neutral tone: "Okay, mind," or "Noted." With practice, the tone often softens into something more compassionate, like speaking to a well-intentioned friend who doesn't always give the most helpful advice.

Welcoming the unwanted is not about liking your pain or pretending it doesn't hurt. It's about recognizing that struggle with your inner world often amplifies suffering, while openness creates the possibility of freedom. Each time you ground yourself, each time you turn toward an anxious thought or a wave of grief with even a sliver of kindness, you are reclaiming energy that once went into battle.

This practice is slow and imperfect. You will forget, resist, and fall back into old patterns. And yet, every moment of willingness plants a seed. Over time, these seeds grow into resilience a steadier nervous system, a broader window of tolerance, and a clearer path back to your values.

References

Bargh, J. A., & Chartrand, T. L. (1999). The unbearable automaticity of being. *American Psychologist*, 54(7), 462–479. https://doi.org/10.1037/0003-066X.54.7.462

Black, D. S., & Slavich, G. M. (2016). Mindfulness meditation and the immune system: A systematic review of randomized controlled trials. *Annals of the New York Academy of Sciences*, 1373(1), 13–24. https://doi.org/10.1111/nyas.12998

Brown, K. W., Goodman, R. J., & Inzlicht, M. (2013). Dispositional mindfulness and the attenuation of neural responses to emotional stimuli. *Social Cognitive and Affective Neuroscience*, 8(1), 93–99. https://doi.org/10.1093/scan/nss004

Chawla, N., & Ostafin, B. (2007). Experiential avoidance as a functional dimensional approach to psychopathology: An empirical review. *Journal of Clinical Psychology*, 63(9), 871–890. https://doi.org/10.1002/jclp.20400

DeLapp, R. C. T. (2025). *Empower yourself against racial and cultural stress: Using skills from the REACH program to cope, heal, and thrive*. Guilford Press. https://www.guilford.com/books/Empower-Yourself-Against-Racial-and-Cultural-Stress/Ryan-T-DeLapp/9781462553082

Gilbert, P. (2009). *The compassionate mind: A new approach to life's challenges*. Constable & Robinson.

Good, D. J., Lyddy, C. J., Glomb, T. M., Bono, J. E., Brown, K. W., Duffy, M. K., Baer, R. A., Brewer, J. A., & Lazar, S. W. (2016). Contemplating mindfulness at work: An integrative review. Journal of Management, 42(1), 114–142. https://doi.org/10.1177/0149206315617003

Gu, J., Strauss, C., Bond, R., & Cavanagh, K. (2015). How do mindfulness-based cognitive therapy and mindfulness-based stress reduction improve mental health and wellbeing? A systematic review and meta-analysis. *Clinical Psychology Review*, 37, 1–12. https://doi.org/10.1016/j.cpr.2015.01.006

Harris, R. (2019). *ACT made simple: An easy-to-read primer on acceptance and commitment therapy* (2nd ed.). New Harbinger.

Hayes, S. C., Strosahl, K. D., & Wilson, K. G. (2012). *Acceptance and commitment therapy: The process and practice of mindful change* (2nd ed.). Guilford Press.

Hayes, S. C., Wilson, K. G., Gifford, E. V., Follette, V. M., & Strosahl, K. (1996). Experiential avoidance and behavioral disorders: A functional dimensional approach to diagnosis and treatment. *Journal of Consulting and Clinical Psychology*, 64(6), 1152–1168. https://doi.org/10.1037/0022-006X.64.6.1152

Hölzel, B. K., Lazar, S. W., Gard, T., Schuman-Olivier, Z., Vago, D. R., & Ott, U. (2011). How does mindfulness meditation work? Proposing mechanisms of action from a conceptual and neural perspective. *Perspectives on Psychological Science*, 6(6), 537–559. https://doi.org/10.1177/1745691611419671

Kabat-Zinn, J. (1990). *Full catastrophe living: Using the wisdom of your body and mind to face stress, pain, and illness*. Delacorte.

Kazantzis, N., Whittington, C., & Dattilio, F. (2010). Meta-analysis of homework effects in cognitive and behavioral therapy: A replication and extension. *Clinical Psychology: Science and Practice*, 17(2), 144–156. https://doi.org/10.1111/j.1468-2850.2010.01204.x

Khoury, B., Lecomte, T., Fortin, G., Masse, M., Therien, P., Bouchard, V., Chapleau, M.-A., Paquin, K., & Hofmann, S. G. (2013). Mindfulness-based therapy: A comprehensive meta-analysis. *Clinical Psychology Review, 33*(6), 763–771. https://doi.org/10.1016/j.cpr.2013.05.005

Najmi, S., Riemann, B. C., Wegner, D. M., & Nock, M. K. (2015). Thought suppression and self-injurious thoughts and behaviors. *Behaviour Research and Therapy, 69,* 9–17. https://doi.org/10.1016/j.brat.2015.03.013

Neff, K. D., & Germer, C. K. (2013). A pilot study and randomized controlled trial of the Mindful Self-Compassion program. Journal of Clinical Psychology, 69(1), 28–44. https://doi.org/10.1002/jclp.21923

Schauer, M., & Elbert, T. (2010). Dissociation following traumatic stress: Etiology and treatment. *Zeitschrift für Psychologie/Journal of Psychology, 218*(2), 109–127. https://doi.org/10.1027/0044-3409/a000018

Shapiro, S. L., Carlson, L. E., Astin, J. A., & Freedman, B. (2006). Mechanisms of mindfulness. Journal of Clinical Psychology, 62(3), 373–386. https://doi.org/10.1002/jclp.20237

Siegel, D. J. (1999). *The developing mind: Toward a neurobiology of interpersonal experience.* Guilford Press.

Stirman, S. W., Miller, C. J., Toder, K., & Calloway, A. (2013). Development of a framework and coding system for modifications and adaptations of evidence-based interventions. *Implementation Science, 8,* 65. https://doi.org/10.1186/1748-5908-8-65

Tol, W. A., Leku, M. R., Lakin, D. P., Carswell, K., Augustinavicius, J., Adaku, A., Brown, F. L., Garcia-Moreno, C., Musci, R., Ventevogel, P., White, R. G., & van Ommeren, M. (2020). Guided self-help to reduce psychological distress in South Sudanese female refugees in Uganda: A cluster randomised trial. *The Lancet Global Health, 8*(2), e254–e263. https://doi.org/10.1016/S2214-109X(19)30504-2

Treleaven, D. A. (2018). *Trauma-sensitive mindfulness: Practices for safe and transformative healing.* W. W. Norton.

Twohig, M. P., & Levin, M. E. (2017). Acceptance and commitment therapy as a treatment for anxiety and depression: A review. *Psychiatric Clinics of North America, 40*(4), 751–770. https://doi.org/10.1016/j.psc.2017.08.009

Wegner, D. M. (1994). Ironic processes of mental control. *Psychological Review, 101*(1), 34–52. https://doi.org/10.1037/0033-295X.101.1.34

Chapter 7

Step 3

Watch Your Words

I truly believe in the transformative power of words. In fact, I've bet my career on words' ability to heal. As a therapist, I've spent countless hours providing talk therapy because language is one of the most powerful tools humans have. It connects us, expresses love, shares knowledge, and imagines futures that don't yet exist. But ACT reminds us that language is a double-edged sword: It can entrap or liberate us, depending on how we wield it and how we relate to the words in our minds (Hayes et al., 2012). Words can also wound, spreading misinformation, fueling propaganda, and reinforcing hate and division. On an individual level, words can activate our threat system, feed self-criticism, and keep us stuck in burnout narratives. Like a machete, language can clear a path or become a weapon. The task here is to learn to use words as guides, not as instruments of harm. We'll take a three-step approach to transforming your relationship with language.

1. **Spot and swap threat-based language.** First, we'll identify words and phrases that inadvertently activate your internal alarm system, drawing on CFT's three-system model of threat, drive, and soothing systems (Gilbert, 2014). Then, we'll explore compassionate word swaps, language that reduces threat and evokes more care, both internally and relationally.
2. **Break free from burnout-amplifying habits.** Next, we'll examine the language habits that sustain burnout, such as venting and complaining. While these can offer short-term relief, over time, they reinforce negative narratives and entrench stress cycles. You'll learn compassionate, action-oriented alternatives that help you process stress without getting stuck in it.
3. **Practice defusion.** Finally, we'll turn to one of ACT's most powerful tools: Defusion. Specifically, we'll focus on cognitive defusion, learning to step back from words, phrases, and stories that narrate your inner world (Hayes et al., 2012). By observing painful thoughts as just words,

DOI: 10.4324/9781003640592-10

not facts, you can create more space between yourself and your burnout narrative, fostering greater flexibility and resilience.

Let's begin by tuning in to how you speak to yourself.

Spot and Swap Threat-Based Language

Certain phrases we use every day can trigger our threat system, activating guilt, shame, fear, or self-criticism. These expressions often reflect rigid thinking, unspoken demands, or internalized expectations. The first step is to notice them. The second is to offer yourself more flexible, compassionate, and values-aligned alternatives.

Before we dive into specific word swaps, it helps to ask: Why does language have the power to activate our threat system in the first place? According to RFT, one of the theoretical foundations of ACT, our minds do not simply store words as isolated definitions; instead, we build complex webs of meaning based on history, context, and associations (Hayes et al., 2001). For example:

- The word *failure* might instantly bring up memories of rejection, shame, or inadequacy, even when no one is criticizing you in that moment.
- Saying *I should be doing more* may trigger guilt and pressure because your brain has learned to associate *should* with performance and expectations.

This process, called *derived relational responding*, describes our ability to relate things through language even without direct experience. It allows us to plan, imagine, empathize, and learn abstract concepts. But it also means that a single word or phrase can cue up a cascade of emotional responses (Törneke, 2010). In other words, language doesn't just describe reality. It shapes it. That's why seemingly innocent thoughts like *I have to do everything* or *I'm so behind* can feel heavy, activating, and even paralyzing.

The goal here isn't to censor your language or plaster affirmations over everything. It's to become more aware of how the words you use impact your nervous system. Once you can see the effect clearly, you can begin making gentle, intentional shifts that support well-being rather than unknowingly fueling burnout.

The Problem with "Have Tos"

We throw around *have tos* all day long: *I have to go to work. I have to update my CV. I have to do laundry.* But this tiny phrase packs a serious psychological punch.

It Communicates Obligation, Not Choice

Have to implies an unbreakable rule, a looming consequence, or even a threat. It removes personal agency. Research shows that the perception of low control and high demand is central to burnout risk (Schaufeli et al., 2009). When everything feels obligatory, life begins to feel like a series of burdens.

The Beyond Burnout Blueprint invites us to reclaim choice and possibility even when options aren't perfect. In reality, very few things are true survival *have tos*: Breathing, eating, drinking, sleeping, and eliminating waste. Ironically, many people sacrifice these genuine needs in service of things they only *think* they "have to" do.

Of course, choices come with consequences. If you don't go to work, you may lose income or face reprimand. If you don't do laundry, your clothes may smell or wrinkle. But underneath most *have tos* lies a values-based choice waiting to be reclaimed:

- "I choose to go to work because earning an income allows me to support my family."
- "I choose to finish this project because it aligns with my career goals."
- "I want to do laundry because I feel better in clean clothes."

It Robs You of Credit

Another subtle cost of *have to* language is that it minimizes your effort. High achievers often dismiss their accomplishments because they "had to" do them. I've seen professionals work 10-hour shifts, respond to crises, hold space for others, and neglect their own needs, yet say, "I did nothing today." If it wasn't optional, it doesn't "count." Meanwhile, their real *have tos*—eating, resting, caring for their body often get ignored, leaving them depleted.

Shifting from *have to* toward *choose to, get to,* or *want to* doesn't mean pretending everything is joyful. It means reclaiming agency and reconnecting with your values. It also helps you give yourself credit for the effort you're already making, while making space for the actual non-negotiables of being human: Rest, care, and nourishment.

Beyond Burnout Exercise: Reclaiming Your Choices

Purpose: To notice where "have to" language shows up in your daily life, uncover the real consequences and values underneath, and reframe those statements to restore agency, flexibility, and self-compassion.

Step 1: Spot Your "Have Tos"

Write down five things you often tell yourself you have to do.
Examples: Finish that grant proposal, respond to emails, cook dinner,
exercise, update your CV.

_____

_____

_____

_____

_____

_____

Step 2: Find the Consequence and Value

For each "have to," briefly note:

- What happens if I don't do this?
- Is that consequence real or internalized pressure?
- What value might be underneath it?

Example:
Have to: Finish the grant application
If I don't: I miss the deadline and lose a funding opportunity
Underlying value: Career growth, impact, financial stability
Now write your own:

Have to: _____
If I don't: _____
Value: _____

Have to: _____
If I don't: _____
Value: _____

Have to: _____
If I don't: _____
Value: _____

Have to: _____
If I don't: _____
Value: _____

Have to: _____
If I don't: _____
Value: _____

Step 3: Reframe with Agency

Rewrite each "have to" using choice-based language: I choose to . . .
I want to . . . I get to . . . It's important to me that . . .
Example:
"I have to go to work" → "I choose to go to work because contributing to my team and supporting my family matter to me."
Now write your own:

I have to _____ → I choose to/want to/get to
_____ because _____.
I have to _____ → I choose to/want to/get to
_____ because _____.
I have to _____ → I choose to/want to/get to
_____ because _____.
I have to _____ → I choose to/want to/get to
_____ because _____.
I have to _____ → I choose to/want to/get to
_____ because _____.

Reflection

Which reframes felt most freeing? Did anything surprise you?

The Shame Spiral of "Should"

If *have to* activates obligation, *should* activates shame. *Should* statements often reflect internalized societal messages about what we must do to be acceptable, successful, or worthy (Beck, 1976). Whether it's the pressure to be more productive, patient, or perfect, *should* language keeps us hustling for worthiness and judging ourselves harshly when we fall short.

From a CFT perspective, *should* activates the drive system. The part that seeks improvement and achievement. But when barriers like fatigue or overwhelm interfere, the threat system takes over, triggering self-criticism and shame spirals (Gilbert, 2014).

- **Forward-facing shoulds:** "I should be working", "I should go to the gym"—these create guilt when unmet, leaving us stuck between inaction and shame.
- **Backward-facing should/should not haves:** "I shouldn't have said that", "I should have already finished this brief", "I shouldn't have eaten that"—these keep us locked in regret and rumination rather than growth.

The antidote is choice and compassion. Instead of berating yourself, choose fully: If you're resting, *really* rest; if you're working, engage fully. Choosing all the way interrupts the shame spiral and restores a sense of agency.

Beyond Burnout Exercise: Shedding the "Shoulds"

Purpose: To recognize the impact of "should" and "should not" language on your nervous system, uncover the values or fears underneath, and practice replacing "shoulds" with empowered, intentional choices.

Step 1: Notice the Shoulds

Take a moment to scan your day, week, or current to-do list. What are the "should" and "should not" statements floating around in your head or coming out of your mouth?
Examples:

- I should be further along in my career.
- I should call them back.
- I shouldn't have said anything in that meeting.
- I shouldn't feel this way.

Write three to five of your own below:
I should

_____

I should

_____

I shouldn't

_____

I should

_____

I shouldn't

_____

Step 2: Pause and Decode

Pick one "should" or "should not" that feels particularly charged. Gently reflect on the following:

- What emotion does this "should" bring up for me? (e.g., guilt, anxiety, shame, frustration)
- What value or need might be underneath it? (e.g., connection, competence, rest, security)
- Am I feeling pressure to perform, belong, or prove something?

- Is there a part of me that's trying to help, even if the message is harsh?

Example:
"Should" or "should not" *statement*: "I should be working on that paper"
Emotion it triggers: Guilt, anxiety
Underlying value: Contribution, competence
What this part of you is trying to protect or do: Keeps me from falling behind.
Now try this with one of your own:
Your "should" or "should not" statement:

_____

Emotion it triggers: _____
Underlying value: _____
What this part of you is trying to protect or do:

Step 3: Reframe with Choice

Now, rewrite that same sentence using empowered, compassionate language:
Try:

- "I choose to . . ."
- "It's important to me that I . . ."
- "Right now, I'm choosing to . . ."
- "I notice the urge to ___, and I'm giving myself permission to ___."

Examples:

- "I should call them back" → "It's important to me to reconnect—I'll reach out when I have the capacity."
- "I shouldn't have skipped my workout" → "I chose to rest today, and I can choose movement again tomorrow."

Now you try:
"I should/shouldn't _____" →
"I choose to/I want to/It's important to me that
I _____"

Step 4: Choose All the Way

If you're caught in "I should be doing ___ but I'm actually doing ___," pause and ask yourself:

- Do I want to keep doing this current activity?
- If yes, can I choose it wholeheartedly?
- If not, what small, values-based action could I take next?

Reflection

- What did you notice about your "shoulds"?
- How does it feel to reframe them with choice and compassion?
- What happens when you fully commit to your current choice, whether it's work or rest?

The Great Invalidation: "But"

Next up in our language detox is a sneaky little word with a big emotional impact: *But.*

But is the great invalidator. Whether we're using it in our self-talk or in our relationships, *but* often negates whatever came before it. It cuts off nuance, replaces connection with contradiction, and subtly communicates: *That first thing you said? It doesn't really matter.*

- *Interpersonally, but* can shut people down: "I know you're upset, but I didn't mean it that way." "You did a great job, but you seemed really nervous." Even when we mean well, *but* tends to create defensiveness because it signals that one truth is trying to cancel out another (Schröder et al., 2017).
- *Internally, but* can invalidate your own experience: "I'm grateful for this opportunity, but I'm exhausted." "I had time to rest today, but I didn't get anything done." These thought patterns feed shame and self-criticism (Gilbert, 2014; Hayes et al., 2012).

Dialectical Behavior Therapy (DBT), a third-wave behavioral therapy developed by Marsha Linehan, combines cognitive-behavioral strategies with mindfulness practices and emphasizes *dialectical thinking* or the ability to hold two seemingly opposing truths at the same time (Linehan, 1993). You can do your best *and* still want to do better. You can love your family *and* feel overwhelmed by them. You can be grateful for your job *and* be completely burnt out.

What if you replaced *but* with *and*? This simple swap validates multiple truths, creating space for complexity, compassion, and growth. Unlike *but*, *and* doesn't force you to choose one truth over another. It honors the full emotional spectrum of your human experience.

- Instead of: "I'm grateful for my job, but I'm overwhelmed."

  Try: "I'm grateful for my job, <u>and</u> I'm overwhelmed."

- Instead of: "I had time to rest, but I didn't get anything done."

  Try: "I had time to rest, <u>and</u> I didn't get to my to-do list."

Beyond Burnout Exercise: But Detox

Purpose: To notice when "but" invalidates your experience (or someone else's) and practice replacing it with more compassionate, dialectical language like "and," "while," or "it's also true that" . . .

Step 1: Notice Your "But" Habits

Reflect on how you use "but" in self-talk, relationships, or at work. Examples:

- "I'm proud of myself, but I still didn't do enough."
- "I hear you, but that's not what I meant."

Write down a few "but" statements you've said or heard:

_____

_____

_____

Step 2: Catch the Invalidation

For each statement, ask yourself:

- What gets dismissed or minimized when you use the word "but"? Are there two truths that deserve space?
- How might it feel to hear this?

Step 3: Reframe with "And" or Similar

Rewrite each sentence using and, while, or it's also true that . . . Example:

"I'm grateful for my job, but I'm overwhelmed." → "I'm grateful for my job, and I'm overwhelmed."

Your turn:

_____ → _____

_____ → _____

_____ → _____

Step 4: Reflect

- What do you notice about how "but" changes the meaning?
- How did it feel to replace it with "and" or another alternative?
- Where in your life could you use more "both/and" thinking?

The Reflexive Shield: "I'm Sorry"

Another common form of threat-based language is *I'm sorry*. For many of us, especially women and people from marginalized identities, apologizing has been conditioned as a form of self-protection (Holmes, 1989; Majeed & Bullock, 2021). Anticipating criticism, rejection, or even mild disappointment, we reflexively say *sorry* to soften ourselves, appear non-threatening, and avoid conflict.

Here's the trouble with chronic apologizing:

1. *It reinforces shame and unworthiness.* Apologizing for existing communicates that simply taking up space requires justification.
2. *It undermines presence and authority.* Over-apologizing can diminish your confidence and the weight of your words, even when you're completely valid (MacGeorge et al., 2003).
3. *It dilutes genuine repair.* When *sorry* becomes reflexive, it loses power. Real apologies for harm, broken trust, or missed responsibilities may no longer land with sincerity.

Instead of apologizing automatically, try these empowered alternatives:

- "Thank you (for your patience, your candor, your time)."
- "I appreciate your understanding."
- "Let me clarify . . ."
- If an apology is warranted: "I apologize for [specific behavior]. Is there anything I can do to make it right?/I'll be mindful of that in the future/ It won't happen again."

Examples:

- "I'm sorry I'm late." → "Thanks for waiting. I appreciate your patience."
- "I'm sorry for asking." → "Thank you for considering this."
- "I'm sorry I'm such a mess today." → "It's a tough day. I appreciate your being here with me."

You're not wrong for saying sorry. It likely grew from a real need for safety. But you don't have to carry that reflex into every room and relationship.

Beyond Burnout Exercise: Sorry Detox

Purpose: Identify patterns of reflexive apologizing, understand what they're protecting, and practice replacing them with grounded, values-based communication.

Step 1: Spot the "Sorry"

Write down a few times you've said "I'm sorry" when no real apology was needed. Think about emails, meetings, texts, or casual conversations.
Examples:

- Sorry for the delay.
- Sorry, I just have a quick question.
- Sorry I'm talking so much.
- Sorry for being emotional.

Your turn:

_____

_____

_____

_____

_____

Step 2: Decode the Message

Choose one example from above and reflect:

- What was I really trying to express or protect?
- Was I avoiding conflict, judgment, or taking up space?
- What value or need might be underneath this?

Example:
Sorry statement: "Sorry for the delay."
What I meant: "I appreciate your patience."
What I was protecting: Avoiding looking unprofessional.
Underlying value: Respect, reliability, connection.
Your turn:
Sorry statement: _____
What I meant: _____
What I was protecting: _____
Underlying value: _____

Step 3: Reframe with Power and Presence

Rewrite your reflexive "sorry" into language that's clear, kind, and rooted in values.

Examples:

- "Sorry I'm late." → "Thank you for waiting—I appreciate your patience."
- "Sorry, I just have a quick question." → "I have a quick question—thanks for your time."
- "Sorry I'm being emotional." → "I'm feeling a lot right now, and I appreciate you holding space."

Your turn:

	→	
	→	
	→	

Step 4: Reflect and Reset

- How does chronic apologizing show up in your life?
- Where do you think it came from?
- What would it look like to communicate your needs, boundaries, or presence without apologizing for them?

Dealing in Absolutes: The Language of "Always" and "Never"

Let's end our language detox with one of the most burnout-amplifying habits of all: Speaking in absolutes.

"I always get passed over."

"No one ever notices what I do."

"Everyone else is handling it better."

"I can't do anything right."

These statements feel heavy and definitive, as if nothing could change. They're also incredibly common when we're in burnout or threat mode. Again, our brain's *negativity bias* wires us to notice, remember, and generalize negative experiences more strongly than positive ones (Rozin & Royzman, 2001). From an evolutionary standpoint, this bias helped us survive, but today, it often turns momentary stress into sweeping, painful narratives.

The noticing may be automatic, but the *language* is what amplifies it. When fleeting emotions get wrapped in absolute terms, they sound like permanent truths. "I feel overwhelmed today" becomes "I'm always overwhelmed." "This task is hard" becomes "I never do anything right." At that point, we're no longer describing a feeling. We're fusing with a story that feels fixed and global.

To loosen the grip of absolutes, we need a two-part shift that is explained in the next two sections.

Zoom In on Painful Absolutes

When you catch yourself using "always," "never" or other generalized language, get specific. What exactly happened? When? Who was involved? What did you feel? Specificity turns a sweeping judgment into a concrete, workable experience.

- "I always get ignored."
  - "Yesterday, during the 2 p.m. meeting, I didn't feel heard when I shared my idea."
- "I'm just burnt out."
  - "Right now, I'm feeling emotionally and physically drained after a week of back-to-back clients."
- "No one ever supports me."
  - "Last week, when I shared that I was struggling, I didn't feel like my supervisor was available to help."

Zoom Out and Savor Positive Moments

Just as we narrow in on pain, we can also *widen our lens* on positives. Too often, when we have pleasant experiences that don't confirm our negativity bias, we dismiss them as flukes; "my boss thanked me, but they were just being nice." Positive psychology research shows that rather than dismissing these experiences, deliberately expanding and *savoring* these moments build lasting resilience.

Savoring is the practice of noticing, appreciating, and prolonging positive experiences. Unlike mere pleasure, savoring is active. It means paying attention to what feels good and letting yourself fully experience it (Bryant & Veroff, 2007). You might:

- Pause to replay a compliment in your mind.
- Share a success story with a trusted colleague or friend.
- Journal about a moment of gratitude at the end of the day.
- Close your eyes and take a deep breath to let an acknowledgment or thank-you really sink in.

Psychologist Dr. Barbara Fredrickson's *Broaden-and-Build Theory* is foundational within Positive psychology *and* shows why this noticing, savoring, and zooming out matter. Positive emotions don't just feel good in the moment; they broaden our perspective and, over time, build enduring psychological, social, and cognitive resources (Fredrickson, 2001, 2013). When we savor and stretch positive moments, we counteract the attentional narrowing of burnout and weave a more balanced, sustaining story.

- "They only acknowledged me in today's meeting because Becky is out."
  - "Over the past few months, I've received positive feedback from several colleagues. I want to take a moment to let myself enjoy how good it feels to be recognized."
- "That client thanked me, but that never happens."
  - "My client expressed gratitude for my support. I can pause to really feel the meaning in those words."
- "I guess today went okay, but it was probably a fluke."
  - "Recently, I've had several days where things flowed well, and I felt grounded. I'm going to notice how steady and calm that feels."

This practice isn't about toxic positivity or denying pain. It's about disrupting global, threat-based language and making space for the full range of your experiences. When you *zoom in* on pain, it becomes specific and workable. When you *zoom out* and savor positives, they become part of the larger story you get to believe.

Beyond Burnout Practice: Zoom In, Zoom Out, and Savor

Purpose: Challenge absolute, threat-based language by zooming in on specific moments and zooming out to notice patterns of support, success, or value. Then, deepen the impact of positive experiences by savoring them, allowing them to broaden your perspective and build lasting resilience.

Step 1: Spot the Absolutes

Write down a few recent thoughts that use absolute or globalizing language (always, never, no one, everyone, I am . . .).
Examples:

- I always mess things up.
- No one ever helps me.
- I'm just not cut out for this.

Your turn:

_____

_____

_____

_____

_____

Step 2: Zoom In (Make It Specific)

Pick one statement and get specific:

- When exactly did this happen?
- Who was involved?
- What was the situation or context?
- How did you feel in that moment?

Example:
Absolute: "I always get ignored."
Zoom In: "Yesterday in the 12 p.m. team meeting, I shared an idea and no one responded. I felt dismissed and frustrated."
Your turn:
Absolute: _____
Zoom In: _____

Step 3: Zoom Out (Balance the View)

Challenge the absolute by widening your lens:

- Have there been times when this wasn't true?
- Have you received support, appreciation, or success that you've minimized?
- What evidence balances the narrative?

Example:
"I've had other meetings where my ideas were well-received. Last month, my supervisor praised my input during a presentation."
Your turn:
Zoom Out: _____

Step 4: Savor (Broaden and Build)

Practice savoring: Intentionally noticing and amplifying the good. Try one of these methods with the positive moment you just identified:

- Pause and replay it in your mind.
- Name what specifically felt good.
- Share it with a trusted friend or colleague.
- Take a deep breath and let the feeling sink in.

Example:
"When my supervisor praised me last month, I felt seen and valued. I'm going to pause, take a breath, and really let myself appreciate that acknowledgment."
Your turn:
Savoring practice: _____

Step 5: Reflect

- How did it feel to zoom in and name one clear moment?
- What shifted when you zoomed out to see the broader picture?
- What happened when you paused to savor the positive experience?
- How might this help you relate differently to your burnout story?

Break Free from Burnout-Amplifying Habits

When we're in peak burnout, our communication often falls into a familiar trifecta: Venting, reassurance seeking, and complaining. In these moments, our words become less about connection and more about control in our attempts to discharge pain, anger, or exhaustion without addressing the deeper needs beneath them.

In burnout, we may feel angry, helpless, invisible, or unappreciated. Instead of sitting with those painful emotions or clarifying our unmet needs, we instinctively pass the emotional hot potato through these burnout-inducing communication habits. These strategies can bring short-term relief, and, in small doses, they can even increase bonding and closeness, sometimes through oxytocin release (Wirth, 2015). But, as with most medicines, the dose makes the poison. When venting becomes chronic, repetitive, or reflexive, it stops helping us process emotions and starts trapping us in rumination (Bushman, 2002; Nils & Rimé, 2012).

Instead of loosening the grip of burnout, the story we tell gets reinforced. We minimize evidence that contradicts our pain, magnify evidence that confirms it, and harden into a role, of being the overlooked, disrespected, or unappreciated one.

As a recovering ventaholic, I know this pattern well. After long workdays, I would start dialing my friend's phone number before I even made it out of the parking lot and would bombard her with my gripes of the day. I replayed every slight, every disappointment, every way I felt undervalued. Beneath the venting was a painful core belief: *I'm the workhorse, not the show pony. I get things done, but I'm not polished or prestigious enough to be celebrated or compensated the way my colleagues are.*

The more I told that story, the truer it felt. My brain built a well-developed neural pathway, one grievance at a time. My friend, wanting to be supportive, validated my pain, but what I heard was confirmation that all my worst assumptions were undeniable truths. This created an echo chamber where outrage drowned out nuance and agency. Instead of helping me move through the pain, repeating it just kept me spinning in it. This doesn't mean my perception wasn't understandable. It means venting didn't release the pain. It amplified it.

To be clear, this isn't about sitting down, shutting up, or silently suffering. Nor is it about tone policing or discouraging voices that challenge injustice. Seeking support, asserting boundaries, and speaking truth to power are critical, especially in systems marked by inequity. Your voice matters. Your anger can be sacred. Your frustration can be fuel. The key difference is *intentionality*.

When we're on burnout autopilot, our threat system drives us into fight-or-flight: We lash out or shut down, blame or disengage. These reactions are human but often ineffective. The goal isn't to suppress your voice; it's to choose how, when, and why you use it.

This conversation carries added complexity for those at the intersection of multiple marginalized identities. Women, people of color, queer folks, and especially Black women are too often criticized, dismissed, or punished for speaking up even when they are assertive, clear, and justified (Wingfield, 2019). To be clear: This is not about code-switching or conforming to dominant norms that silence or dehumanize. It's about using your voice in ways that are effective, authentic, and values-driven, so your energy and truth land in ways that serve you.

Beyond Burnout Exercise: Venting Versus Values-Based Expression

Purpose: Increase awareness of emotional habits and shift from reactive venting to intentional, values-aligned communication.

Step 1: Reflect on a Recent Venting Moment

Think of a time you vented to a friend, coworker, or partner.

- What did you say or share?
- What emotion(s) were you feeling?
- What did you need or want underneath that emotion?
- Did venting help move you toward getting that need met, or did it keep you stuck?

Step 2: Try a Reframe

What could you have said if you had paused, grounded yourself, and spoken with intention and values in mind?

Examples:

Venting: "I'm so sick of no one listening to me in meetings."

→ Values-based reframe: "It's important to me that my contributions are heard. Can you help me think through how to assert that more clearly?"

Venting: "I'm always doing everything and no one helps."

→ Values-based reframe: "I'm feeling overwhelmed and just need some space to share what's on my mind before I start brainstorming solutions. Would you be willing to hear me out?"

Venting: "I hate how they treat me. They don't respect me."

→ Values-based reframe: "I'm noticing a pattern that's painful, and I want to find a way to advocate for myself while staying aligned with my integrity."

Your turn:

Venting: _____

→ Values-based reframe: _____

From Complaining to Communicating: Don't Let Burnout Speak for You

We all know that one person at work who's always complaining. Their negativity starts to feel contagious, shifting team energy from engaged to defeated. The harder truth? Sometimes, we don't realize when *we've* become that person.

Burnout has a way of making everything feel personal, global, and permanent. When we're living in threat mode, our communication tilts toward sweeping blame, cynical criticism, and nonconstructive feedback. The concerns may be real, but the delivery is often ungrounded, unfiltered, and ineffective. It feels good in the moment, but it rarely creates change. I know because I've been there.

A colleague and friend once experienced harassment at our workplace. I had a strong emotional reaction to how it was handled. I was hurt on her behalf, worried about what it signaled to the rest of our staff about safety and accountability, and deeply triggered by my own history of sexual trauma. Memories of not being believed, not being protected, and not feeling safe were reawakened in my nervous system.

My feedback was valid. My concerns were real. But my communication? Dysregulated AF. I didn't just speak up. I raged up. I cc'd the entire leadership team and launched what can only be described as a multi-email, all-caps spiritual indictment of the institution. I invoked patriarchy, white supremacy, institutional betrayal, every layer of injustice I had ever witnessed or endured. In the subtext of those emails, I laid bare my unprocessed scars around harm and silence.

The frameworks weren't wrong, but my delivery came out condemning and, frankly, self-righteous. There was space for dialogue. There may even have been willingness to listen. But I missed it, blinded by the fog of activation. And there were consequences.

Afterward, I felt embarrassed for a long time, not days or weeks, but months and years. Even now, nearly half a decade later and on the other side of the country, I sometimes cringe when it comes to mind. Relationships I had worked hard to build were permanently altered.

Sometimes, there is no speaking up without risk. Even if I had communicated skillfully, there still could have been backlash. But the irreparable damage wasn't caused by *what* I said, it was caused by *how* I said it. That distinction has stayed with me, not as shame but as wisdom. I don't regret taking the risk. I don't regret using my voice. I do regret going scorched earth.

The truth I was trying to express was buried beneath a storm of blame and pain that couldn't be metabolized by the people who most needed to hear it. With distance and a lot more self-compassion, I can see it for what it was: My email crusade was a control strategy. The situation didn't just make me angry. It also flooded me with fear, shame, and sadness from an earlier chapter of my life. Instead of making space for those emotions, I tried to control them by controlling others. It was experiential avoidance dressed up as moral fire.

Yet, beneath the reaction, there were values: Justice, safety, advocacy, voice, and friendship. I wanted to be effective. I wanted to be heard. I wanted to stand up for my friend. All of that was true. But because I was in threat mode, the avoidance hijacked the values. Instead of leading with intention, I led with intensity. And the clarity of my message got lost in the chaos of my delivery.

This is why learning to speak up without spiraling matters. Your voice deserves to be heard. Not just echoed in your own head, but received. And you already have the tools to do it. Many of the strategies you've practiced to manage burnout like grounding, willingness, mindfulness from Step 2 of the Blueprint (Welcome the Unwanted) are the very same tools that help you slow down, regulate, and communicate with clarity instead of reactivity.

Once grounded, that's your moment to reach for burnout word swaps: Those small but mighty language shifts that disarm your threat system and create space for intention. Looking back at the emails I regret, they were riddled with *shoulds, have tos, buts, sweeping absolutes,* and more than a few *sorry-not-sorrys.*

But now, you have a different option. You can pause. You can choose language that reflects your growth, not just your grievance. And even more, you can return to Step 1 of *the Beyond Burnout Blueprint*: Your compelling vision.

- Who are you becoming on the other side of burnout?
- What does the Beyond Burnout version of you sound like when you speak up?
- How do you want people to feel when you give feedback, advocate for change, or stand up to power?
- What do you want to stand for?
- What impact do you want your words to leave behind?

This isn't about being perfect. It's about being intentional. It's about using your words as instruments of alignment, advocacy, and authenticity.

Beyond Burnout Exercise: Speak Up Without Spiraling

Purpose: Practice speaking up about what truly matters to you in a way that reflects your values, even when emotions are running high.

Step 1: Reflect on a Time You Spoke Up and Regretted It

Think of a time when you voiced something important but felt it didn't go well. Maybe your tone was sharper than intended, the message got lost in emotion, or it caused a rupture.

- What happened?
- What was I trying to protect? (e.g., integrity, my boundaries, someone else, safety)
- What was I trying to change or ask for?
- What emotions were fueling my words? (e.g., anger, helplessness, grief, shame)
- How did I feel afterward? (e.g., proud, embarrassed, dismissed)
- Was my message grounded in values, or overtaken by pain or avoidance?

Step 2: Language Check

Looking back, did I use burnout-triggering language?

- Should
- Have to
- But

- Sorry (reflexive)
- Absolutes (always, never, no one, everyone, I am . . .)

Note any that applied:

_____

_____

Step 3: Reimagine the Moment

If I were grounded in my values and regulated in my nervous system, how might I have expressed this?
Old version:

_____

New version (values-based, intentional):

_____

What would I want my words to do, not just express? (e.g., inform, invite change, set a boundary, advocate for justice)

_____

_____

Step 4: Anchor the Lesson

This experience taught me that:

_____

Next time I feel emotionally activated but compelled to speak, I can:

- Take a breath.
- Identify what I'm feeling.
- Clarify the value I want to speak from.
- Check for burnout-triggering language.
- Speak with both courage and clarity.

Practice Defusion

ACT is full of paradoxes, and here comes another one. I've just spent most of this chapter talking about the incredible, transformative, burnout-buffering power of your words. And now I'm going to tell you . . . your words are also completely meaningless.

That's right. Words are just sounds. Just letters. Just symbols. They only have the power we give them. And sometimes, we give them way too much.

Think of words as spells. Across cultures, incantations, chants, and mantras have long been believed to shape reality. Modern science shows something similar: The placebo and nocebo effects reveal how our beliefs and expectations, often carried through words, can trigger measurable changes in pain, healing, and physical functioning (Colloca & Barsky, 2020). In other words, it isn't the words themselves that carry power. It's the meaning and belief we attach to them. I see cognitive defusion, one of ACT's core processes, as a way to break these spells, a practice that loosens the grip of words so they no longer dictate our reality.

Clinical Vignette: Benny

Benny's story illustrates how burnout can intertwine with trauma and moral injury. Moral injury occurs when experiences in high-stakes environments violate a person's core values, leading to shame, guilt, and a sense of betrayal that can contribute to post-traumatic stress (Litz et al., 2009). Benny, a frontline health-care worker in a New York City hospital during the first wave of COVID-19, carried all of these burdens at once. Like so many of his colleagues, he showed clear signs of burnout alongside post-traumatic stress disorder (PTSD) symptoms: Nightmares, hypervigilance, numbness, and intense emotional reactivity.

What stood out most was the weight he placed on a single word: *Hero*. Everyone was calling him a hero, his family members, leadership, the news, even strangers who dropped off pizza and ice cream with "thank you healthcare heroes" signs. But Benny didn't feel proud. He felt furious, guilty, and ashamed.

"I'm no hero," he told me. He had watched person after person die, often feeling overwhelmed, under-resourced, and misinformed. He resented being separated from his wife. He envied the "nonessential" workers at home, posting TikToks and banging pots and pans.

When the hospital began playing *Empire State of Mind* over the hospital's loud speaker every time a patient was discharged, what was meant to be uplifting felt like a gut punch to Benny. At first, few patients survived to hear it. Later, when survival improved, the song played daily but for Benny, it only deepened the wound. Soon, even the word *New York,* central to the chorus of the song, triggered a full-body reaction.

I didn't try to convince him he was a hero. Instead, we worked on defusion practices: Creating space between Benny and the words fused with his trauma. We started small:

- "I'm having the thought: I'm not a hero."
- "I'm having the feeling of anger."
- "I'm noticing the tension in my hands and jaw."

These small linguistic shifts helped Benny *observe* his experience rather than be consumed by it. We named the loop his *Anti-Hero Story*. From there, we worked directly with the triggers: Slowing the song to half speed until the words lost their shape, looking at the sheet music as symbols, even reading the lyrics backwards. Step by step, we stripped the spell-like power from the language.

Defusion didn't erase Benny's pain, but it loosened its grip. The word *hero* and the sound of *Empire State of Mind* no longer dictated his reaction. He could notice the surge of thoughts, sensations, and emotions and still choose how to respond.

Breaking the Spell: The Practice of Defusion

Words can feel like incantations, but they only carry the power we grant them. Defusion is the practice of breaking the spell. It doesn't mean silencing or suppressing thoughts. It means changing our relationship to them.

Here are a few simple ways to practice:

- Prefixing thoughts with "I'm having the thought that . . ."
- Saying a loaded word slowly until it loses meaning.
- Naming the thought or thought pattern.
- Seeing words as sounds, shapes, or ink on a page.

The goal isn't to eliminate thoughts, but to see them for what they are—sounds and symbols, not truths or commands.

Words are everything, and they are nothing. They can wound, heal, deceive, or inspire. But ultimately, they are not you. They are not your values. They are not your future. When you break the spell, you get to choose what story you live.

Beyond Burnout Practice: Breaking the Spell with Thought Defusion

Purpose: Shift your relationship to difficult thoughts so they feel less like commands or truths and more like what they are—just words. This creates space to move toward your values without being pulled off course by your inner narrative.

Step 1: Name the Thought

Bring to mind a thought that's been hooking you lately something that fuels self-doubt, shame, overwhelm, or burnout.
Write it exactly as it shows up:

_____

_____

_____

Step 2: Create Distance

Reframe the thought using one of these phrases:

- "I'm having the thought that _____."
- "I notice I'm telling myself the story that _____."

This small shift moves you from being inside the thought to noticing it from the outside.

Step 3: Label the Pattern

What kind of thought is it—self-criticism, fear, burnout script?
"This sounds like my _____ story."
(e.g., "My imposter syndrome loop," "My 'never enough' script")
If it feels right, give it a nickname or persona. Humor can loosen its grip but be gentle if the thought is tied to deeper pain.

Step 4: Play with It

If it's not too raw or triggering, try:

- *Saying it in a cartoon or robot voice*
- *Repeating it quickly until it sounds like nonsense*
- *Whispering it, stretching it out, or imagining it in helium voice*

This reminds you it's just a sound in your mind.

Step 5: Watch It Drift By

Visualize the thought floating past you like leaves on a stream, clouds in the sky, a text bubble fading away, a subtitle scrolling off-screen, or a song lyric playing in the background. Notice that you're still here, and the thought has already moved on.

Reflection

- What shifted when you stopped fighting the thought?
- How did it feel in your body before and after?
- Where could you use this skill in your daily life?

There's no one-size-fits-all defusion technique. Experiment. Notice what helps. You can mix, match, or invent your own. What works may change from day to day or thought to thought. Some will find that compassion softens the edges; others will need irreverence to snap out of the spell. The point is choice. Notice your thoughts. Name them. Play with them. Thank them for trying to protect you. Then return to the present moment and what matters most.

Burnout has a way of stealing our voice, twisting it into complaint, collapsing it into silence, or turning it against ourselves. The work we've done here is about finding our way back to language that feels like us.

This is what it means to *Watch Your Words*. Not to police yourself, but to stay awake to how your language shapes your reality. It's about noticing the stories you tell, loosening the ones that keep you stuck, and choosing words that move you closer to the life you want to live.

References

Beck, A. T. (1976). *Cognitive therapy and the emotional disorders*. International Universities Press.

Bryant, F. B., & Veroff, J. (2007). Savoring: A new model of positive experience. Lawrence Erlbaum Associates, Publishers.

Bushman, B. J. (2002). Does venting anger feed or extinguish the flame? Catharsis, rumination, distraction, anger, and aggressive responding. *Personality and Social Psychology Bulletin, 28*(6), 724–731. https://doi.org/10.1177/0146167202289002

Colloca, L., & Barsky, A. J. (2020). Placebo and nocebo effects. *New England Journal of Medicine, 382*(6), 554–561. https://doi.org/10.1056/NEJMra1907805

Fredrickson, B. L. (2001). The role of positive emotions in positive psychology: The broaden-and-build theory of positive emotions. *American Psychologist, 56*(3), 218–226. https://doi.org/10.1037/0003-066X.56.3.218

Fredrickson, B. L. (2013). Positive emotions broaden and build. In J. M. Olson & M. P. Zanna (Eds.), *Advances in experimental social psychology* (Vol. 47, pp. 1–53). Academic Press. https://doi.org/10.1016/B978-0-12-407236-7.00001-2

Gilbert, P. (2014). The origins and nature of compassion focused therapy. *British Journal of Clinical Psychology, 53*(1), 6–41. https://doi.org/10.1111/bjc.12043

Hayes, S. C., Barnes-Holmes, D., & Roche, B. (2001). *Relational frame theory: A post-Skinnerian account of human language and cognition*. Kluwer Academic/Plenum.

Hayes, S. C., Strosahl, K. D., & Wilson, K. G. (2012). *Acceptance and commitment therapy: The process and practice of mindful change* (2nd ed.). Guilford Press.

Holmes, J. (1989). Sex differences and apologies: One aspect of communicative competence. Applied Linguistics, 10(2), 194–213. https://doi.org/10.1093/applin/10.2.194

Linehan, M. M. (1993). Cognitive-behavioral treatment of borderline personality disorder. Guilford Press.

Litz, B. T., Stein, N., Delaney, E., Lebowitz, L., Nash, W. P., Silva, C., & Maguen, S. (2009). Moral injury and moral repair in war veterans: A preliminary model and intervention strategy. *Clinical Psychology Review, 29*(8), 695–706. https://doi.org/10.1016/j.cpr.2009.07.003

MacGeorge, E. L., Graves, A. R., Feng, B., Gillihan, S. J., & Burleson, B. R. (2003). The myth of supportive communication competence. Human Communication Research, 29(3), 377–398. https://doi.org/10.1111/j.1468-2958.2003.tb00845.x

Majeed, N. M., & Bullock, M. (2021). How race and gender shape the dynamics of apologizing. Social Psychological and Personality Science, 12(5), 823–832. https://doi.org/10.1177/1948550620947354

Nils, F., & Rimé, B. (2012). Beyond the myth of venting: Social sharing modes determine the benefits of emotional disclosure. *European Journal of Social Psychology*, 42(6), 672–681. https://doi.org/10.1002/ejsp.1880

Rozin, P., & Royzman, E. B. (2001). Negativity bias, negativity dominance, and contagion. Personality and Social Psychology Review, 5(4), 296–320. https://doi.org/10.1207/S15327957PSPR0504_2

Schaufeli, W. B., Bakker, A. B., & Van Rhenen, W. (2009). How changes in job demands and resources predict burnout, work engagement, and sickness absenteeism. Journal of Organizational Behavior, 30(7), 893–917. https://doi.org/10.1002/job.595

Schröder, T., Dawel, A., & Kehoe, J. (2017). The influence of language on interpersonal evaluations: The case of "but." *Journal of Language and Social Psychology*, 36(1), 3–21.

Törneke, P. (2010). *Learning RFT: An introduction to relational frame theory and its clinical application.* New Harbinger Publications.

Wirth, M. M. (2015). Hormones, stress, and social support: The underpinnings of oxytocin and venting. *Social and Personality Psychology Compass*, 9(6), 315–325. https://doi.org/10.1111/spc3.12175

Wingfield, A. H. (2019). *Flatlining: Race, work, and health care in the new economy.* University of California Press.

Chapter 8

Step 4

Identify Your Unique Gifts

This step in *the Beyond Burnout Blueprint* is about something deceptively simple but profoundly transformative: Recognizing your unique gifts. It is an opportunity to amplify what is already strong within us. But before we can do that, we must first learn to see our strengths clearly and name them without hesitation. For many of us, this is the hardest part.

Many of us were never taught how to claim our strengths without apology. In fact, women and those from historically marginalized identities are often socially conditioned to downplay what makes them powerful. Research shows that women, in particular, are more likely to attribute success to external factors and to hesitate in self-promotion, a pattern influenced by cultural norms around modesty and gender roles (Exley & Kessler, 2019; Rudman, 1998). We are taught to wait for external validation from someone with more authority or power to tell us what we are good at. We shrink under the guise of humility. We mistake the acknowledgment of our strengths as arrogance rather than accuracy.

Reclaiming your gifts is not about ego; it is about alignment. It is about stepping fully into who you are and what you are here to contribute. Positive psychology research supports that identifying and using one's strengths foster greater well-being, engagement, and resilience in both personal and professional domains (Niemiec, 2013; Seligman et al., 2005).

Despite working in a largely female-dominated field, I was not immune to this conditioning, and neither were my colleagues. During a gender equity panel I participated in at a large academic medical center, we explored this paradox directly. We were a panel of women in a department that was mostly female yet still contending with deeply entrenched inequities, reminders that systemic and cultural barriers persist even in spaces where women are numerically in the majority (Carnes et al., 2008).

We spoke candidly about the persistent and systemic barriers to women's equity in our workplace: Lack of representation in senior leadership positions, inequitable distribution of emotional and administrative labor,

DOI: 10.4324/9781003640592-11

vague or ineffective policies, and ongoing experiences of harassment and dismissal.

I had been asked to provide the final remarks at the panel. I wanted to offer something that felt empowering, compassionate, and forward-moving, but I struggled. I wanted to inspire others, but I also found myself caught in that familiar tangle of doubt. I felt the pull to self-minimize, to qualify my authority, to be careful not to take up too much space. I found myself editing and softening the truth of what I wanted to say.

During preparation, one of my colleagues noticed I was struggling with the draft. She challenged me to speak to my strengths plainly, a request that felt deeply uncomfortable, but necessary. Here's the version I ultimately delivered: It began with a quote from Gloria Steinem: *The truth will set you free, but first it will piss you off* (Steinem, 1992, p. 25).

And this was the truth I shared:

Today we have heard experiences from our colleagues that are upsetting and unfair—we have heard from women in the Department of Psychiatry; our friends and colleagues that they have been injured, ignored, demeaned, and passed over largely because of their gender.

The experiences may feel shocking to you, or familiar. Either way, I imagine feeling "pissed off" may be a likely emotional state for many in this room. However, you relate to what has been shared, this is the truth.

Accepting that we are not as far along as we should be, or want to be, is vitally important. Even the most well-intentioned among us are deeply embedded in a system of patriarchal values that are not easy to extract ourselves from. To acknowledge who and where we are is the first liberating step of becoming who we want to be.

When sharing a draft of this closing statement with my co-panelists, one of my fearless and eternally optimistic colleagues pulled me aside and gently confronted me about how my draft was peppered with self-deprecation and self-doubt. She called upon me to use this opportunity to speak to my strengths, my abilities, and the value I bring to the department.

When she challenged me to this, I felt embarrassed to even think of standing in front of a room full of colleagues and rattling off my attributes. How conceited would I sound? How out of context? How would I come off?

And then I thought of my daughter.

My amazing daughter Lily, who the nurses described as "defiant" when she came into this world screaming, flailing, and wild. Lily's favorite thing in the world is to pretend she's a dinosaur—including growling and chasing after people. I won't lie and say I haven't gotten a call or two about her biting a fellow toddler at daycare, to which she justifiably exclaims, "Grrr, I am dinosaur."

If I fast forward a decade or two, while I pray she is no longer biting people, I will be devastated if she loses her unapologetic strength and confidence, which has been ever-present from her first seconds on this planet. I hope that if she were challenged to speak to her strengths in front of a room full of people, she would do so proudly and without reservation. And I would hope that she wouldn't have to be coaxed to speak about herself at all, because she would never undermine her own power.

While there may be no one better equipped to shatter the glass ceiling than my daughter the dinosaur, I hope she doesn't have to. I hope people like myself, and all of you in this room, can help change what it means to be a woman in power. I hope we can prevent her from internalizing the thousands of direct and indirect messages about how a woman must conceal and downplay their own worth.

Like all of you, I have to start with myself.

So, my name is Shaina Siber. For the past several years I have been honored to serve as the Director of Ambulatory Psychiatry and Emergency Services where I have administrative and clinical oversight of multiple programs. I have developed the Department's Social Work Academy, the first program in this hospital to be recognized as an accredited continuing education provider for New York State Department of Education for social workers. I have initiated the Social Work Wellness Committee to increase training, support, and serve as a mechanism for burnout prevention for social work staff. I am one of very few social workers that lectures in the psychiatry residency training programs and have worked extensively to expand knowledge and competency in working with gender-diverse patients all throughout the department. I have been closely involved in curriculum development for Structural Humility and LGBTQ+ Care. I am routinely called upon because I am knowledgeable, hardworking, and work tirelessly to hold on to both the clinical and administrative frames when exercising decision-making. I am committed to enhancing our patients' experience and providing support to our staff, and most of the time, in the face of great systemic barriers—I do a damn good job.

After I leave work every day, I move to what's affectionately referred to as the second shift, where I pick up, bathe, feed, play with, and read to my two joyful, messy children, usually alone, as my husband works nights as a doorman. After the kids are tucked away, and my six-year-old son comes up to ask for water or to use the bathroom no less than seven–eight times, I start what I less affectionately call the third shift—where I finish the professional work of the day, sometimes to ungodly hours of the night. This is typically when I see many of my female colleagues too—responding to emails, submitting drafts, finalizing projects.

This ongoing cycle of care and commitment has never let up and neither have I, no matter the shift or season. My work ethic hasn't wavered, not through growing programs or growing children. But what I'm realizing now is that it's time to extend that same care and commitment to myself.

So, the commitment I make to myself today is this: I will advocate for myself related to my worth, I will speak up when I witness or experience gender-based microaggressions, and I will push through my fear of overstepping the invisible line of who I am expected to be. I know confronting these truths about myself is essential to facilitating change, not only for me, but to shift the culture for my female colleagues who hold less privilege in the system than I do.

My hope is that initiating this important dialogue is a first step in crystallizing our vision for the future of our department. A future in which transparent action is taken to ensure equal pay, and to close gender-based wage gaps. A future in which women do not carry the immense pressure of repeatedly proving their worth. A future in which women in power positions are not constantly plagued with trying to fit in an impossible and ever-narrowing space between not being taken seriously and not being likable. A future in which "office housework" including office birthdays, filing, taking notes, and answering the phones is not automatically assigned to the women of the workplace. A future in which we have strict and effective policies for harassment, that serve to prevent and eradicate physical, sexual, and emotional injury to our female colleagues. A future in which all women of a certain age aren't assumed to be on the verge of a family medical leave. A future in which being a mother is not used as an evaluative measure of a woman's professional commitment. A future in which we call out and interrupt gender bias when we see it and when we experience it, without fear of judgment or repercussion. A future in which women are empowered to showcase their skills, competency, and knowledge without apology.

Arriving at this future requires an honest look inward to examine the attitudes that make daily life for women more challenging. We must take inventory of the systemic practices around hiring, promotions, the delineation of work responsibilities, the provision of feedback and ensure these practices are aligned with our mission to promote gender equity. We must take responsibility for how we interact with and talk about women in the workplace—in their presence and in their absence. And we, as women, must see where we may be holding ourselves back.

I invite you to get pissed off with me and to use these feelings of anger and disappointment as a call to action.

I was blown away by the feedback I received after giving this speech. While I had intellectually known I wasn't alone in these feelings, I realized in that moment just how much I had been carrying an emotional disconnect. I believed that perhaps I was the only one struggling to speak my value out loud. The response made something undeniably clear: This wasn't just my experience. It was something collective.

And it wasn't only the women in the room. The discomfort, the exhaustion, the simultaneous pressure to perform and to shrink, it was everywhere. That's when it hit me: Discovering your strengths is not simply a professional exercise; it is an act of resistance against years of social conditioning that taught many of us to downplay our abilities, wait for permission, and confuse humility with self-erasure.

Research shows that women and members of marginalized groups are disproportionately penalized for behaviors that deviate from traditional stereotypes of modesty and deference (Rudman, 1998; Williams & Tiedens, 2016). Over time, this conditioning can lead to self-silencing including suppressing authentic self-expression to maintain relationships or avoid conflict (Jack & Ali, 2010).

Reclaiming our strengths means disrupting these patterns. It means refusing to wait for external validation or for someone in power to grant us permission. That recognition begins with us.

Beyond Burnout Exercise: What Would You Say If You Weren't Afraid to Take Up Space?

Purpose: This exercise is designed to help you dismantle internalized messages about staying small, silent, or self-effacing. Burnout thrives in environments where your worth goes unnamed by others or yourself. By naming your strengths, reclaiming your voice, and embracing your impact, you begin to heal from burnout and move toward a life anchored in authenticity and courage.

Reflection Prompts

What strengths have you been waiting for someone else to name for you?

_____

_____

_____

What stories have you told yourself or absorbed from others about why you shouldn't speak about your value?

_____

_____

_____

If you could stand up in front of a room and share your truth, what would you say about the work you do, the person you are, and the value you bring?

_____

_____

_____

What kind of example do you want to set for the people who are watching you—your children, your peers, your younger self?

_____

_____

_____

We tend to think of strengths as the qualities others have validated. We think of them as what we've been praised or paid for, the accolades on our resumes, the skills noted in performance reviews, or LinkedIn headlines. Yet, some of our most essential strengths never appear in those places.

Many strengths go unrecognized not because they aren't real, but because they are so deeply embedded in who we are that we overlook them. They feel too natural to count. We assume, *doesn't everyone do this?* Often, the answer is no.

Sometimes, our strengths are not only unseen but also misinterpreted. Assertiveness is labeled aggression. Sensitivity is dismissed as weakness. Emotional depth is reduced to overreacting. Creativity is cast as impractical. The very qualities that make us powerful, intuitive, or visionary are often misunderstood by those who don't value them. And because we often wait for people in authority to reflect our strengths back to us, we may never hear them spoken aloud. That doesn't mean they aren't there.

Clues to our strengths can be found not only in feedback or job titles but also in the moments when we feel most ourselves. Psychologist Mihaly Csikszentmihalyi (1990) described these experiences as *flow states*, when we are so absorbed in what we're doing that time seems to disappear. Flow is not always effortless, but it is deeply engaging, a signal that we are working in natural alignment with our values and abilities. Neurobiologically, flow involves what is called *transient hypofrontality*, a temporary quieting of the prefrontal cortex, the part of the brain responsible for self-criticism and time awareness. In simpler terms, it's when the mental chatter that judges and second-guesses us takes a back seat. At the same time, the brain releases a cocktail of chemicals like dopamine, norepinephrine, and endorphins, which sharpen focus, fuel motivation, and create a sense of energy and enjoyment (Dietrich, 2004; Ulrich et al., 2014). Flow tends to occur when challenge and skill are closely matched, pushing the brain into a state of optimal performance.

To begin uncovering your strengths, it helps to ask: *When do I feel most alive or focused? What tasks make me forget to check the clock? What challenges feel invigorating rather than draining?* The answers often reveal not just what you can do but also how you show up when you are at your best.

Beyond Burnout Exercise: Follow the Flow

Purpose: Sometimes, our strengths are hiding in plain sight, tucked into what we enjoy, what comes naturally, or what holds our attention without effort. Use these questions to explore the rhythms of your energy, curiosity, and growth.

Part 1: What Comes Easy to Me?

- What are three things I do that feel natural or intuitive but I've never thought of as a strength?
- What do people come to me for help with, even outside of my job description?
- What feels "light" to me that seems difficult or overwhelming to others?

Part 2: What Do I Like to Do?

- What kinds of tasks or interactions make me feel energized afterward?
- When I think about my favorite part of a workday or project, what is it?

Part 3: What Puts Me in a Flow State?

- When do I lose track of time?
- What type of problem-solving or creativity pulls me in, even when it's challenging?
- When have I felt fully "in it"—clear, focused, alive?

Part 4: What I'm Curious to Learn More About?

- What topics or skills do I find myself researching, bookmarking, or thinking about at night?
- If I had a completely free day, what would I choose to learn or explore?
- If I weren't afraid of failing, what new area would I dive into?

Part 5: Look for Patterns

- Jot down anything that surprised you.
- Notice where there's an overlap between what comes easy, what you enjoy, and what excites your curiosity.
- Ask yourself: Where in my life or work am I already doing these things and where might I want to do more of them?

The Oaktree Within the Acorn

You don't have to be the best at something for it to be your gift. It doesn't need a trophy, a platform, or a published piece to be real. Gifts don't usually show up fully polished. Sometimes, they sit quietly for years, like an acorn holding the promise of a giant oak tree. The potential is there from the start, it just needs some care, a little attention, and space to grow.

For me, one of those gifts has been words, spoken and written, but it took me decades to own it. Writing didn't feel like a gift when it was tied to academic essays or journal articles (I did plenty of those and hated every minute). It showed up in something smaller and more personal: Emails. Emails that made complicated things clearer. Emails that comforted, encouraged, or connected. Long before ChatGPT, colleagues would come to me saying, *Can you help me find the right words for this?* And most of the time, I could. My gift wasn't living in the spotlight, it was living in those everyday exchanges.

That's how gifts often work. They don't always announce themselves, and they don't need someone else's stamp of approval to count. We tend to miss them when we compare ourselves to someone else's "oak tree," already in full bloom. But no oak tree starts that way. It starts as an acorn—small, unassuming, and full of potential.

And just like an acorn, your gifts need time. You don't get mad at an acorn for not having branches yet or for not offering shade. You know that becoming a tree takes patience, care, and the right conditions. The same is true for your strengths.

Sometimes, nurturing your gifts looks messy. It means giving yourself permission to be awkward, uncertain, or imperfect while you figure it out. So if something inside you keeps tugging at your attention, a curiosity, a spark, a pull might be your acorn. Even if it's not polished. Even if no one else sees it yet. You don't need to prove it's good enough. You just need to let it grow.

Beyond Burnout Exercise: The Oaktree Within

Purpose: This exercise is an invitation to notice the gifts that may still be in acorn form—quiet, hidden, or waiting to be nurtured. Some may be sprouting already. Others may need sunlight, time, and trust.

Step 1: Remember the Acorn

Reflection Prompts

- *What's something I used to love doing as a child or teen that made me feel connected, alive, or at ease?*
- *What's a quality or skill I've quietly carried that others might not have seen or that I didn't know was valuable?*
- *Has anyone ever come to me for help with something I'm good at but don't think of as "special"?*

Step 2: Notice the Soil

Growth doesn't happen in a vacuum. For an acorn to become a tree, it needs safety, space, and nourishment. Consider what conditions helped or hindered your gift's development.

Reflection Prompts

- *What environments or people have helped this gift grow, even if just a little?*
- *Where did this part of me get stifled, ignored, or dismissed?*
- *What do I need now to help this gift take root more fully? (Time? Encouragement? Boundaries? Practice?)*

Step 3: Honor the Sprout

Whether you've been practicing this gift for years or it's just starting to emerge, your growth counts. A sprouting oak is still an oak.

Reflection Prompts

- *What's one way I've used this gift in the past year?*
- *How does this gift show up in the way I connect, lead, work, or care for others?*
- *What would it feel like to name this as a strength, even if it still feels new or vulnerable?*

Step 4: Nurture the Growth

- What's one way you can support this gift today? It doesn't have to be big.
- Water the roots. Give it sun. Speak to it kindly. Commit to one small action this week to use or protect your gift.

From Strengths to Confident Stances

By now, you've hopefully begun to name some of your strengths and maybe even dared to say them out loud. The next step is letting them shine: Creating opportunities to practice, refine, and amplify them in your daily life. One of the most important ways we do this is by stepping into confidence.

Confidence is one of the most overused and misunderstood concepts in modern culture. We're told to "just be confident," "fake it till you make it," or "stop doubting yourself," as though it's a switch we can flip.

Confidence is often defined in terms of self-efficacy, our belief in our ability to organize and carry out the actions needed to reach specific goals (Bandura, 1997). Others come to see it more as a relationship with themselves, a stance of self-trust that shapes how they move through doubt and challenge. Put simply, confidence isn't a permanent state or a personality trait you either have or don't. It's the belief that you can take the next step and figure things out along the way.

Yet, many of my clients describe confidence not as a steady belief but as a feeling they're chasing, hoping it will finally arrive once they've achieved enough or proved themselves.

Much like the myth that happiness is a lasting destination, we often chase confidence like a carrot on a string: *Once I do enough, prove enough, become enough then I'll feel confident.* But confidence doesn't arrive as a reward at the end of a to-do list. It isn't a badge of worthiness you unlock once you've stopped making mistakes. From a CFT perspective, our sense of confidence is rooted in early attachment experiences and our biological wiring for safety, connection, and survival (Gilbert, 2005, 2014). If confidence feels elusive, there is usually a very good reason.

Many of us learned to downplay ourselves as a way of staying safe in early relationships. We scanned for signs of rejection, anticipated others' needs, and silenced our own. We kept our gifts quiet so we wouldn't risk disconnecting. In this light, self-consciousness isn't weakness, it's a survival strategy, shaped by a nervous system trying to protect us (Mikulincer & Shaver, 2016).

But survival strategies aren't ideal for creating thriving personal and professional lives. You deserve confidence. And you can reclaim it not as an identity you either have or don't, but as a stance you practice and way you relate to yourself.

What Confidence Is (and Isn't)

Confidence is often confused with fearlessness, perfection, arrogance, or extroversion. It's not waiting to speak until you're 100% sure, nor is it the absence of discomfort. Confidence is a practice. A set of small, repeatable habits that build self-trust over time (Bandura, 1997). When we stop chasing the illusion of constant confidence and start practicing grounded self-belief, everything shifts. We take more values-aligned risks, collaborate more effectively, and loosen perfectionism's grip.

Habits of Confident People

Some of the habits of confident people include:

- Acting before they feel ready, knowing clarity comes through action.
- Modeling behaviors of people they respect.
- Naming and owning their strengths without minimizing them.
- Asking for help and seeing collaboration as strength, not weakness.
- Setting boundaries and saying "no" without unnecessary apology.
- Celebrating growth, not just outcomes.
- Speaking to themselves with kindness after setbacks.
- Embracing imperfection and treating failure as feedback.
- Uplifting others without seeing their success as a threat.

Building Confidence Through Personal Agency

When overwhelm or self-doubt strikes, confidence can be reclaimed by shifting focus through the three lenses of personal agency identified in Step 2 of the Blueprint, *Welcome the Unwanted*:

1. *Focus—What am I paying attention to?*

   - Am I scanning for mistakes or noticing growth?
   - Am I replaying the "not enough" story or honoring the effort I've made?

2. *Meaning—What am I telling myself this means?*

   - Does this challenge signal failure or a growth edge?
   - Does a misstep mean I don't belong or that I'm learning?

3. *Behavior—How am I showing up?*

   - Am I acting like someone I respect?
   - Am I keeping the commitments I make to myself?
   - Am I showing up with integrity and aligned with my personal values?

Confidence grows in the practice of these questions, not in the absence of fear or doubt. It isn't something you wait to feel. It's something you build, step by step.

Perfectionism: The Confidence Killer

Perfectionism is one of the fastest routes to burnout and one of the surest ways to erode confidence. When we convince ourselves we have to be great at everything, we enter a performance spiral that's unsustainable, unrewarding, and deeply isolating. It's the HOV lane to burnout, and no one wants to carpool with you there.

In part fueled by social media, cultural narratives that glorify achievement and wealth, and the weight of parental and societal expectations, perfectionism appears to be on the rise (Curran & Hill, 2019). Psychologists describe three primary forms of perfectionism (Hewitt & Flett, 1991):

1. **Self-oriented perfectionism:** Demanding perfection of yourself, setting rigid and unrealistic internal standards.
2. **Socially prescribed perfectionism:** Believing that others expect perfection from you, often rooted in fear of rejection or negative comparison.
3. **Other-oriented perfectionism:** Imposing unrealistic expectations on others, which can lead to strained relationships and chronic dissatisfaction.

You may recognize yourself in one or in all of these. But no matter the form, perfectionism has a cost. It kills collaboration. When we're striving to be all things to all people, there's no room to ask for help, share the load, or let others shine. The unintended message is that we don't trust others to contribute meaningfully. Over time, that makes us less connected, less creative, and less enjoyable to work with.

And here's the truth: An acorn will never grow into a lemon tree. It's not meant to. In the same way, you're not meant to master every skill or role. You're meant to grow in alignment with your own gifts. The more you pressure yourself to be everything, the further you drift from the things you are actually built to become.

For me, one of those lessons came through my writing. My brain works fast often in hyper-focused bursts. I can synthesize information, generate ideas, and build something cohesive out of chaos in a short amount of time. That speed, that intensity, that's one of my gifts. But here's what I'm not: Polished. I'm not the person who will triple-check for typos or catch every missing word. Things that require advanced organizational skills and attention to detail are not in my wheelhouse. Editing slows me down in a way that feels like cognitive glue.

For years, I treated that gap as a flaw to fix. I worked closely with a physician in a leadership role who almost always circled back with comments on a missing comma, an awkward phrase, or a typo. And it stung. I would rage internally: *How are you missing all the work I put into this? All you see are the mistakes.*

I tried harder. I re-read drafts, slowed myself down, poured hours into catching every error. And yet, inevitably, something slipped through, and the sting came again.

Eventually, I had to face the truth: This isn't my gift. Editing isn't where I shine. It drains me. But what if that wasn't a moral failure? What if his fixation on details wasn't criticism, but contribution? He was an editor. I was an idea generator. I could produce the first draft; he could refine it. That didn't mean I was sloppy or inadequate. It meant that we were different. It meant that I didn't have to be everything.

That's when things shifted. I stopped wasting energy trying to force myself into someone else's gift and instead invested in protecting the energy I needed to use to my own benefit. Ironically, our collaboration improved because I wasn't trying to do his job. I was letting both of us bring our strengths fully to the table.

Beyond Burnout Exercise: What's Mine to Grow, What's Not Mine to Hold

Purpose: This exercise is here to help you name where perfectionism is showing up in your work or life, how it might be killing your confidence, and what you're ready to release.

Step 1: Where Is Perfectionism Showing Up?

List three areas where you feel pressure to "get it perfect" or be great at everything.
Examples: Writing, parenting, being liked at work, responding to emails, scheduling, presenting, being "low maintenance," etc.

1.
2.
3.

Now ask yourself:

- What does "perfect" look like in this area?
- What unwritten rules or standards have I created in this area?
- Why does that feel so important to me?
- Do I have this rule or standard for others?
- Who told me that's what I needed to be?
- What societal messages have influenced this belief?
- What happens (emotionally, mentally, physically) when I try to meet that standard?

Step 2: What's the Cost?

What do I lose when I aim for perfection here?

☐ Time
☐ Energy
☐ Joy
☐ Collaboration
☐ Confidence
☐ Creativity
☐ Other: _____

Is trying to be perfect here actually helping me or just keeping me from being seen, supported, or satisfied?

Step 3: Reframe the Expectation

Pick one area above and answer:

• What would it feel like to do this well, not perfectly?
• What's the core need underneath my perfectionism here? (To feel safe? Respected? Loved? In control?)
• Is there a more compassionate or collaborative way to meet that need?

Step 4: Let Something Be Not Yours

Name one task, skill, or role that you've been trying to perfect that might simply not be your strength:
"I've been trying to be good at_____, but maybe that's not mine to master."
Now reframe it:

• "Instead of trying to fix this, I can let someone else shine here."
• "My gift is _____. I want to grow that."

From Confidence to Collaboration

Once you start recognizing your own strengths, you may no longer feel like you have to hold everything. That's where both power and relief live. When you trust what you bring to the table, you can begin to celebrate what others bring too.

Understanding your own strengths doesn't just help you grow; it reframes how you see others. Instead of defaulting to comparison, you can practice appreciation. You start noticing and valuing the gifts others carry, which makes collaboration, not competition, the natural outcome. This shift moves us out of a threat state and into a more sustainable, connected, and compassionate drive (Gilbert, 2014; Edmondson, 1999).

So how do we practice this in daily life? We talk behind people's backs in the best way possible. Send a quick note to a supervisor about a colleague's contribution. Talk up the new hire. Mention how helpful Yolanda has been. Celebrate people even when they're not in the room.

When you speak kindly about others and name their strengths, you build a reputation as someone uplifting, supportive, and emotionally generous. People feel good around you, and that presence is powerful. Of course, appreciation doesn't stop behind someone's back. Don't let kind thoughts go unspoken. Shine a light on their gift and name the strength you see. Instead of "Great job," say: *You're so creative*, or *Your clarity brought order to a messy conversation.* Connect the gift to its impact: *Your creativity opened a new revenue stream* or *Your rigor caught errors before launch.*

Now flip it: What happens when the spotlight turns on you? Many of my clients feel starved for acknowledgment, but when someone finally offers it, they shut it down.

Oh, it wasn't a big deal, I could've done better, It was nothing, really.

When you deflect a compliment, it doesn't just diminish you. It can make the giver feel awkward or rejected, which discourages them from offering praise again. That reinforces the cycle of feeling unseen.

These days, I try something simple but sincere: *Wow, thank you! You just made my whole day.* Not only is that true, but also it honors the effort the other person made to notice and affirm me. While this chapter is about not relying on external validation to define your worth, acknowledgment still matters. And when you receive it well, you reinforce the behavior, making it more likely to happen again, for you and for others.

These practices don't just create a positive work culture; they activate the brain's soothing system, interrupt biases that make some people less visible, and set the stage for equity (Gilbert, 2009). This is where amplification comes in, particularly for those of us with privilege.

During the administration of President Barack Obama, the first African American president of the United States, elected in 2008 and taking office in 2009, there was a unique sense of possibility for equity and inclusion. His presidency carried enormous symbolic weight in a country with a dark history of slavery, segregation, and systemic racism. Against that backdrop, women staffers in the Obama White House noticed how often their contributions were overlooked or attributed to others, a reflection of long-standing gender inequities in politics and professional life.

To counter this, they created what became known as the "amplification pact": When a woman made a strong point, another woman would repeat it, credit her by name, and reinforce its value (Eilperin, 2016). For example: *I want to circle back to what Aisha said. Her suggestion about improving the back-end processes will save time and improve the customer experience.* This intentional practice ensured that women's voices could not be sidelined or forgotten.

In CFT terms, this is compassion flowing outward, care translated into deliberate, structural action. When you name and elevate someone's gift out loud, by name, and in front of others, you're not just being nice. You're disrupting invisibility, building psychological safety, and giving people a mirror to see what you already see in them.

Real confidence isn't just claiming your own power; it's using that power to uplift others. Recognizing and voicing both our own gifts and those of others move us from isolation to interconnectedness. This is how we move beyond burnout: By refusing to shrink, allowing ourselves to be seen, and ensuring others are seen too. Naming strengths is both a personal act of courage and a cultural intervention. Each time we speak value into the room, ours or someone else's, we plant seeds of belonging, equity, and resilience. Over time, those seeds grow into workplaces where confidence is contagious, collaboration thrives, and collective growth becomes inevitable.

References

Bandura, A. (1997). *Self-efficacy: The exercise of control.* W.H. Freeman.

Carnes, M., Morrissey, C., & Geller, S. E. (2008). Women's health and women's leadership in academic medicine: Hitting the same glass ceiling? *Journal of Women's Health, 17*(9), 1453–1462. https://doi.org/10.1089/jwh.2007.0688

Csikszentmihalyi, M. (1990). *Flow: The psychology of optimal experience.* Harper & Row.

Curran, T., & Hill, A. P. (2019). Perfectionism is increasing over time: A meta-analysis of birth cohort differences from 1989 to 2016. *Psychological Bulletin, 145*(4), 410–429. https://doi.org/10.1037/bul0000138

Dietrich, A. (2004). Neurocognitive mechanisms underlying the experience of flow. *Consciousness and Cognition, 13*(4), 746–761. https://doi.org/10.1016/j.concog.2004.07.002

Edmondson, A. (1999). Psychological safety and learning behavior in work teams. *Administrative Science Quarterly, 44*(2), 350–383. https://doi.org/10.2307/2666999

Eilperin, J. (2016, September 13). White House women want to be in the room where it happens. *The Washington Post.* https://www.washingtonpost.com/politics/white-house-women-want-to-be-in-the-room-where-it-happens/2016/09/13/14e4bafc-79dd-11e6-bd86-b7bbd53d2b5d_story.html

Exley, C. L., & Kessler, J. B. (2019). The gender gap in self-promotion. *The Quarterly Journal of Economics, 134*(3), 1623–1675. https://doi.org/10.1093/qje/qjz009

Gilbert, P. (2005). Compassion and cruelty: A biopsychosocial approach. In P. Gilbert (Ed.), *Compassion: Conceptualisations, research and use in psychotherapy* (pp. 9–74). Routledge.

Gilbert, P. (2009). *The compassionate mind: A new approach to life's challenges.* Constable & Robinson.

Gilbert, P. (2014). The origins and nature of compassion focused therapy. *British Journal of Clinical Psychology, 53*(1), 6–41. https://doi.org/10.1111/bjc.12043

Hewitt, P. L., & Flett, G. L. (1991). Perfectionism in the self and social contexts: Conceptualization, assessment, and association with psychopathology. *Journal of Personality and Social Psychology, 60*(3), 456–470. https://doi.org/10.1037/0022-3514.60.3.456

Jack, D. C., & Ali, A. (2010). *Silencing the self across cultures: Depression and gender in the social world.* Oxford University Press. https://doi.org/10.1093/acprof:oso/9780195398090.001.0001

Mikulincer, M., & Shaver, P. R. (2016). *Attachment in adulthood: Structure, dynamics, and change* (2nd ed.). Guilford Press.

Niemiec, R. M. (2013). VIA character strengths: Research and practice (The first 10 years). In H. H. Knoop & A. Delle Fave (Eds.), *Well-being and cultures: Perspectives from positive psychology* (pp. 11–29). Springer. https://doi.org/10.1007/978-94-007-4611-4_2

Rudman, L. A. (1998). Self-promotion as a risk factor for women: The costs and benefits of counterstereotypical impression management. *Journal of Personality and Social Psychology, 74*(3), 629–645. https://doi.org/10.1037/0022-3514.74.3.629

Seligman, M. E. P., Steen, T. A., Park, N., & Peterson, C. (2005). Positive psychology progress: Empirical validation of interventions. *American Psychologist, 60*(5), 410–421. https://doi.org/10.1037/0003-066X.60.5.410

Steinem, G. (1992). *Revolution from within: A book of self-esteem.* Little, Brown and Company.

Ulrich, M., Keller, J., & Grön, G. (2014). Neural signatures of experimentally induced flow experiences identified in a typical fMRI block design with BOLD imaging. *Social Cognitive and Affective Neuroscience, 9*(10), 1681–1687.

Williams, M. J., & Tiedens, L. Z. (2016). The subtle suspension of backlash: A meta-analysis of penalties for women's implicit and explicit dominance behavior. *Psychological Bulletin, 142*(2), 165–197. https://doi.org/10.1037/bul0000039

Chapter 9

Step 5

Be Kind to Yourself and Others

One of the things we talk about the least when we're suffering from burnout is how hard it is to be kind. When exhaustion sets in, kindness is often the first casualty. We stop offering warmth to ourselves or others. We snap at loved ones, go cold at work, and berate ourselves. Our minds spin stories: *They're arrogant, I'm lazy, they're out to get me, I'm an embarrassment, they're stupid.* Burnout can make it feel like us against the world, while, painfully, we aren't even on our own side.

Dr. Kristin Neff (2003, 2011), one of the leading researchers on self-compassion, identifies three core elements of self-compassion: (1) self-kindness, (2) shared humanity, and (3) mindfulness. Yet, kindness, especially when directed inward, often gets some of the worst PR imaginable.

When we turn kindness toward ourselves, we may fear it will make us lazy, weak, or self-indulgent, that it's just "making excuses." We tell ourselves that we must stay harsh to stay sharp, motivated, and worthy. Even kindness from others can be mistrusted: Brushed off as pity or, worse, suspected as manipulation. For many with histories of abuse or betrayal, kindness wasn't safe—it was a tactic, a trap, a warning sign that danger was near (Germer & Neff, 2013; Gilbert, 2014). Extending kindness outward can feel equally risky, as though softening makes us naïve or unprotected.

And sometimes, even when we try to accept or practice kindness, it hurts before it heals. This is called *backdraft*, a term borrowed from firefighting, describing what happens when oxygen hits a smoldering fire, and it flares up. Psychologically, backdraft occurs when opening the door to compassion allows old grief, anger, or shame to rush in (Neff & Germer, 2018). Backdraft isn't inevitable, though. With the regulation skills you've been practicing, staying within your window of tolerance, grounding your body, and widening your attention, you can let warmth in without being engulfed in flames. Compassion steadies the nervous system, supports clearer thinking, and strengthens relationships (Kirschner et al., 2019; Kirby et al., 2017).

DOI: 10.4324/9781003640592-12

If compassion feels complicated, you're not broken, but you're likely guarded. Most of us recruited an inner critic long ago to protect us when protection was scarce. It worked the lonely night shift, doing its best, often harshly. In this chapter, we'll unpack that protector while also giving it support: Practices that allow you to nurture yourself without abandoning self-protection.

To kick-start kindness, we'll move in two directions:

1. How to be kind to yourself (and receive kindness) even when it feels unnatural or undeserved.
2. How to extend kindness to others, especially those who frustrate you or misunderstand you while still holding firm boundaries.

Study Your Inner Critic

Before we can extend kindness toward ourselves, we need to understand the part of us that often resists it: The inner critic. The inner critic refers to the internal voice that judges, undermines, and attacks our sense of worth. From a CFT perceptive, we can see that the inner critic is not merely a bad habit but an evolved strategy linked to our survival wiring (Gilbert, 2010, 2014). CFT encourages us to transform our relationship with our inner critical voices through self-compassion, while also examining the functions it serves.

As we've discussed, our brains evolved for survival, not happiness. The threat detection system continuously scans for danger, mobilizing us to respond whether the threat is a lion in the bushes or a critical email (Gilbert, 2009; McEwen, 2007). The inner critic is essentially this same threat system turned inward. Instead of monitoring the external environment, the critic scrutinizes *you*; your behavior, emotions, and body for perceived mistakes or weaknesses that might jeopardize belonging, safety, or status. This part of you believes that it is helping by warning you before others can or by motivating you through fear and shame. Its logic is simple: If you are harsh enough with yourself, you'll stay in line, productive, lovable, and safe (Gilbert & Irons, 2005).

The inner critic works with urgency. Its goal is to hijack your attention by activating strong emotions: Anger, fear, shame, or disgust. Like a propaganda campaign, it appeals to emotion, reinforces biases, and builds a belief system about your inadequacy. It catastrophizes ("If you don't fix this, you'll lose everything"), pushes all-or-nothing thinking ("You're either perfect or worthless"), and engages in character assassination ("You're lazy. You're broken. You're a fraud"). With repetition, these attacks begin to feel like the truth.

Despite its harshness, the inner critic isn't trying to destroy you. It believes that it is protecting you from failure, rejection, humiliation, or abandonment. But threat-based motivation only works in the short term. Over time, these inner critical voices erode resilience; corrode self-trust; and fuel hypervigilance, exhaustion, and burnout (Beaumont et al., 2012; Gilbert, 2014). Safety does not come from self-punishment. Your critic may be relentless, but underneath, it is an outdated survival strategy. It doesn't hate you; it fears for you. If we want it to lower its volume, we first have to study it and then offer it a better job.

Beyond Burnout Practice: Study Your Inner Critic

Purpose: The goal of this practice is not to silence or destroy your critic. The goal is to meet it with curiosity.

Let yourself answer the following questions honestly, without judgment:

- *Who is your inner critic?*
- *How old is your inner critic? How long has it been with you?*
- *Why is it there? What is it trying to do for you?*
- *What does it sound like?*
- *Is it sharp, sarcastic, mocking, cold, urgent?*
- *Does it sound suspiciously like someone you once knew? (A parent, a teacher, a boss, a peer?)*
- *When does your inner critic get loudest? (After making mistakes? When you feel vulnerable? After a success? In moments of rest or slowing down? During conflict or risk-taking?)*
- *What is your critic trying to get you to do more of? (Work harder? Be perfect? Stay small and out of trouble? Earn love or approval?)*
- *What is it trying to get you to do less of? (Take risks? Speak your truth? Slow down and rest? Set boundaries?)*
- *In what ways has it been helpful?*
- *In what ways has it been unworkable or kept you from what's deeply important to you?*

Complete these sentences to deepen your understanding:

My inner critic sounds like:

_____

_____

My inner critic usually shows up when:

_____

_____

My inner critic wants me to do more of:

_____

_____

My inner critic wants me to do less of:

_____

_____

When I listen to my inner critic, I feel:

_____

_____

An Invitation, Not an Exorcism: Appreciating Your Inner Critic

The inner critic isn't a demon to exorcise. It is a protector caught in an outdated role. While some compassion literature encourages "befriending" the critic, that language can feel off-putting. You don't have to like your critic. But you can learn to appreciate what it has been trying to do. Think of it like routine maintenance, getting an oil change or undergoing a necessary but uncomfortable medical screening. You may not enjoy the process, but you recognize its utility. The inner critic is similar: Not pleasant, not a best friend, but a long-standing and often clumsy part of you that has been working overtime to keep you safe.

That voice, painful as it may be, often took shape early in life, echoing caregivers, teachers, cultural norms, or religious messages. Its goal was to keep you striving, acceptable, and attached (Gilbert & Irons, 2005; Gilbert, 2010). While its strategies are harsh, its motives are rooted in protection. And when we approach the critic with compassion instead of contempt, something important happens, it begins to soften. The critic doesn't disappear, but it evolves (Germer & Neff, 2013).

By now, you've studied your critic and begun to understand where it came from, what it wants, and how it has tried, however clumsily, to keep you safe. The next step is shifting its role. Seen through this lens, the critic resembles a familiar leader: The boss who means well but manages poorly. They micromanage, highlight every mistake, rarely acknowledge growth, and keep you in a constant state of fear. Many of our inner critics function this way: Overbearing managers using outdated strategies in desperate need of leadership training.

The good news is that, just as a struggling boss can improve with the right mentorship, your critic can be retrained into a trusted advisor, one who provides constructive feedback, fair evaluation, and genuine encouragement rather than constant attack. You don't have to fire your critic. You can promote it to a better role.

Beyond Burnout Exercise: Giving Your Inner Critic Leadership Training

Purpose: Imagine your inner critic as an overworked, undertrained boss who's been running your internal company with outdated methods: Fear, shame, criticism. Today, you are not firing them.
You're inviting them to leadership training. This exercise helps you reset the terms of your relationship with humor, strength, and compassion.

Step 1: Picture Your Inner Critic as a Manager

If your inner critic were a manager, what would they look like?
(Sharp suit? Frazzled clipboard? Megaphone?)
What's their leadership style?
(Micromanager? Fear-monger? Perfectionist taskmaster?)

Step 2: Identify Their Management Missteps

Think about how your critic "manages" you right now:

- What's their go-to strategy when something goes wrong?
- How do they try to "motivate" you?
- How do they react when you need rest, support, or encouragement?
- What are your inner critic's bad habits?

Step 3: Design the Leadership Training Program

Now imagine you're offering your inner critic a chance to become a better leader. A leader who builds trust, not fear.
Answer these questions:

- What new skills do they need to learn?
  (e.g., encouragement, realistic goal-setting, patience)
- What words or phrases should they start using instead of harsh criticism?
  (e.g., You're learning, Mistakes are part of growth, Your effort matters)
- What's the new vision you want them to help you pursue?
  (Thriving, not just surviving. Consistency, not perfection.)

Design a few "training goals":
Leadership Training Goals for My Inner Critic:
(1) _____
(2) _____
(3) _____

Step 4: Draft Their New Job Description

Imagine handing your inner critic a new contract.
What are the updated expectations?
Examples:

- Offer constructive feedback, not personal attacks.
- Motivate through encouragement, not fear.
- Support risk-taking and learning, not just perfect outcomes.
- Protect my well-being, not just my achievements.

Write your version:
My Inner Critic's New Job Description:

_____
_____
_____

Clinical Vignette: Alex

When I began working with Alex, he didn't name his struggle as burnout, but that's exactly what it was. He described feeling exhausted, angry, and worn down, trapped in a cycle of stress, resentment, and survival mode with no clear way out.

Alex worked as a security guard in a busy hospital where stress and danger were daily realities. His role extended far beyond checking IDs at the front desk. He was called to manage patients in agitated psychotic states, severely intoxicated individuals, grieving family members lashing out at staff, and violent altercations in overcrowded emergency rooms. He had been sworn at, threatened, shoved, and once, years earlier, seriously injured on the job.

After the injury, Alex returned to work carrying both physical and emotional scars, but he didn't feel supported. The unspoken expectation was to "toughen up and move on." Over time, resentment became his armor. It hardened him, protected him, and isolated him. But the most brutal battles were internal. Alex was furious with himself for not finishing college; angry about financial struggles; and consumed by comparisons to classmates, neighbors, and social media influencers who seemed to be living the life he wanted. His inner critic was merciless. If anyone had suggested self-compassion then, it would have felt insulting. Kindness carried risk in his world, with vulnerability experienced as diametrically opposed to safety.

Before we could begin burnout recovery, we had to redefine compassion. Alex needed to see that compassion wasn't weakness, indulgence, or letting his guard down. Instead, it was a different kind of strength: One that could soothe wounds while protecting his worth. I introduced him to Dr. Kristin Neff's framework of self-compassion, which has two faces: *Yin* and *yang*. Yin compassion is tender, nurturing, and often directed inward, comforting ourselves in pain. Yang compassion is fierce, protective, and outward, standing up for ourselves, setting boundaries, and taking action (Neff, 2016). Alex didn't have to choose between being strong and self-compassionate. True compassion could fortify him for the life he deserved (Germer & Neff, 2013).

Alex began experimenting with both sides of compassion in his daily life.

- *Yin compassion* meant acknowledging the weight he carried, grieving his injury, and offering himself gentleness he had never received: *Of course this hurts. Of course you're tired. It makes sense.*
- *Yang compassion* meant setting clearer boundaries with coworkers, advocating for himself at work, and reframing goals not as proof of worth but as investments in his future.

Healing required both: Yin tenderness to comfort his pain, and yang strength to take meaningful steps forward. For Alex, each act of compassion, soft or fierce was an act of courage.

Beyond Burnout Exercise: Finding Your Yin and Yang Response

Purpose: Think about a situation in your own life where you're feeling stuck, stressed, hurt, or overwhelmed right now. This exercise helps you explore the gentle and fiercely compassionate ways you can show up.

Step 1: Describe the Situation

- Take a few moments to bring the situation to mind.
- Briefly describe the situation you're struggling with in your own words.

Step 2: Practice Your Yin Response

Imagine responding to yourself with yin compassion—tender, soothing, nurturing.

Ask yourself:

- *What would a truly kind and understanding friend say to me right now?*
- *How can I offer myself comfort instead of criticism?*
- *How can I honor my emotional experience, without minimizing it or judging it?*

Write your Yin Response here:

_____

_____

_____

Step 3: Practice Your Yang Response

Now imagine responding with yang compassion—fierce, protective, action-oriented.
Ask yourself:

- *What boundary needs to be set here?*
- *What would standing up for myself look like?*
- *What small but powerful action could move me toward healing, strength, or justice?*

Write your Yang Response here:

_____

_____

_____

Step 4: Reflect

Which response (yin or yang) felt easier for you to access?
Which response felt harder?
What might it feel like to allow both sides to exist?

Our Inherent Worth

At first, Alex struggled to connect with compassion. Survival mode had cut him off from moments of receiving or offering it. That made sense: Compassion can feel foreign if it hasn't been safe. But compassion is less about invention than remembrance. In CFT affiliative drives, our pull toward connection, belonging, and emotional safety is considered core to being human (Gilbert, 2009, 2010). The task is not to manufacture compassion but to reconnect with it, clearing away what blocks its warmth.

Other therapies echo this truth. Internal Family Systems (IFS) identify *self-energy*—qualities such as compassion, curiosity, and calm as innate resources available beneath our defenses (Schwartz, 2013). ACT describes a similar stance as *self-as-context*: The stable sense of awareness that observes and endures beyond thoughts, feelings, or history (Hayes et al., 2011).

This deeper self is the same presence that existed the day you were born, untouched by scars or circumstances. Civil rights lawyer Bryan Stevenson, founder of the Equal Justice Initiative, has dedicated his life to advocating for people society has often discarded: Those who are incarcerated, condemned, or forgotten. Many of these individuals have not only been harmed by systemic injustice but also caused harm to others. Stevenson's work is rooted in the radical belief that even in those situations, dignity and worth remain. His call is not about denying responsibility, but about refusing to reduce a person to their worst act.

He captures this truth when he reminds us: "Each of us is more than the worst thing we've ever done" (Stevenson, 2014, p. 290). For people who feel consumed by shame or defined by failure, this statement is a lifeline. It embodies a hope that extends even to those our culture deems unworthy of redemption. In therapy, this reminder has been adapted into an ACT exercise originally developed by Drs. Yash Bhambhani and Laurie Gallo as a compassionate, mindfulness-based intervention within their trauma-informed, culturally adapted ACT manual for racially and economically marginalized clients with chronic pain and opioid use disorder (Bhambhani et al., 2025). The exercise has been modified here for burnout recovery, while retaining the core intention: inviting you to hold yourself in a wider, more compassionate frame.

Beyond Burnout Practice: You Are More Than . . .

Purpose: This practice helps you reconnect with your inherent worthiness. The part of you that exists beyond mistakes, criticism, or circumstances. When burnout and shame cloud your perspective, this exercise widens the frame, reminding you that compassion is not indulgence but truth-telling.

Step 1: Ground Yourself

Find a comfortable position, sitting upright but relaxed. Place one hand over your heart, or rest both hands gently on your lap. Take three slow, steady breaths in through your nose, out through your mouth. With each exhale, imagine releasing a little of the tension you're carrying.

Step 2: Repeat the Reflections

Silently or aloud, say to yourself:

- *I am more than the worst choice I've ever made.*
- *I am more than the harshest criticism anyone has thrown at me.*
- *I am more than my paycheck, my title, or the debt I carry.*
- *I am more than what was done to me, more than my lowest moment, more than my survival strategies.*

Step 3: Pause and Notice

After each statement, pause for a breath. Notice what comes up: Resistance, sadness, relief, or even nothing at all. There's no right response. Simply acknowledge what arises.

Step 4: Anchor the Truth

Take one final breath in, holding the last statement: I am more than . . . As you exhale, imagine this truth settling into your body like a steady, quiet warmth.

Reflection Questions

- *Which statement felt easiest to accept?*
- *Which felt hardest?*
- *What shifts, even subtly, when you hold yourself in this wider frame?*

Foundational Self-Care: Loving Yourself, Not Fixing Yourself

Self-care is a core expression of self-compassion. Before we explore deeper practices, we need to ground ourselves in the basics. Foundational self-care includes the daily actions that support the brain and body: Drinking water, getting adequate sleep, moving your body, exposure to sunlight, reducing the consumption of distressing content, and limiting substances that disrupt regulation (Germer & Neff, 2013; Porges, 2017).

That's easier said than done—not just emotionally but also structurally. Many people face systemic and environmental barriers that make even basic care difficult: Food deserts, poor air quality, unsafe neighborhoods, lack of green space, or limited access to health care (Algren et al., 2020; Braveman et al., 2011). These are not personal failings. They are a public health crisis.

When I lived in the Bronx, it took effort, creativity, and money to access fresh air, safe places to walk, or affordable food. After moving to a suburb of Phoenix, the difference was striking—walking paths, green belts, parks, and citrus trees on every corner. It became exponentially easier to care for my body, not because I changed, but because my environment did. That's why self-care must never be reduced to individual willpower or framed as a moral failure. Even when accessible, we need to understand our orientation to self-care practices. For many, what we deem as healthy behaviors are pursued as punishment for not being "fit enough" or "disciplined enough." But you can't hate yourself into healing. When self-care is driven by shame, it reinforces depletion, self-criticism, and avoidance (Kelly et al., 2010).

We are most successful when foundational self-care is guided by compassion, not perfection. It's not about fixing yourself; it's about protecting yourself, lovingly and realistically in the context you live in. Sometimes that means asking: *What's accessible to me right now? What small shift might help?*

Examples of foundational self-care include:

- Drinking more water
- Getting seven to nine hours of sleep most nights
- Moving your body in ways that feel safe or manageable
- Seeking natural light, even through a window
- Reducing exposure to distressing media
- Eliminating or reducing substance use or engaging in substance use in safer ways (harm reduction practices)
- Consistently taking prescribed medications
- Feeding yourself regularly

Practiced with compassion and intention, these basics stabilize the nervous system and create a platform for deeper healing. They are not rewards for being "good." From a human rights perspective, they are vital needs for all people. When systems fail to support those needs, it is the structure that is broken, not you (WHO, 2014).

Self-Care Is Neuroscience, Not Self-Indulgence

Self-care is not self-indulgence; it is biology. With consistency and intention, caring for yourself activates systems that recover, regulate, and rewire the brain (Davidson & McEwen, 2012). Burnout disrupts these systems, leaving people feeling depleted, but intentional self-care can help restore balance. The body uses different kinds of chemical messengers to communicate and regulate functions such as neurotransmitters, hormones, and neuropeptides.

- *Neurotransmitters* are fast-acting messengers that carry signals between nerve cells in the brain.
- *Hormones* are slower-acting messengers released into the bloodstream, influencing organs and tissues throughout the body.
- *Neuropeptides* are small protein-like molecules that can act as both neurotransmitters and hormones, often with longer-lasting effects on mood, pain, and stress.

Some messengers, like oxytocin and endorphins, function across these categories, working in both the brain and body. When self-care practices are consistent, they stimulate these systems in ways that directly counteract the effects of burnout:

- *Oxytocin* (neurotransmitter and hormone): Supports bonding, trust, and emotional safety (Heinrichs et al., 2009).
- *Dopamine* (neurotransmitter): Fuels motivation and goal-directed behavior (Berridge & Kringelbach, 2015).
- *Serotonin* (neurotransmitter): Regulates mood, confidence, and well-being (Young, 2007).
- *Endorphins* (neuropeptides/hormones): Provide physical relief and emotional uplift (Boecker et al., 2008).
- *Gamma-aminobutyric acid (GABA)* (neurotransmitter): Promotes calm and nervous system downregulation (Cryan & Kaupmann, 2005).

Together, these messengers form the body's built-in recovery system. They remind us that self-care is a way of directly supporting biology that makes resilience, healing, and engagement possible.

The Four Pillars of Sustainable Self-Care

Each pillar supports different aspects of nervous system regulation and psychological well-being. You don't need to do all four daily, but aiming to engage each category across the week helps restore balance (Porges, 2017).

1. Rest—physical and mental recovery

- *Purpose:* Restores baseline functioning, improves cognition, reduces inflammation, strengthens immunity
- *Neurobiology:* Activates parasympathetic nervous system, increases GABA and serotonin
- *Examples:* Deep breathing, screen-free wind-down, naps, stretching, warm baths, quiet time

2. *Connection—relational safety and support*

- *Purpose:* Fosters belonging, intimacy, and care
- *Neurobiology:* Boosts oxytocin and endorphins
- *Examples:* Hugging, calling a trusted friend, snuggling with a pet, joining a community, sharing truth with someone safe

3. *Presence—mindful engagement*

- *Purpose:* Anchors attention in the present, increases awareness, reduces reactivity
- *Neurobiology:* Enhances GABA and serotonin, strengthens attentional networks
- *Examples:* Mindful walking or eating, journaling, grounding, sensory noticing, single-task focus

4. *Meaningful pursuit—vitality, growth, and purpose*

- *Purpose:* Reconnects you with agency, joy, and motivation
- *Neurobiology:* Activates dopamine, serotonin, and endorphins
- *Examples:* Small steps toward goals, creative expression, volunteering, planning something exciting, reflecting on values

Beyond Burnout Practice: The Self-Care Science Project

Purpose: Try this weekly experiment to intentionally support your nervous system across the four pillars of self-care. Each category targets a specific set of neurotransmitters, hormones, or brain systems that burnout often disrupts.

This week, try doing one activity in each pillar that supports the associated neurobiology. Afterward, reflect on how it made you feel.

Rest

Supports GABA and serotonin
What I will try to support physical or mental recovery:

_____

_____

How I felt after:

_____

Connection

Supports oxytocin and endorphins

What I will try to increase relational safety and support:

_____

_____

How I felt after:

_____

Presence

Supports GABA, serotonin, and attentional regulation
What I will try to practice mindful engagement:

_____

_____

How I felt after:

_____

Meaningful Pursuit

Supports dopamine, serotonin, and endorphins
What I will try to reconnect with growth, purpose, or agency:

_____

_____

How I felt after:

_____

You can repeat this practice weekly or return to it anytime your system feels dysregulated or depleted. With time, you'll start to notice which categories help restore you most and where you may be undernourished.

Part 2: Rebuilding Bridges—Forgiveness, Shared Humanity, and Compassion for Others

As you reconnect with compassion, another layer often rises to the surface—anger, hurt, or resentment. These emotions may be directed toward yourself, toward others, or even toward life itself. They are not mistakes.

They are natural responses to being wounded, betrayed, disappointed, or overwhelmed (Enright & Fitzgibbons, 2015). But when left unprocessed, they can harden into barriers that block compassion from fully reaching you.

This is where forgiveness can become a powerful practice. Forgiveness is often misunderstood. It is not about letting someone "off the hook," pretending harm wasn't real, or excusing injustice. Instead, forgiveness is a willingness to face the wound without gripping it so tightly that it defines you (Wade et al., 2014).

When resentment takes hold, our minds loop on questions without satisfying answers: *Why did they hurt me? Why was I overlooked? Why did they think so little of me?* In the search for meaning, blame often turns inward (*Maybe I wasn't good enough*) or outward into broad mistrust (*I can't trust anyone. Everyone's out to get me*). Resentment keeps us tethered to the injury, as if staying hurt long enough might force recognition or undo the past. But in reality, remorse from others is not guaranteed, nor is it required for your healing. Remaining in resentment rarely brings safety and often costs you in terms of your physical, mental, and emotional well-being (Toussaint et al., 2015).

Not all wounds weigh the same. Some feel lighter to release; others remain too raw. That's why forgiveness is best approached as a gradual, self-paced process, starting where it feels possible and building courage for deeper work overtime (Enright & Fitzgibbons, 2015). To make this process tangible, you can map it visually using the *Forgiveness* Ladder (see Figure 9.1). On its lower rungs are the people, situations, or parts of yourself that feel easier to release. Higher rungs hold the injuries still carrying the most weight. Forgiving yourself might mean acknowledging you were doing the best you could with the knowledge and resources you had. Forgiving others may involve releasing the expectation they will change or make amends. Forgiving life might mean grieving for what could have been while choosing to live fully with what is.

You don't have to climb this ladder all at once. Even loosening your grip on one small hurt is an act of courage. Over time, forgiveness becomes less about changing the past and more about reclaiming your present and protecting your future.

Beyond Burnout Practice: The Forgiveness Ladder

Purpose: This practice is designed to help you gently engage in forgiveness—not as a demand to instantly release everything, but as an experiment in loosening your grip on pain. Forgiveness here is about protecting your energy, honoring your boundaries, and reclaiming agency. It's about practicing compassion for yourself and others, not achieving a perfect state of release.

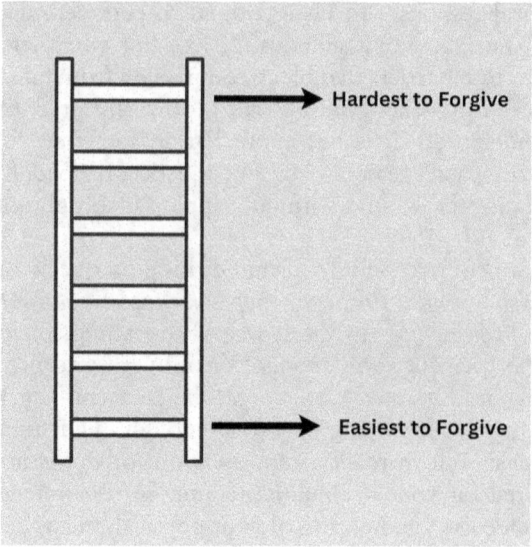

Figure 9.1 The Forgiveness Ladder. Original figure created by the author.

Step 1: Build Your Ladder

Draw a simple vertical ladder with eight rungs. At the bottom, write down the grievances, situations, or parts of yourself that feel easiest to forgive. As you move upward, list those that feel increasingly difficult. This creates a visual guide for your journey, showing that forgiveness is a process that happens in stages.

Step 2: Identify the Domains

As you fill in the rungs, notice which area each item belongs to:

- *Yourself*: Releasing self-blame, softening harsh self-criticism, and remembering that your worth is intact.
- *Others*: Letting go of the expectation that someone else will change, apologize, or understand.
- *Life itself*: Grieving what could have been and finding ways to make peace with what is.

Step 3: Choose Your Rung

From your ladder, select one or two items in each category (yourself, others, life) that feel workable. Choose those on the lower or middle rungs, where practicing forgiveness feels possible, not overwhelming. Starting where the ground is steadier helps build trust in the process.

Step 4: Experiment with Forgiveness Practices

Spend a few moments with each chosen item, using whatever compassionate approach feels most accessible. The goal is not to force complete forgiveness in one sitting, but to practice showing up in ways that keep the door open to compassion. Try one of the following:

- *Journal on the Hurt*: Write freely about the injury, betrayal, or disappointment, completely unfiltered. Let yourself name the anger, sadness, or grief without censoring. When finished, write an intention to forgive, followed by a reflection on what might be freed up if you released this pain like your energy, joy, clarity, or peace.
- *Write a Release Statement*: Capture in words what you are ready to set down. For example: "I release the pressure to carry this" or "I release the resentment that no longer serves me." Writing helps anchor intention and communicates it clearly to yourself.
- *Visualize Release*: Use imagery to symbolically let go. You might picture pulling back a bow and releasing an arrow into the sky, watching it soar away. Imagine placing a heavy stone in a river and seeing the current carry it downstream. Or exhale smoke or mist and watch it dissolve into air. These metaphors give your mind and body a felt sense of release.
- *Affirmations of Forgiveness*: Repeat phrases that extend compassion toward yourself or others. Examples include:
- *I forgive myself for being imperfect and learning.*
- *May I find peace, and may you find peace too.*
- *Even if we cannot reconcile, I choose not to be defined by this pain.*
- *Write a Letter about What You Needed to Hear*: Imagine the person who hurt you saying exactly what you needed. Write their words as if they were speaking: "I am sorry. I see how my actions hurt you. You did not deserve that. You are worthy of love and safety." This surfaces unmet needs and creates space for healing, even if reconciliation is not possible.

Shared Humanity: Seeing Ourselves in Others

Once you begin loosening the grip of resentment toward yourself, others, and even life itself, you create space for something deeper to take root: Another of Dr. Kristin Neff's three core elements of self-compassion, *shared humanity* (Neff, 2003). Shared humanity means recognizing that pain, fear, and imperfection are universal experiences. Everyone you meet carries invisible wounds. Everyone struggles with unmet needs, defensive walls, and injuries that shape how they show up in the world.

This recognition does not excuse harm. It does not mean that you accept mistreatment or abandon your boundaries. Instead, it softens the isolating belief that you are alone in your suffering. Research shows that when people connect to a sense of shared humanity, they experience lower levels of shame, greater resilience, and stronger interpersonal connections (Neff & Germer, 2013; Barnard & Curry, 2011). Seeing others through this wider lens also shifts how we interpret difficult behavior. People often operate from their *threat system* more than we realize—lashing out, shutting down, betraying, or disappointing. These reactions are less about your worth and more about their own nervous system being hijacked by fear, shame, or scarcity (Gilbert, 2014). In the next section, we'll practice building this lens of compassion even toward the people we find most difficult.

Beyond Burnout Practice: Seeing the Difficult Person Through the Lens of Compassion

Purpose: This exercise is not about excusing harm. It's about reclaiming your ability to see people in a less threatening lens to optimize your agency in your interpersonal decision-making.

Step 1: Choose a Difficult Person

Think of someone who stirs anger, sadness, or resentment inside you. This could be someone from your past or present. Choose someone with whom it feels safe to explore this exercise—not someone who poses an active danger to you.
Name or Describe: _____

_____

_____

Step 2: Imagine Their Early Story

Now imagine this person as a child. Not the adult version you know today, but the vulnerable child they once were.
Ask yourself:

- *What might they have needed that they didn't get?*
- *What fears might have shaped them?*
- *Who taught them how to survive, and what did survival look like for them?*

You don't have to know the exact details. Trust your intuition to fill in the blanks with compassionate imagination.

Their early vulnerabilities might have been: _____

_____

_____

Step 3: Identify Threat-Based Behaviors

Now think about their actions that have hurt or frustrated you.
Ask yourself:

- *Could these behaviors be coming from fear?*
  (Fear of inadequacy, fear of being controlled or dominated, fear of abandonment, fear of losing status)
- *Are they stuck operating from a threat state rather than their best self?*

Threat behaviors I notice:

_____

_____

_____

Step 4: Speak to Them (Silently) from Fierce Compassion

In your mind or on paper, speak to them from your compassionate, empowered self.
You might say something like:

- I see your pain, even if you don't.
- I see how fear has shaped you.
- I choose compassion for me, and for the part of you that never learned another way.

Write your own version if you like: _____

_____

_____

Mirrors and Meaning: Seeing Ourselves and Others

One of the hardest truths about compassion is that people are mirrors for us, just as we are mirrors for them. Their reactions aren't always about who we are personally, but often about what we represent. When I first stepped into a director role, one of the administrative secretaries on the leadership team seemed to dislike me almost immediately. I could feel it in her tone, her body language, the clipped way she spoke. I tried all the cognitive skills I taught others—check the facts, consider alternative explanations, don't jump to conclusions.

Then one day, in a meeting, she looked me in the eye and said bluntly: *Look, I don't like you, and you don't like me.* I was taken aback. I had grown used to socially acceptable passive-aggression, but here the tension was spoken aloud. The truth was, I hadn't disliked her, but I had grown increasingly uncomfortable around her. I avoided interactions when I could, leaning on colleagues who were easier to connect with. I wasn't immune to the tension.

In that moment, I had a choice. I could have called her out for being "unprofessional," defended myself, or reminded her I was her supervisor. But something in me knew that wasn't the path. I was in a position of power, not just from my leadership role but also from aspects of my social identity. I was a white woman in my early thirties stepping into leadership, while she was an older woman of color who had been part of the program for decades. She had been indispensable to my predecessor, but with new leadership, everything was changing. She didn't know where she stood, and that uncertainty carried real fear. Her reaction wasn't just about me; it reflected broader histories of inequity and exclusion in institutions where fairness and dignity had not always been guaranteed (Sue et al., 2007; Williams & Mohammed, 2009).

In that moment, she didn't need me to assert control. She needed to feel safe. I chose to meet her with non-defensiveness and curiosity. I chose to see the human being in front of me, not just her behavior. Over time, we built a strong working relationship rooted in growing trust, mutual respect, and shared investment. By the time I left, we genuinely liked and respected one another. That relationship didn't heal because I demanded respect, but because I practiced humility instead of superiority. I held space for the fear in the room, both hers and mine while recognizing that our interaction wasn't just interpersonal. We cannot always fix the systems we inherit, but we can choose how we show up within them. When we remember that people's reactions are often shaped by battles we cannot see—grief, exclusion, attachment wounds, trauma histories—we can respond with strength, grace, and boundaries that uphold everyone's dignity, including our own (Germer & Neff, 2013; Gilbert, 2014).

Beyond Burnout Practice: Compassionate Detachment

Purpose: Sometimes when someone treats us with judgment, hostility, or indifference, we absorb it as truth about who we are. But often, their reaction says more about their internal world or systemic stressors than it does about our worth. This exercise helps you practice holding their behavior with compassion without letting it fuse to your identity. It's important to note that this is not for situations where your rights or physical or emotional safety are being violated. It's also not to avoid taking responsibility or making a repair when that may be the correct course of action. In both of those instances, fierce compassion practices may be more appropriate.

Step 1: Recall a Situation

Think of a recent or memorable situation where someone reacted negatively to you, whether through criticism, withdrawal, coldness, or anger.
Situation (briefly describe):

_____

_____

_____

Step 2: Name What You Represented

Instead of asking, "What's wrong with me?"
Ask,

- *How might they be in pain?*
- *What might I represent to them?*

Consider:

- *Did you represent change?*
- *Did you trigger feelings of jealousy, fear, shame, or abandonment?*
- *Did you remind them of something painful from their past?*

What I might have represented:

_____

_____

_____

Step 3: Offer Compassion at a Distance

Imagine gently saying to yourself:

- *Their reaction belongs to them.*
- *Their pain belongs to them.*
- *I can hold understanding without holding blame.*

Now, complete this prompt:
One thing I can release:

_____

_____

_____

One thing I choose to hold on to about my worth:

_____

_____

_____

People-Pleasing Versus Kindness

Extending compassion toward others does not mean losing yourself. It does not mean abandoning your needs, tolerating mistreatment, or saying yes when you want to say no. Many people navigating burnout identify as chronic givers, helpers, or empaths. Underneath, there is often a well-worn pattern of people-pleasing. This is sometimes mistaken for kindness, but it is not the same thing.

People-pleasing is a coping strategy rooted in fear, shame, or the need for external validation. It involves prioritizing others' comfort or approval at the expense of your own needs, boundaries, or truth (Ciarrochi et al., 2016; Lynch & Kilmartin, 2013). For some, this is most closely related to the "fawn" response in the trauma literature, the instinct to appease or placate as a means of ensuring safety in threatening environments (Walker, 2013). While it often becomes an entrenched habit, in certain contexts, this strategy remains necessary. What may look like people-pleasing from the outside can actually be an act of self-preservation. In those cases, people may even feel "bad" or angry afterward about needing to act nice to people who may pose a threat to them, but those emotions don't mean that the choice was inappropriate or ineffective. They reflect the painful reality that protecting oneself sometimes requires strategies that come at an emotional cost and that choosing survival is a valid, compassionate act.

This distinction is particularly important for Black, Indigenous, and People of Color (BIPOC), trans, and other marginalized individuals whose self-expression is often policed and sometimes met with violence (Comas-Díaz et al., 2019). "Being nice" may not reflect a lack of boundaries but rather a deliberate survival strategy when navigating spaces where asserting needs could trigger punishment, discrimination, or danger. In these instances, feigning niceness may be the most values-aligned decision available.

Cultural forces also shape these patterns. Gender socialization teaches many women that being accommodating, pleasant, and self-sacrificing is not only virtuous but also expected in some collectivist contexts; and respecting and putting others first are deeply ingrained, making boundary-setting feel selfish or wrong (Cross & Madson, 1997). While not universal, these norms repeatedly pressure individuals, especially women and marginalized groups, to conflate "niceness" with worthiness, even when it comes at a personal cost. Many women will recognize the familiar experience of walking down the street only to be told by a stranger, almost always a man, to "Smile!" As if not performing agreeableness for others warrants correction. The message is clear: Your comfort matters less than others' perception of your pleasantness (Calogero & Tylka, 2014).

Healing from burnout requires reclaiming kindness as something that includes you, too. Genuine kindness arises from compassion, not compulsion. A practical step is to notice the difference between compassionate behavior and people-pleasing in daily choices: Am I acting from fear of disapproval, or from a grounded desire to connect?

Beyond Burnout Practice: The People-Pleasing Pulse Check

Purpose: Sometimes, it's hard to tell if you're acting from care or from fear. This pulse check helps you pause and tune into your motivation before you act. The goal isn't to judge yourself, but to notice your patterns with compassion.

When you feel pulled to say yes, offer help, or "be nice," pause and move through the following steps.

Step 1: Assess for Safety

Is there a perceived imminent threat to my physical or psychological safety?
If the answer is yes, then choosing to be agreeable may be the most values-aligned option in that moment. If the answer is no, review the next series of reflection questions.

Step 2: Reflect

- *What's my motivation?* Am I acting because it aligns with my values and I genuinely want to, or because I'm afraid of rejection, conflict, or being seen as "bad"?
- *How will I feel afterward?* Will I feel peaceful, grounded, and proud of my choice, regardless of how it's received, or resentful, drained, and anxious about how I came across?
- *Am I respecting my own needs?* Am I honoring my limits or pushing past my discomfort and ignoring what I need?
- *Do I need a certain response?* Can I offer this kindness without expecting a praise, approval, or reassurance?
- *Am I being authentic?* Am I showing up as my real self, even if it means being misunderstood, or am I trying to appear "nice," "easy," or "helpful"?
  The more you practice this check-in, the easier it becomes to act with compassion in a way that includes you.

Beyond Burnout Compassionate Commitments

To really solidify the teaching of step five of the Blueprint, consider making the following commitments to yourself. These aren't rigid rules, but agreements to return to.

1. *I will turn toward my inner compassion*, even when I can't feel it clearly, I will trust that it's still there—steady, warm, and waiting.
2. *I will lead my inner world with strength and kindness.* I will offer leadership, not warfare, to the parts of me that struggle.
3. *I will consider forgiveness to free myself, not excuse others.* I will loosen my grip on pain when I'm ready, not to erase the past, but to reclaim my future
4. *I will see others through the lens of shared humanity.* I will recognize that others' behaviors often reflect their own struggles, not my worth.
5. *I will act with compassion without abandoning myself.* I will extend kindness without erasing my needs, my boundaries, or my voice.

You will forget these commitments at times. The practice is in noticing when you've drifted and choosing to come back. Over time, they become less like a checklist and more like muscle memory, guiding how you meet yourself and others. Compassion, especially self-compassion, isn't a finish line you cross once. It's a lifelong relationship you tend to, one choice, one breath, one moment at a time. When burnout tries to strip away your energy or your hope, these commitments are how you find your way back.

References

Algren, M. H., Bak, C. K., Berg-Beckhoff, G., & Andersen, P. T. (2020). Health-risk behaviour in deprived neighbourhoods compared with non-deprived neighbourhoods: A systematic literature review of quantitative observational studies. *PLOS ONE, 15*(4), e0230937. https://doi.org/10.1371/journal.pone.0230937

Barnard, L. K., & Curry, J. F. (2011). Self-compassion: Conceptualizations, correlates, & interventions. *Review of General Psychology, 15*(4), 289–303. https://doi.org/10.1037/a0025754

Beaumont, E., Galpin, A., & Jenkins, P. (2012). 'Being kinder to myself': A prospective comparative study, exploring post-trauma therapy outcome measures, for two groups of clients, receiving either cognitive behaviour therapy or compassion focused therapy for post-traumatic stress disorder. *Counselling Psychology Review, 27*(1), 31–43.

Berridge, K. C., & Kringelbach, M. L. (2015). Pleasure systems in the brain. *Neuron, 86*(3), 646–664. https://doi.org/10.1016/j.neuron.2015.02.018

Bhambhani, Y., Gallo, L., McNamara, E. O., Stotts, A. L., & Gabbay, V. (2025). Persisting with purpose: Using Acceptance and Commitment Therapy to target comorbid opioid use disorder and chronic pain in a racially and economically marginalized population. *Journal of Contextual Behavioral Science, 36*, 100888. https://doi.org/10.1016/j.jcbs.2025.100888

Boecker, H., Sprenger, T., Spilker, M. E., Henriksen, G., Koppenhoefer, M., Wagner, K. J., & Tölle, T. R. (2008). The runner's high: Opioidergic mechanisms in the human brain. *Cerebral Cortex*, *18*(11), 2523–2531. https://doi.org/10.1093/cercor/bhn013

Braveman, P., Egerter, S., & Williams, D. R. (2011). The social determinants of health: Coming of age. *Annual Review of Public Health*, *32*, 381–398. https://doi.org/10.1146/annurev-publhealth-031210-101218

Calogero, R. M., & Tylka, T. L. (2014). Sanctioning resistance to objectification: A test of the sanctions, internalization, and resistance model. *Psychology of Women Quarterly*, *38*(3), 271–285. https://doi.org/10.1177/0361684313510111

Ciarrochi, J., Bilich, L., & Godsell, C. (2016). Psychological flexibility as a mechanism of change in acceptance and commitment therapy. In R. D. Zettle, S. C. Hayes, D. Barnes-Holmes, & A. Biglan (Eds.), *The Wiley handbook of contextual behavioral science* (pp. 327–346). Wiley.

Comas-Díaz, L., Hall, G. N., & Neville, H. A. (2019). Racial trauma: Theory, research, and healing. *American Psychologist*, *74*(1), 1–16. https://doi.org/10.1037/amp0000442

Cross, S. E., & Madson, L. (1997). Models of the self: Self-construals and gender. *Psychological Bulletin*, *122*(1), 5–37. https://doi.org/10.1037/0033-2909.122.1.5

Cryan, J. F., & Kaupmann, K. (2005). Don't worry 'B' happy!: A role for GABA(B) receptors in anxiety and depression. *Trends in Pharmacological Sciences*, *26*(1), 36–43. https://doi.org/10.1016/j.tips.2004.11.004

Davidson, R. J., & McEwen, B. S. (2012). Social influences on neuroplasticity: Stress and interventions to promote well-being. *Nature Neuroscience*, *15*(5), 689–695. https://doi.org/10.1038/nn.3093

Enright, R. D., & Fitzgibbons, R. P. (2015). *Forgiveness therapy: An empirical guide for resolving anger and restoring hope* (2nd ed.). American Psychological Association. https://doi.org/10.1037/14526-000

Germer, C. K., & Neff, K. D. (2013). Self-compassion in clinical practice. *Journal of Clinical Psychology*, *69*(8), 856–867. https://doi.org/10.1002/jclp.22021

Gilbert, P. (2009). *The compassionate mind: A new approach to life's challenges*. Constable.

Gilbert, P. (2010). *Compassion focused therapy: Distinctive features*. Routledge.

Gilbert, P. (2014). The origins and nature of compassion focused therapy. *British Journal of Clinical Psychology*, *53*(1), 6–41. https://doi.org/10.1111/bjc.12043

Gilbert, P., & Irons, C. (2005). Focused therapies and compassionate mind training for shame and self-attacking. In P. Gilbert (Ed.), *Compassion: Conceptualisations, research and use in psychotherapy* (pp. 263–325). Routledge.

Hayes, S. C., Strosahl, K. D., & Wilson, K. G. (2011). *Acceptance and commitment therapy: The process and practice of mindful change* (2nd ed.). Guilford Press.

Heinrichs, M., von Dawans, B., & Domes, G. (2009). Oxytocin, vasopressin, and human social behavior. *Frontiers in Neuroendocrinology*, *30*(4), 548–557. https://doi.org/10.1016/j.yfrne.2009.05.005

Kelly, A. C., Zuroff, D. C., Foa, C. L., & Gilbert, P. (2010). Who benefits from training in self-compassionate self-regulation? A study of smoking reduction. *Journal of Social and Clinical Psychology*, *29*(7), 727–755. https://doi.org/10.1521/jscp.2010.29.7.727

Kirby, J. N., Tellegen, C. L., & Steindl, S. R. (2017). A meta-analysis of compassion-based interventions: Current state of knowledge and future directions. *Behavior Therapy*, *48*(6), 778–792. https://doi.org/10.1016/j.beth.2017.06.003

Kirschner, H., Kuyken, W., Wright, K., Roberts, H., Brejcha, C., & Karl, A. (2019). Soothing your heart and feeling connected: A new experimental paradigm to study the benefits of self-compassion. *Mindfulness*, 10(3), 461–480. https://doi. org/10.1007/s12671-018-0981-7

Lynch, L., & Kilmartin, C. (2013). Over-concern for others: A review of the self-sacrificing schema. *Journal of Clinical Psychology*, 69(12), 1168–1181. https://doi.org/10.1002/jclp.22043

McEwen, B. S. (2007). Physiology and neurobiology of stress and adaptation: Central role of the brain. *Physiological Reviews*, 87(3), 873–904. https://doi. org/10.1152/physrev.00041.2006

Neff, K. D. (2003). The development and validation of a scale to measure self-compassion. *Self and Identity*, 2(3), 223–250. https://doi.org/10.1080/15298860309027

Neff, K. D. (2011). Self-compassion, self-esteem, and well-being. *Social and Personality Psychology Compass*, 5(1), 1–12. https://doi.org/10.1111/j.1751-9004.2010. 00330.x

Neff, K. D. (2016). The yin and yang of self-compassion. In M. Z. Zeidner & G. Matthews (Eds.), *Handbook of self-compassion* (pp. 1–19). Springer.

Neff, K. D., & Germer, C. K. (2013). A pilot study and randomized controlled trial of the mindful self-compassion program. *Journal of Clinical Psychology*, 69(1), 28–44. https://doi.org/10.1002/jclp.21923

Neff, K. D., & Germer, C. K. (2018). *The mindful self-compassion workbook: A proven way to accept yourself, build inner strength, and thrive*. Guilford Press.

Porges, S. W. (2017). *The pocket guide to the polyvagal theory: The transformative power of feeling safe*. Norton.

Schwartz, R. C. (2013). *Introduction to the Internal Family Systems model*. Trailheads Publications.

Stevenson, B. (2014). *Just mercy: A story of justice and redemption*. Spiegel & Grau.

Sue, D. W., Capodilupo, C. M., Torino, G. C., Bucceri, J. M., Holder, A., Nadal, K. L., & Esquilin, M. (2007). Racial microaggressions in everyday life: Implications for clinical practice. *American Psychologist*, 62(4), 271–286. https://doi.org/10. 1037/0003-066X.62.4.271

Toussaint, L., Worthington, E. L., & Williams, D. R. (2015). *Forgiveness and health: Scientific evidence and theories relating forgiveness to better health*. Springer. https://doi.org/10.1007/978-94-017-9993-5

Wade, N. G., Hoyt, W. T., Kidwell, J. E. M., & Worthington, E. L. (2014). Efficacy of psychotherapeutic interventions to promote forgiveness: A meta-analysis. *Journal of Consulting and Clinical Psychology*, 82(1), 154–170. https://doi.org/ 10.1037/a0035268

Walker, P. (2013). Complex PTSD: From surviving to thriving: A guide and map for recovering from childhood trauma. (1st ed.). Azure Coyote.

Williams, D. R., & Mohammed, S. A. (2009). Discrimination and racial disparities in health: Evidence and needed research. *Journal of Behavioral Medicine*, 32(1), 20–47. https://doi.org/10.1007/s10865-008-9185-0

World Health Organization. (2014). *Social determinants of mental health*. WHO Press.

Young, S. N. (2007). How to increase serotonin in the human brain without drugs. *Journal of Psychiatry & Neuroscience*, 32(6), 394–399.

Chapter 10

Step 6

Let Your Values Take the Wheel

Values are the pillars of your Beyond Burnout life. Throughout the prior five steps of the Blueprint, you've been laying the groundwork to bring your values into sharper focus, integrating them into your language, reflections, and daily choices.

This chapter is about what comes next: Learning how to let your values take the wheel, every day, in real time, especially when it's hard. It's about practicing the skill of placing your values at the helm of your decision-making, not only in hindsight or during calm moments but also in the middle of life's noise, stress, and overwhelm. It's also about rerouting when you inevitably drift off course.

When burnout dominates, it's like a reckless, intoxicated driver insisting on the keys. This final step in *the Beyond Burnout Blueprint* teaches you how to ensure your values become the designated driver, the steady guide you can return to again and again.

Other emotions and motivators are still in the car. They're allowed to ride along. Sometimes, they'll be loud backseat drivers. Fear might slam the brakes, anger might try to take the wheel, or shame might throw the car in reverse. Occasionally, those reactions are adaptive. But more often, they're false alarms. In your beyond burnout life, they've been demoted to eternal passenger princesses, still present, sometimes dramatic, but no longer steering the course. Your task is to pivot quickly, take a breath, and hand the wheel back to your values. When your values drive, you may not always take the smoothest or fastest route, but the journey will be worthwhile.

If your values are the driver, then your GPS destination is your compelling vision. While vision and values are deeply connected, within *the Beyond Burnout Blueprint*, they serve slightly different functions. Values are the enduring qualities you want to embody like integrity, creativity, compassion, justice, which guide moment-to-moment actions (Hayes et al., 2012). Your vision is bigger and more vivid: The imagined life that emerges when your values are consistently enacted. It reflects not just what matters to you but also why it matters, shaping the emotional and relational

DOI: 10.4324/9781003640592-13

texture of your future, including your goals and aspirations (Kashdan & Ciarrochi, 2013).

Importantly, it's not enough to keep this vision in the background. You must intentionally center it. Like holding onto the anticipation of reaching a long-awaited destination, reconnecting with your vision energizes both the journey and the arrival. When held with compassion rather than pressure, it becomes a steady source of meaning instead of another impossible standard (Neff & Germer, 2018). A compelling vision sustains you not by demanding perfection, but by gently reminding you where you are headed, why it matters, and who you are becoming along the way.

The Blueprint has equipped you with the tools to navigate the road ahead. Mindfulness and present-moment awareness help you read the road and adjust to what's unfolding (Hayes et al., 2012). Cognitive defusion quiets the backseat commentary that tells you you're lost or not enough. Willingness keeps the engine running even when the road gets steep (Vilardaga et al., 2009). And compassion is your fuel, and without it, the tank runs dry, no matter how hard you press the accelerator.

Here is the central takeaway of this chapter, and perhaps the whole Blueprint: *Direction is far more important than speed.*

Beyond Burnout Practice: Select Your Top Drivers

Purpose: This exercise helps you identify and prioritize the values that guide your choices and actions. In *the Beyond Burnout Blueprint*, values act as your drivers, they determine your direction, help you navigate challenges, and keep you moving toward a life that feels meaningful. By clarifying which values are your "all-stars" versus those that play a supporting role, you'll be better equipped to make decisions that align with what matters most, even under stress.
Not all drivers have the same role:

- *All-Star Drivers:* Your most important values that fuel your biggest choices and inspire action.
- *Mid-Level Drivers:* Somewhat important values that you care about, but that don't lead every day.
- *Back-Up Drivers:* Less important values that might only show up in certain situations or seasons of life.

Driver Selection Pool

(Adapted from the Values Card Sort, Miller et al., University of New Mexico)

Acceptance • *Achievement* • *Adventure* •
Altruism • *Assertiveness* • *Authenticity* •
Autonomy • *Beauty* • *Belonging* • *Caring* •
Challenge • *Comfort* • *Commitment* •

Compassion • Community • Connection • Connection to Nature • Collectivism • Contribution • Cooperation • Creativity • Curiosity • Dependability • Duty • Economic Security • Equity • Excellence/Quality • Excitement • Fairness • Family • Fitness • Flexibility • Forgiveness • Freedom • Friendship • Fun • Generosity • Genuineness • Gratitude • Growth • Harmony • Health • Honesty • Humility • Humor • Independence • Individualism • Industry • Inner Peace • Integrity • Intimacy • Justice • Kindness • Knowledge • Learning • Leisure • Love • Mastery • Mindfulness • Moderation • Openness • Order • Passion • Patience • Persistence • Pleasure • Power • Purpose • Respect • Responsibility • Romance • Security • Self-Acceptance • Self-Awareness • Self-Development • Self-Esteem • Sensuality • Service • Sexuality • Simplicity • Skillfulness • Social Justice • Spirituality • Stability • Sustainability • Trustworthiness

Table 10.1 is an author-created table inspired by values card-sort methodologies.

Add Your Own Drivers

Rank your drivers in the all-star, mid-level, and back-up driving categories below.

Table 10.1 Select Your Top Drivers

All-Star Drivers (Most Important)	Mid-Level Drivers (Somewhat Important)	Back-Up Drivers (Less Important)

Values' Roadblocks

The prior chapters have outlined many of the internal and external forces that block us from living in alignment with our values. These are the classic energy-drainers, compassion-zappers, and the protective processes that can also trap us:

- Avoidance of unwanted emotions
- Fusion with painful beliefs or self-narratives
- Threat-based thinking that fuels comparison and self-criticism
- A nervous system locked in survival mode, narrowing our behavioral options to fight, flight, freeze, fawn, or flop (Walker, 2013)

While these factors are significant, two of the most common and convincing forces I see push values out of the driver's seat are guilt and obligation.

Guilt and obligation often masquerade as values. They appear as familiar, internalized scripts: "You should do this, they'll be upset if you don't" or "If you say no, they'll think you're not grateful." On the surface, such thoughts sound morally sound, but they are often fear-driven rather than values-driven. The underlying fear is usually of disappointing others, being misjudged, or losing connection. Beneath that fear sits an internalized belief: *I am responsible for other people's emotions.* This belief is especially common in people with histories of insecure attachment, relational trauma, or roles that demanded caretaking or appeasement to stay safe and connected (Mikulincer & Shaver, 2016).

When those expectations inevitably cannot be met, guilt can quickly escalate into shame. Guilt arises when we evaluate a specific behavior: *I made a mistake, I let someone down.* Shame, by contrast, is a judgment of the self: *I am selfish, I am lazy, I am a bad friend or person* (Tangney & Dearing, 2002).

Guilt can be constructive. From an evolutionary standpoint, it promotes prosocial behavior, reciprocity, and social cohesion, mechanisms that historically increased survival for both individuals and groups (Baumeister et al., 1994). In everyday life, guilt can serve as a moral compass, signaling misalignment with our values and motivating repair or clarifying aspects of our identity. The problem arises when guilt becomes reflexive or collapses into shame. Whereas guilt points to *what I did*, shame attacks *who I am*, often leading to withdrawal, secrecy, or self-criticism rather than growth.

At this point, guilt and obligation stop functioning as guides and instead become control strategies, attempts to manage how others see or feel about us, often at the expense of authenticity and well-being. For those raised in environments where love felt conditional or earned, guilt can morph into a survival tool: A way to avoid rejection, overextend to feel worthy, or stay silent and compliant to maintain safety (Gilbert, 2014).

Sometimes, guilt and obligation are not only internalized but also actively reinforced by systems that strip away power or choice. Health-care workers, for example, often navigate rigid, hierarchical, or under-resourced settings where asserting their needs risks punishment in the form of exclusion, missed opportunities, or negative evaluations. They are told to speak up, but, when they do, they risk being labeled as ungrateful or difficult. In turn, they learn to self-censor, over-function, and push themselves harder until burnout becomes inevitable.

Cultural context also matters. For many first-generation Americans and immigrants, guilt and obligation are not distortions of values but part of deeply rooted intergenerational narratives of sacrifice and belonging. When parents have crossed borders, left behind dreams, or endured hardships to create opportunities for their children, it is not so simple to say, "Just choose what feels aligned". Western mental health frameworks, including my own, can fall short here. For many, the real conflict is not between values and guilt, but between competing values: Personal desire and collective responsibility, individual choice and cultural loyalty (Chentsova-Dutton & Ryder, 2020).

So, what can you do with guilt and obligation? I often encourage clients to pause and ask themselves: *If guilt or obligation is my only reason for saying yes (or no), can I find at least one other values-based reason to support my choice?* If the answer is no, it is a cue to slow down and sit with what is surfacing. Sometimes, what feels like guilt is actually a longing to act with integrity. Sometimes, what we call obligation is in fact an expression of love. That is why we do not dismiss these feelings. Instead, we slow them down, get curious, and explore them with care.

This process might involve asking: What value am I protecting here? What relationship am I trying to honor? Is a cultural or religious commitment at play? What part of me is afraid, and what do I fear will happen if I choose differently? Am I attempting to manage how others perceive me, or am I taking responsibility for their emotional reactions? And crucially, is this guilt, shame, or both?

Being considerate of others' feelings is not the same as being responsible for them. Compassion asks us to care about how our actions impact others, but values-based living requires holding that care alongside boundaries without assuming full responsibility for someone else's disappointment or discomfort (Neff & Germer, 2018). When we blur that line, we often abandon ourselves in an attempt to control how we are seen or how others feel.

The goal is not to eliminate guilt or override obligation but to approach them gently and choose from a place of grounded alignment. You are not bad for feeling guilty. You are not selfish for having boundaries. You are human. And you deserve to make decisions that reflect not only who others want you to be but also who you want to be.

Clinical Vignette: Sally

Let me introduce you to Sally, a dedicated pediatric intensive care unit (PICU) nurse and a mother of three. She came to therapy in the thick of burnout, not just from the grueling hours and emotional labor of her work but also from the invisible weight she carried with her long after she left the hospital: Guilt. Guilt over not doing enough at work. Guilt over not being home enough. Guilt that followed her like a shadow, even in the rare moments when she tried to rest.

The PICU is where some of the sickest children receive lifesaving or life-sustaining care. These are often children with complex medical needs, trauma, congenital illness, or conditions with no known cure. Many are so sick that they spend months in the hospital, with a minimal quality of life. For health-care workers, this is a sacred and agonizing space.

At home, the pressure shifted but didn't ease. Her three children needed her in ways that felt impossible to meet when her emotional reserves were running on empty. Her days off were rare and often filled with the pressure to entertain her kids, as well as complete a never-ending to-do list of errands, all with a smile on her face.

So, when she received an invitation to attend the funeral of a child she had cared for and recently died, it cracked something open. The bereaved family had told her how much her presence had meant to them. She cared for them deeply. And when she looked at the date, her heart sank even further . . . She was off that day.

Somehow, that made it worse. She had been quietly hoping she would be working, so she could let herself off the hook. If she were at the hospital, that would be a *worthy* reason to say no. But a day off? That felt harder to defend. *What kind of person skips a child's funeral to sit on the couch?,* guilt screamed.

We slowed it all down in therapy. We listened to what the guilt was trying to protect—her deep compassion, her sense of integrity, her identity as a caregiver. But we also got curious about what else was there. Beneath the guilt was the realization that participating in the funeral was not how she wanted to grieve. She had her own grieving rituals and boundaries that were protective from the regular occupational occurrence of losing patients in the PICU. Beneath the obligation was exhaustion. Her physical and emotional battery was so drained that figuring out the logistics of getting to the funeral and being in the presence of dozens of grieving family members were simply overwhelming. And layered alongside her desire to honor the family was a very real need to honor herself.

Sally made the values-aligned choice to decline the invitation and to write a heartfelt letter to the family instead. But that didn't make the guilt disappear. And when the day off arrived, the weight of the loss, the funeral she wasn't attending, the child she couldn't stop thinking about, hit her harder than expected.

She was home with her children, who had been excited to finally have her to themselves. But what she actually needed wasn't structured time or a perfect day of connection. She needed space. She needed to rest. Yet, there was that other voice: *You owe them this. Don't disappoint them.*

This, too, was obligation. Not rooted in resentment, but in love and her strong family values. Still, it didn't leave room for her own humanity. So, Sally was honest with her kids. She told them she was feeling heavy and sad, and she was grateful to be with them, but she did not have a lot of energy. She also explained she needed some time alone. They agreed to a movie. She asked her oldest to order pizza. They spent a few hours shoulder to shoulder on the couch, with no pressure to perform or entertain. Later, she gave herself the quiet space she needed in solitude.

The guilt and obligation didn't vanish. But they didn't get to drive the day. Sally chose her values. Not just the values others expected of her but also the ones that were calling her from within. Living in alignment with your values isn't about erasing discomfort. It's about learning to listen to it and then choosing, intentionally, what gets to lead.

Flexible Perspective-Taking: You Are More Than One Thing

Sally's story is a powerful example of something many of us struggle with: Honoring the different parts of ourselves, especially when they seem to be pulling us in opposite directions. This is one of the hardest parts of burnout.

Burnout doesn't just come from doing too much. It comes from being only one thing for too long. When your professional identity overtakes everything else—your needs, your relationships, your rest, your inner life, it can feel like a hostile takeover. The nurse, therapist, executive, entrepreneur, teacher, parent, or helper in you begins to push all the other parts of you out of the driver's seat.

I've lived this tension myself. I love my kids more than I love my career, full stop. And yet, if you looked at my schedule on any given day, it might not reflect that. I often spend more hours working than I do with them. But time isn't always the most accurate measure of love. My work helps sustain our family, financially, yes, but also emotionally. It connects me to purpose and fulfillment in ways that allow me to show up as a more present version of myself at home.

This is where the practice of *compassionate prioritization* becomes essential. Compassionate prioritization is the intentional act of making thoughtful, values-based decisions when multiple important values are competing at once. It means making space for all parts of yourself while choosing, with care and flexibility, which value needs to lead right now (Kashdan & Ciarrochi, 2013).

Honoring all of you requires listening with compassion instead of judgment and being willing to shift when needed, without losing sight of what matters most in the larger arc of your life. Values can coexist, shift, and share space. Sometimes that means I'm the one who leaves work to pick up my child when they're sick. Sometimes it means showing up for a school concert or a small everyday moment. Other times, if my husband can step in, I let him. If a client is in crisis, I take the call. It isn't about perfect balance. It's about aligning with what matters most in that moment, knowing there will be other opportunities to realign again. Values-aligned living is a pattern over time, not a single decision (Hayes et al., 2012; Vilardaga et al., 2009).

This book itself was written in those in-between spaces: On weekends, late at night, during long stretches of focus, and in tiny windows while my daughter did cartwheels across the bedroom floor as I typed in bed. I felt that same tug-of-war between guilt and obligation with every chapter. Sometimes, I felt guilty for writing, missing time with my family. Other times I felt guilty for not writing, as though I were falling short on a promise to myself. At different times, I felt obligated to my kids, my husband, my clients, or my deadline. And often, all of those feelings showed up at once.

In those moments, I kept asking myself: *What value is most alive right now? What part of me wants to lead today?* Sometimes creativity and contribution won out, and I locked the door and wrote for hours. Sometimes family and dependability led, and I put the work down for days or weeks. Sometimes self-compassion and rest took the wheel, and I gave myself permission to pause (Neff & Germer, 2018). It wasn't perfect, but it was intentional. It was values-guided. That's what compassionate prioritization is all about.

Here's my hot take: Work–life balance is a myth. Balance implies an ideal 50/50 split, where everything gets equal weight on a perfectly level scale. That's not real life. What we need instead is *work–life flexibility*, the ability to adapt, to shift focus, to give different values more space at different times (Kossek & Lambert, 2005). It's about choosing with compassion who gets to lead right now, knowing that the other values and priorities are still present, waiting to be honored in their time.

This flexible perspective-taking allows you to see your full self and affirm: *I am not just a professional. I am not just a parent. I am not just a helper. I am not just a partner, friend, sibling, or child. I am a whole person, with many values, many roles, and many ways to live a meaningful life.* When those parts of you feel like they're in conflict, it doesn't mean something is wrong, it means you care. The work isn't to erase the tension but to meet it with compassion and choose your next step with clarity.

Beyond Burnout Practice: Who's Driving Today?

Purpose: To practice compassionate prioritization—the skill of making intentional, values-based decisions when multiple important parts of you are asking to lead.

Step 1: Pause and Reflect

Take a moment to check in with the many parts of yourself:

- *What role or identity has been in the driver's seat lately?*
- *Which part of you has been getting most of your time, energy, or attention?*
- *Which part has been sitting quietly in the backseat, waiting to be noticed?*
- *What value might that quieter part be trying to bring forward?*

Step 2: Choose with Compassion

Ask yourself:

- *Who do you want to lead today?*
- *What would it look like to let that part take the wheel just for this stretch of road?*

Remember: You don't have to be everything to everyone at once. You just have to choose what matters most right now and trust that you can always re-route.

What to Do When You Drift: The Reset Ritual

Let's normalize something right now: You will drift. You will fall out of alignment with your values. That's not failure, it's feedback. It's part of the process. Even airplanes don't fly in a perfectly straight line. For most of the journey, they're slightly off course, making small, continuous adjustments for wind, weather, and other variables. Pilots don't see this as a mistake; it's expected. The destination is reached not through rigidity, but through ongoing responsiveness.

Many of us, however, don't reset; we get swept away once we notice we are off track. We tell ourselves, *next year, next week, next time.* We miss the moment and spin it into a story. We say things like, *I was going to be courageous and ask for that raise in my review, but I didn't . . . maybe next year.* Or, *I was going to honor my health and cut out sugar, but then I downed two Krispy Kremes . . . January 1st isn't far.* Or, *I was going to focus on connection and do a no-screens activity with my kids after work, but I'm exhausted . . . maybe next week.*

Alignment doesn't require perfection. It requires permission to begin again with compassion. This is what I call *compassionate recalibration*: The practice of noticing you've drifted, releasing judgment, and gently steering yourself back toward your values. It's not a hard reset or a harsh correction. It's a soft, steady re-centering.

Present-moment awareness, a core process in ACT, reminds us that the only place we can choose differently is now (Hayes et al., 2012). Burnout often pulls us into mental time travel: Replaying the past, catastrophizing the future, or checking out altogether. But the moment you notice you've drifted is not a detour, it's a doorway. A cue to return, recalibrate, and begin again.

Beyond Burnout Practice: Back to Me in 15—A Compassionate Recalibration Ritual

Purpose: This practice is a quick, compassionate recalibration. Like a plane constantly adjusting its flight path, this ritual helps you make micro-corrections and return to your values, no matter how far off-course you feel. You can choose one or more steps of this process to help you reroute when you hit an inevitable detour.

Step 1: Move (3–5 Minutes)—Shift Your Body and Energy

Choose any (or all the following): *Stretch, take a short walk, shake out your arms or legs, dance to one song, or do a few yoga poses.*
The goal is to move your physical state to interrupt inertia and signal transition.

Step 2: Reset (1–3 Minutes)—Reground in the Present

Choose one or more of the activities below:

- *Take some soothing rhythmic breaths.*
- *Run cold water on your wrists, take a 2-minute shower or use an ice roller on your face.*
- *Drink a full glass of water.*
- *Say a grounding mantra out loud or silently, for example, I am allowed to begin again or This moment matters.*

Step 3: Refocus (5–7 Minutes)—Realign with Your Values

Grab your journal or the notes app on your phone or simply reflect on the following:

- *What was a meaningful moment today, big or small?*
- *What's the next step I want to take from a place of values?*
- *What's one word I want to embody for the rest of the day?*

From Autopilot to Aligned Action

Letting your values take the wheel isn't just about identifying what matters most, it's about building a life that reflects those values in motion. This is where committed action comes in. In ACT, committed action refers to the ongoing, values-driven steps we take in our daily lives. It's not a single achievement but a consistent pattern of behavior that moves us toward what matters (Hayes et al., 2012). Committed action can take many forms such as setting goals, breaking them down into mindful action steps, or cultivating systems and habits that serve your deeper commitments.

You already have habits. Even when you feel unmotivated or burned out, your life is stitched together by routines. Snoozing your alarm three times? Habit. Hitting your vape pen after a long day? Habit. Collapsing onto the couch and scrolling for two hours? Also a habit. So is making coffee first thing in the morning, walking your dog, getting to work on time, or automatically saying "yes" when someone asks for your help. If you do it consistently and without much thought, it counts as a habit. The real question isn't whether you're disciplined, it's whether your discipline is aligned with your values.

Burnout often convinces us that we're failing. But more often, the issue isn't a lack of willpower, it's that we're stuck in routines that no longer serve us. Add decision fatigue, the mental drain from making countless choices throughout the day, and it's even easier to slide into autopilot (Baumeister et al., 1994). That's why even the smallest values-based tweaks matter. When your existing routines reflect what matters most, your habits begin to carry you through the hard moments, so you don't have to white-knuckle it every step of the way. Your habits do the heavy lifting, leaving you with more energy for what truly matters.

Beyond Burnout Practice: One Small Shift

Purpose: You don't have to overhaul your life to live in line with your values. You just have to make tiny, intentional tweaks to the things you're already doing. This practice helps you spot one easy win.

Step 1: Spot a Daily Anchor

Think of one to three things you do almost every day without fail. These are your "anchors," the moments you can build on without adding more to your plate.

Choose from the following, or identify your own:

- *Making coffee*
- *Brushing your teeth*
- *Commuting to work*
- *Eating lunch*
- *Checking your phone in the morning*

Step 2: Choose a Value to Infuse

Pick one value you want to embody more today or this week. Examples: Presence, connection, rest, curiosity, courage, creativity.

Step 3: Make the Micro-Tweak

Ask: What's one tiny thing I could add, change, or swap in this moment to better reflect that value?
Examples:

- While making coffee → take three mindful breaths
- While brushing teeth → think of one thing you're grateful for
- While commuting → listen to an uplifting podcast instead of the news
- At lunch → eat without screens and look out a window
- While checking your phone → text one person "thinking of you" first

Step 4: Try It

Pick just one tweak and try it. Notice how it feels.
One tweak I'll try this week: _____

Step 5: Give Yourself Credit

Even the smallest change is a win. End the day by noticing and naming how you showed up for yourself.

Committed Action, Work Edition

Committed action isn't about grinding yourself into the ground. It's about showing up in ways that serve your long-term well-being and reflect what matters most even when the steps are small. In the last section, you explored everyday tweaks you could make in your personal routines. Now we're shifting the lens to your professional world.

Committed action shapes how you show up at work: The choices you make, the boundaries you set, the risks you take, and the habits you commit to that move you toward a more sustainable, values-aligned career. It's not about piling more onto your plate. It's about making sure the way you work reflects what matters most, so your professional life supports you instead of draining you.

The following ten examples aren't exhaustive, but they highlight common ways values can come alive in a professional setting. Some might feel energizing, while others might stir discomfort. Both reactions are worth noticing. You don't need to do them all at once. Start with the one that feels most meaningful or perhaps most overdue.

1. **Taking Risks.** Stepping into something new, vulnerable, or bold in service of what matters. This might mean pitching a project that reflects your creative vision, volunteering for a leadership role that excites you, or sharing an unconventional idea in a meeting.

2. **Repairing and Owning.** Acknowledging mistakes and taking responsibility to maintain trust and integrity. For example, apologizing to a colleague after a misunderstanding, being transparent about a missed deadline, or initiating a repair conversation with a client.

3. **Quiet Consistency.** Showing up reliably for the tasks and commitments that matter, even without recognition. This could look like completing your case notes each day to a "good enough" standard, keeping up with weekly team check-ins, or maintaining a steady workflow during busy seasons.

4. **Saying No.** Declining opportunities, projects, or requests that don't align with your values, capacity, role, or broader vision. Sometimes, the most values-aligned choice is passing on a "stretch" assignment so that you can give your best to what truly matters.

5. **Advocacy.** Speaking up for yourself, your team, or those you serve. This might include requesting equitable pay, raising concerns about unfair policies, proposing redistribution of work, or calling out bias in decision-making.

6. **Letting It Be.** Accepting that not every problem can be solved or every process perfected and safeguarding your energy accordingly. That might mean allowing a colleague to complete a task in their own way, resisting the urge to overedit a project that's already good enough, or letting go of outcomes that aren't fully yours to control.

7. **Choosing Rest or Play.** Building in intentional moments of restoration and joy. Examples include taking your full lunch break, using vacation days for an adventure, or carving out an afternoon for creative

brainstorming, instead of packing your schedule with back-to-back meetings.

8. **Creative Expression.** Bringing creativity into your role in ways that are authentic and energizing. This might be designing a new resource for clients, experimenting with facilitation styles, or developing a project that reflects your unique perspective.

9. **Investing in Growth.** Seeking out experiences, feedback, and education that keep you engaged and evolving. This could mean joining a peer consultation group, pursuing advanced training, or working with a mentor or coach.

10. **Boundaries.** Protecting your time, energy, and integrity so that you can sustain your work in the long term. That might involve not checking email after work hours, setting realistic response expectations, or blocking off focus time in your calendar. (We'll go deeper into boundaries in the next section.)

Protecting Your Values Through Boundaries

Living in alignment with your values isn't just about moving in the right direction. It's also about protecting your ability to stay on that path. That's where boundaries come in. Boundaries are one of the most vital and most misunderstood forms of committed action. Many people think of them only in terms of how others treat us, but boundaries are ultimately about how we treat ourselves. They reflect the choices we commit to and the ways we communicate our responses to both welcome and unwelcome behaviors.

In the workplace, where expectations often blur and burnout creeps in, boundaries function as a line of self-respect: A clear statement of what you will and won't participate in, based on what truly matters to you. Research shows that blurred work–life boundaries predict declines in well-being, while clear limits around workload and communication protect mental health and enhance job satisfaction (Pluut, 2020; Vanderbilt University, 2025). When organizations and leaders model healthy boundaries, employees report greater creativity, productivity, and overall well-being (U.S. Surgeon General, 2025).

Some people struggle to set boundaries at all. Others set them but fail to enforce them. In both cases, resentment builds. We might think, *How dare they email me after hours* or *You can't talk to me like that*, while outwardly replying, *No worries!*. That mismatch often hides a deeper plea: *Please respect me. Please see me. Please treat me with care.*

For those with attachment wounds or trauma histories, these struggles often trace back to early experiences of being unseen, dismissed, or violated by people they depended on. In adulthood, this can manifest fawning behaviors, people-pleasing, or using boundaries as unspoken tests or ultimatums, hoping finally to get the care or respect that was once withheld. Clinical research shows that attachment insecurity is strongly associated with boundary difficulties, as early relational patterns shape how safe it feels to assert needs and limits (Mikulincer & Shaver, 2016).

Here's the essential shift: True boundaries aren't about getting others to comply. They don't depend on whether someone listens, agrees, or changes. A true boundary is a committed action you take to stay aligned with your values, regardless of how others respond.

To create values-aligned boundaries, it helps to distinguish between three common but often conflated forms of communication: (1) Seeking understanding, (2) stating preferences, and (3) setting a boundary.

- *Seeking understanding* is information sharing: "I can give my best at work when my workload is manageable, and I have weekends to recharge."
- *Stating a preference* is making a request: "Please don't contact me after hours or on weekends."
- *Setting a boundary* is committing to your own behavior: "I don't answer emails after 6 p.m. or on weekends."

All three are valuable in professional relationships, and ideally you use them all. The difference lies in where the control rests. Seeking understanding and stating a preference depend on the other person's willingness to hear or honor your words. Setting a boundary relies only on you.

When we blur these categories, communication becomes unclear. Workplace frustrations often occur when we voice a preference but expect it to be honored like a boundary. When that doesn't happen, we feel disappointed or disrespected even though we never followed through with our own commitment. This pulls us into trying to control others instead of focusing on our personal agency: The meaning we make of our experiences and the choices available to us in the moment.

Getting clear on whether we're sharing information, making a request, or committing to a boundary helps us communicate more effectively and act in alignment with our values.

It's also worth remembering that boundaries aren't threats. Saying "If I don't get a raise, I'll quit," when you don't intend to leave or when you don't have control over the raise, isn't a boundary. It's an ultimatum, and it usually backfires. A values-aligned boundary, on the other hand, might sound like: "I'm looking to grow in my career and want to explore leadership opportunities here. If that's not possible, I'll pursue other options that align with my long-term goals." This isn't manipulative. It's honest. It's not about forcing someone else's hand. It's about taking your next step.

Beyond Burnout Exercise: Protecting What Matters

Purpose: Get clarity on your preferences and boundaries to communicate and protect your values.

Step 1: Use These Prompts to Reflect on Where Your Values Might Need Clearer Protection without Needing Anyone Else to Change First.

Where in your life are you currently saying "yes" to things that pull you out of alignment with your values?

_____

_____

What is one value-aligned boundary you could clarify for yourself?

_____

_____

Can you identify a place where you've been using the language of boundaries to try to control someone else's behavior? What would it look like to shift back into your own agency?

_____

_____

_____

Step 2: Identify What You're Protecting

What value are you trying to honor?
My value: _____

Step 3: Clarify Your Intention

What are you actually trying to do? Be respected? Protect your time? Preserve your energy? Get space?
I'm trying to . . .

_____

_____

_____

Step 4: Sort It Out. Is It a Request, Preference, or Boundary?

Sometimes, we confuse these three categories, which makes it harder to communicate clearly. Here's the difference:

- **Request to be understood**—Sharing information so others know what supports you.
  Example: "I'm feeling frustrated about the pattern of the meeting starting late. When everyone is running on time, it communicates commitment and respect."
- **Preference**—Letting someone know what you'd like them to do.
  Example: "I'd appreciate it if we could start meetings on time."
- **Boundary**—A clear limit you will act on, regardless of other people's choices.
  Example: "If the meeting hasn't started within 10 minutes, I will log off."

Now try yours:
What I want to say: _____

This is a: Request to be understood/Preference/Boundary

Step 5: Refine Your Language

Use this template to make sure that your boundary stays grounded in agency, not control.
Boundary Starter Template: To honor my value of [value], I've decided [specific action I will take or avoid].
Examples:
- To honor my value of family, I don't schedule work meetings after 5 pm.
- To honor my health, I've decided to decline weekend work events.
- To support my value of growth, I'm exploring leadership roles even if that means stepping outside my current organization.
- Your boundary statement:

_____

_____

_____

Reflection Questions

- How does this boundary help protect what matters most to you?
- Where might you anticipate pushback or discomfort?
- How will you stay grounded in compassion and clarity when enforcing this?

Once you've explored a specific boundary and reflected on how it aligns with your values, it can be helpful to identify broader patterns. Many of us struggle to articulate or uphold boundaries not because we lack motivation, but because we haven't named the categories that most often drain us. By recognizing common types of professional boundaries and the values they protect, you can begin to spot where your energy leaks occur and where more structure or clarity might help. Let's look at some of the key boundary domains that come up in professional settings.

Professional Boundary Types

1. Time Boundaries

Value: Balance, Rest, Sustainability

- Setting work hours and not responding to emails after hours
- Blocking calendar time for deep work, lunch, or transitions
- Saying "I need to reschedule" rather than overextending

2. Workload Boundaries

Value: Integrity, Quality, Self-respect

- Pushing back when assigned tasks exceed capacity
- Asking for prioritization: "Which project takes precedence?"
- Declining additional responsibilities that compromise your performance or well-being

3. Emotional Labor Boundaries

Value: Self-compassion, Emotional safety

- Not absorbing others' distress as your responsibility to fix
- Naming when a dynamic feels unsustainable (e.g., constant venting or crisis cycling)
- Refusing to be the workplace therapist if that's not your role

4. Role Clarity Boundaries

Value: Integrity, Fairness, Leadership

- Redirecting tasks outside your scope: "That's actually handled by [X]"
- Naming scope creep respectfully
- Advocating for updated job descriptions or fair expectations

5. Feedback and Communication Boundaries

Value: Respect, Transparency, Accountability

- Addressing inappropriate, microaggressions, passive-aggressive communication
- Declining to engage in gossip or triangulation
- Requesting clarity in roles, decisions, or expectations

6. Upward Boundaries (with Leadership)

Value: Growth, Courage, Honesty

- Naming unmet needs for mentorship, growth, or feedback
- Expressing when expectations feel misaligned with your role or values
- Advocating for systemic change, not just personal accommodation

7. Downward/Peer Boundaries (If You're in Leadership)

Value: Justice, Boundaried Care, Professionalism

- Saying no to over-functioning for your team
- Modeling values-based time off and rest
- Setting norms that honor the needs of employees, customers, and leadership

When Making It Work Isn't Workable

Sometimes, the ultimate boundary that needs to be set is leaving our current roles. In some burnout journeys, "making it work" is no longer workable. In these moments, resigning can be more than a last resort. It can be a powerful act of committed action in service of your values. But not all resignations are created equal. Leaving a job under the grip of panic, fear, or resentment can be a form of experiential avoidance, an attempt to escape rather than to move toward something meaningful. On the other hand, resigning with clarity, dignity, and intentionality can reflect fierce self-compassion. It's not a cure for burnout, and it won't eliminate all pain or uncertainty. But in some cases, it is exactly how we walk into our values, reclaim our personal agency, and make space for the life we're longing to build.

Beyond Burnout Exercise: A Values-Based Exploration of Resigning

Purpose: This exercise helps you discern whether leaving your job might be a values-aligned choice.

Step 1: Reconnect with Your Values

Reflect on the following:

- *What are your three to five most important values right now?*
- *How is your current job aligned with those values?*
- *How is it actively interfering with or violating them?*

Step 2: Scan for Nonnegotiables

Check in with the following indicators that "making it work" might be harming more than helping:

- ☐ Ongoing symptoms of chronic stress (e.g., insomnia, migraines, GI issues)
- ☐ Emotional numbing or dread each day
- ☐ Repeated boundary violations or ethical/moral injury
- ☐ Leadership or organizational culture that is unresponsive to your needs or concerns
- ☐ Failed attempts to make change despite reasonable, values-based efforts
- ☐ Feeling unable to show up as the parent, partner, or person you want to be outside of work

Step 3: Consider Real-World Logistics

Logistics and material realities matter. Use this list of questions to assess what resources and protections you have in place:
Finances

- Do I have enough savings for a buffer (ideally three to six months)?
- Are there income streams I can tap or adjust?
- What would a temporary bridge job or consulting option look like?

Health Insurance

- What are my Consolidated Omnibus Budget Reconciliation Act (COBRA) or marketplace options?
- Can I obtain coverage through a partner or public program?

Benefits

- Am I forfeiting paid time off (PTO), tuition reimbursement, retirement vesting, or bonuses by leaving now?
- Are there benefits I need to use before I go (e.g., therapy, flexing spending account (FSA) funds, leave)?

Step 4: If I Leave, How Do I Leave with Integrity?

Leaving can be a radical act of love but only if it's done in service of what you care about.

Reflection Prompt

"If I were to leave in a way that honored my values of [insert values], what would that look like?"
Possibilities:

- Giving thoughtful notice with transparency and professionalism
- Creating a smooth transition plan for your clients or team
- Speaking truthfully, but not vindictively to leadership
- Saying goodbye to colleagues with appreciation

Step 5: Try the Decision On

Close your eyes and picture two paths:

- Path A: You stay.
- Path B: You leave.

In your body, where is there tightness? Where is there release? Six months from now, what would each version of you thank you for?

Step 6: Envision the Transition—Not Just the Exit

Leaving one job doesn't always mean immediately finding your dream role, but it does open space to build toward something more aligned. This step helps you think through the transition practically and meaningfully.

Reflection Prompts

- If I left this role, what kind of job would feel more aligned with my values?
- What qualities would I want in my next workplace (e.g., leadership style, flexibility, mission, size, population served)?
- What do I need to feel supported in the transition (e.g., mentorship, time off, temporary work, reskilling)?
- Who could I talk to for support, perspective, or networking?

Also consider:

- Could this be a sabbatical period for recalibration?
- Would part-time work or consulting offer breathing room?
- Is this time to prioritize parenting, health, or caregiving needs?

Compassionate Urgency

I know my refrain throughout this chapter has been that direction matters more than speed. Healing, alignment, and transformation aren't sprints but paths to be walked with intention. Yet, as we wrap up this final step of *the Beyond Burnout Blueprint*, I want to introduce something that complements that steady, deliberate pace: *Compassionate immediacy.*

Compassionate immediacy, a concept articulated by Dr. Robyn Walser, one of ACT's foremost clinicians and teachers, is described as the act of "leaning in" with presence and care, bringing a sense of urgency that is not fear-driven but rooted in compassion and commitment.

It's understanding that life is finite, and we move with urgency not because life is an emergency, but because it is precious. It's the realization that your life is happening now, and the time to align with your values isn't someday–it's *this day*. You don't need to finish healing before you begin. You don't need to wait until you are no longer burnt out. You just need to recognize that your time is sacred and limited, and that every moment is an invitation to live on purpose.

I didn't expect to be writing this book while my best friend of 25 years was being diagnosed with stage III breast cancer. Miriam has seen me through some of the hardest, most defining moments of my life. She's as vibrant, full of life a person as you can find. Alongside the heartbreaks and hardships of her life when we are together, I could count on her laughing (very loudly), dancing, and her hugging me tightly. She's raising two amazing sons, leading in corporate America; navigating the complexities of co-parenting; and still showing up with humor, heart, and late-night phone calls full of dating stories and life updates.

Just a week before her diagnosis, we were on the phone cackling about something ridiculous misadventure in her New York City dating life. Days later, we were planning chemo schedules and figuring out how she'd tell her kids.

In the wake of this shocking news, an overnight, earth-shattering diagnosis, for a vibrant, seemingly healthy woman came an overwhelming outpouring of love and support. Friends, family, coworkers, even acquaintances, and kind strangers showed up with care and compassion. I found myself marveling aloud at how deeply loved she was, and how incredible her community had become. She agreed but noted: "I just wish it didn't take all of this."

And she's right. It shouldn't take illness or collapse to bring our lives into focus. It shouldn't take heartbreak or burnout to make us rest. It shouldn't take a diagnosis to teach us how to live.

That's the invitation of compassionate immediacy. We don't have to wait for a devastating diagnosis to access our connection to vitality and love. All it takes is intentionally holding this perceptive.

So, if you knew, truly knew you had 40 years left . . . how would you live? What about 20?

10? 5? What would you stop putting off? What would you say, or do, or finally stop struggling with?

What would shift if you stopped waiting and started living with both direction and urgency, guided not by fear, but by fierce compassion? Let this be your turning point. Let your values take the wheel, and compassionate immediacy set the pace.

References

Baumeister, R. F., Stillwell, A. M., & Heatherton, T. F. (1994). Guilt: An interpersonal approach. *Psychological Bulletin, 115*(2), 243–267. https://doi.org/10.1037/0033-2909.115.2.243

Chentsova-Dutton, Y. E., & Ryder, A. G. (2020). Cultural models of normalcy and deviancy. *Asian Journal of Social Psychology, 23(2),* 187–204. https://doi.org/10.1111/ajsp.12413

Gilbert, P. (2014). The origins and nature of compassion focused therapy. *British Journal of Clinical Psychology, 53*(1), 6–41. https://doi.org/10.1111/bjc.12043

Hayes, S. C., Strosahl, K. D., & Wilson, K. G. (2012). *Acceptance and commitment therapy: The process and practice of mindful change* (2nd ed.). Guilford Press.

Kashdan, T. B., & Ciarrochi, J. (Eds.). (2013). *Mindfulness, acceptance, and positive psychology: The seven foundations of well-being.* Context Press.

Kossek, E. E., & Lambert, S. J. (2005). *Work and life integration: Organizational, cultural, and individual perspectives.* Psychology Press.

Mikulincer, M., & Shaver, P. R. (2016). *Attachment in adulthood: Structure, dynamics, and change* (2nd ed.). Guilford Press.

Neff, K. D., & Germer, C. K. (2018). *The mindful self-compassion workbook: A proven way to accept yourself, build inner strength, and thrive.* Guilford Press.

Pluut, H. (2020). Not able to lead a healthy life when you need it the most: A study of work–life interference and well-being during COVID–19. *BMC Public Health, 20*(1), 1–12.

Tangney, J. P., & Dearing, R. L. (2002). *Shame and guilt.* Guilford Press.

U.S. Surgeon General. (2025, January 24). *Workplace mental health & well-being.* U.S. Department of Health & Human Services. https://www.hhs.gov/surgeongeneral/reports-and-publications/workplace-well-being/index.html

Vanderbilt University. (2025, February 3). *Setting boundaries at work: A key to well-being.* Vanderbilt University News. https://news.vanderbilt.edu/2025/02/03/setting-boundaries-at-work-a-key-to-well-being/

Vilardaga, R., Hayes, S. C., Levin, M. E., & Muto, T. (2009). Creating a strategy for progress: A contextual behavioral science approach. *The Behavior Analyst, 32*(1), 105–133.

Walker, P. (2013). *Complex PTSD: From surviving to thriving: A guide and map for recovering from childhood trauma.* Azure Coyote.

Part III

Broader Applications for the Beyond Burnout Blueprint

Chapter 11

Flexible, Compassionate Leadership

You made it through *the Beyond Burnout Blueprint*. This chapter is about what comes next: You as a leader. Maybe you're tempted to skip ahead, perhaps thinking the word "leader" doesn't apply to you. But stay with me, this chapter isn't about titles, promotions, or corner offices. What the world needs now are more compassionate, visionary leaders willing to influence and shape families, workplaces, cultures, and communities in both small and big ways. Whether you're running a business, raising children, working on a team, or showing up for a cause, you hold influence and thus leadership potential. Even if you don't yet identify as a leader, I invite you to keep reading. We'll explore the practical challenges and meaningful opportunities of leading formally or informally with integrity, courage, and care.

Money, Power, and Influence

One thing often absent from the discussions of leadership and burnout is money. Not just paychecks or budgets, but our relationship with money. How it shapes our sense of safety, values, leadership choices, and capacity to serve. Like Voldemort, we dare not speak its name as if most of us aren't deeply influenced by the money (or lack thereof) in our bank accounts. Yet, it's everywhere: In how we price our work, set boundaries, advocate (or don't), and evaluate our worth. Money and power and how we relate to them are not side notes in the burnout story: They're main characters.

Burnout, Money Worries, and Mental Health

Living with financial instability takes a tremendous toll on the body, mind, and nervous system. Research shows that financial scarcity imposes a heavy "cognitive bandwidth tax," narrowing attentional capacity and diminishing self-control when resources are limited (Mani et al., 2013; Mullainathan & Shafir, 2013). In the United States, money anxieties are widespread.

DOI: 10.4324/9781003640592-15

Forty-two percent of adults report that financial concerns negatively affect their mental health, and those under financial stress are more distracted, absent more, and less engaged at work (TIAA Institute, 2024).

Recent findings show that ongoing money-management worries among U.S. employees are linked to increased burnout and reduced job satisfaction (University of Georgia, 2025). More broadly, high levels of subjective financial worry are consistently associated with psychological distress, especially among vulnerable groups such as low-income households, renters, and the unemployed (Ryu, 2022).

If you employ others, remember that how you pay people matters: Fair (even generous) wages, plus benefits like health insurance, paid time off, and family leave aren't perks, they're lifelines. One serious medical expense can derail even insured individuals financially, creating chronic stress that undermines performance and well-being in the workplace.

When people are financially depleted, they're more vulnerable to quick fixes and predatory promises. Scarcity hijacks cognitive bandwidth, disrupts sleep, heightens inflammation, and diminishes one's capacity to be present, regulated, and well (Mani et al., 2013). It becomes nearly impossible to show up as your best self when your basic needs remain uncertain.

Reframing Money: From Goal to Conduit

Our relationship with money is shaped by messaging from caregivers, culture, and larger economic structures. For some, money is tied to prestige or legacy; for others, it's about survival, security, or escaping debt. The pursuit of wealth isn't inherently wrong. It's the function of that pursuit that matters.

In my view, "make as much money as possible" is an empty goal if untethered from meaning. We're not Scrooge McDuck gratuitously diving into a pool of gold coins. Accumulating wealth without vision can become hoarding, often born from scarcity and threat. Unchecked growth in the human body is akin to a virus or cancer. Yet, we glorify it in business. From a Social Rank Theory perspective, resource acquisition is tied to perceived social position. If we feel "below" in the hierarchy, less successful, admired, or secure, we may default to competitive, status-driven behaviors: More clients, revenue, reach . . . but to what end?

Reflect on your money's role in your business or in your life. Do you want it?

- To pay your team well and create a workplace culture you're proud of?
- To reach more people with life-changing services or meaningful products?

- To rest, be present with family, or build generational wealth?
- To travel, enjoy beauty and culture, invest in health, or savor everyday life?
- To support community, fund passion projects, or create space for creativity?
- To invest in education or fuel bold, impactful ventures?
- To back causes that matter, become a philanthropist in your own way, or simply feel stable enough to breathe?

There's no right or wrong answer. Your financial vision must be compelling to you.

In our society, money matters. Income provides a standard of living that positions people to have a better shot at health and well-being, but its effects are not uniform. Earlier research suggested that emotional well-being plateaued around $75,000 in U.S. data (Kahneman & Deaton, 2010), roughly equivalent to the low $100,000s today when adjusted for inflation. More recent findings, however, show a more nuanced picture: While the benefits of additional income diminish, they do not disappear. For those under greater strain, higher income reduces distress up to a point, while for many others, well-being continues to rise, albeit modestly, even beyond this threshold (Killingsworth, 2021; Killingsworth et al., 2023). And sufficiency thresholds are shifting: Housing costs have far outpaced inflation in many markets, with renter cost burdens reaching record highs (Harvard JCHS, 2024).

Beyond this point of sufficiency, money's role becomes more complex. I would argue that money is not the goal. Money is a conduit: A tool, a resource, a potential expression of our values, if we're intentional (Mullainathan & Shafir, 2013). Some people worship money. Some people see money as evil. But it is our relationship with money that really reveals the role money will ultimately play in our lives. Like much of the messaging of this book, context is everything. The real question becomes: What is money's function in your life and business? How much do you need emotionally, physically, relationally, and operationally to live your values and execute your vision?

Beyond Burnout Exercise: Money and Meaning Audit

Purpose: Let's reframe your relationship with money using values, not fear, as your guide. This reflection is designed for leaders, entrepreneurs, creatives, and mission-driven professionals.

Take a few quiet minutes. Reflect. Journal. Be honest. There are no wrong answers.

1. What does money represent to you right now?
   Safety? Freedom? Status? Control? Legacy? Survival? Adventure?
2. When you imagine earning more, what values come up?
   What would that money allow you to build, have, do, offer, or change?
3. Do you feel shame, guilt, or fear around wanting more money?
   Where did those messages come from? Are they still serving you?
4. How do you want to earn your income?
   What kind of labor, leadership, or creativity feels values-aligned?
5. What are the ethical or emotional limits of your ambition?
   When does accumulation turn into hoarding? When does growth become misalignment?
6. Finish this sentence:
   "I want my business to generate enough income so that I can _____
   _____."

Let's Talk About Power: To Do What, With Whom, and Why?

Just like money, the word power can make people squirm. It's loaded. We often associate it with control, domination, or oppression. But power can also mean voice, agency, influence, protection, and possibility (Clegg et al., 2006; Keltner et al., 2003). Power isn't the problem. The problem is when we pursue it blindly or avoid it entirely without asking deeper questions.

Are you seeking power to dismantle inequity? To protect your team or your time? To make space for others at the table . . . or to make sure no one takes your seat?

These are hard questions. But they're essential ones. Because when we don't investigate our motives around power, fear tends to fill in the gaps. Many burnt-out leaders, especially in high-stakes, high-performance fields, secretly believe: *If I don't stay in control, everything will fall apart*. Research supports that fear of losing control amplifies stress and accelerates burnout, particularly in organizational cultures that equate leadership with constant vigilance and dominance (Maslach & Leiter, 2016).

In burnout culture, we often frame power in binary terms: Those who have it and those who don't. But the truth is more complex. You can have power in one area of your life and feel disempowered in another. You can hold positional authority but feel emotionally powerless. You can accumulate power in ways that inadvertently reinforce toxic systems, especially when the social environment rewards dominance, status, and control (Haslam et al., 2011).

Power can be wielded as a personal asset or shared as a collective resource. Which kind of leader do you want to be? If your team doesn't know your values around power, they'll project their own fears. But when power is wielded with transparency, intention, and vision, it becomes a force for transformation (Keltner, 2016).

Beyond Burnout Exercise: Power and Purpose Audit

This reflection will help you clarify your relationship to power and how you want to use it in your work, leadership, and relationships. Take a moment to slow down. Reflect on the following:

What Kind of Power Do You Want to Have?

Think: Decision-making, autonomy, influence, platform, creative freedom. Where do you feel you lack power, and why is that important to you?

Power to Do What?

- What change, boundary, impact, or opportunity do you want to create with this power?
- What would this power allow you to say yes or no to?

Power with Whom?

- Who are you building this power with or for?
- Are you using power to consolidate control or to distribute voice, care, and responsibility?

Why This Power?

- What values or lived experiences are driving your desire for this kind of power?
- How does this connect to your bigger vision?

Red Flags to Watch For

- Am I using power to avoid vulnerability?
- Am I hoarding power out of fear, scarcity, or imposter syndrome?
- Am I assuming I know what's best without collaboration?
- Was anyone harmed or disempowered in the process?
- Did my use of power reinforce unethical systems or challenge them?

Complete the Sentence

"I want to use my power to _____, in partnership with
_____, because I believe _____."

From Jungles to Gardens

Some advice you remember because it changes you. Other advice you remember because it makes you pause and think, *Wait . . . what?* Years ago, a supervisor I genuinely like and respect was leading a training for managers and said, with good intentions: *You've just got to get the monkey off your back.*

She was referring to the classic *Harvard Business Review* article, "Management Time: Who's Got the Monkey?" (Oncken & Wass, 1974). The idea was that every time a direct report brought you a problem, it was like a monkey jumping off their shoulders onto yours. As a leader, your job was to delegate, to empower others to tend to their own monkeys, rather than letting them pile onto you. Her essential leadership message was about ensuring your employees' problem didn't become your (the leader's) problem.

It was meant to be a lesson in boundaries, delegation, and maybe even empowerment. But in practice, I didn't feel empowered, I felt ashamed. At the time, I was deep in burnout. I didn't have one monkey on my back. I had an entire menagerie. Rhesus macaques of reactivity. Spider monkeys of unmet expectations. Gibbons of shifting priorities. And one particularly grumpy silverback, my monkeyless supervisor's approval I was constantly seeking. Instead of feeling supported in how to lead through complexity, I felt like I had to hide the chaos. I internalized the message that if I was carrying too much, it must mean I was doing leadership wrong.

I didn't feel like a leader. I felt like a barely functioning zookeeper. I've learned, so often people aren't trying to pass off responsibilities. They are overwhelmed. The system is overstretched. The problem isn't delegation, it's design.

The real leadership question isn't *how do I get the monkey off my back?* The question is *why is there a monkey on anyone's back at all?* And what kind of ecosystem creates perpetual overpopulation of these pesky primates? Because as a leader, you're not meant to be a zookeeper. You're the steward of an ecosystem (Senge, 2006).

If the monkey metaphor left me feeling like I was just managing chaos, it's because I was. Everything felt reactive, overgrown, and urgent. And in hindsight, that's exactly what it was: A leadership jungle.

In a jungle, things grow wild, tangled, unpredictable, and hard to navigate. No matter how well-intentioned you are, it's impossible to lead with clarity when you're hacking your way through the brush. But a garden? A garden is intentional. Things are planted on purpose. There's rhythm, care, pruning, and composting. Mistakes become soil. Beauty has room to grow. In a garden, your job isn't to control everything, it's to tend what matters most.

Garden-style leadership means:

- Prune what no longer serves your mission or people
- Compost failures and stress into learning and growth
- Plant thoughtful systems, roles, and rituals
- Water the values, relationships, and skills you want to cultivate

This shift from zookeeper to gardener is not just a change in mindset; it is a transformation in how power is held, how labor is shared, and how the daily life of the team is shaped. A zookeeper's goal is containment—keeping the monkeys under control, problems out of sight, and chaos at bay. A gardener, by contrast, accepts that challenges are not failures but part of the natural order. Weather will shift, pests will arrive, some crops will wither, and others will flourish. Losses are expected, even inevitable, yet they coexist with moments of growth, beauty, and harvest. In this frame, leadership is not about eliminating difficulty but about cultivating conditions where resilience can take root, where setbacks are anticipated and absorbed, and where triumphs, whether small blossoms or abundant harvests, are genuinely celebrated.

Beyond Burnout Exercise: Mapping Your Leadership Ecosystem

Purpose: Use this reflection to reimagine your leadership style through the lens of stewardship, not survival.

1. Spot the Monkeys

- What situations feel like constant crises?
- Are they truly urgent or signs of unclear roles, unmet needs, or broken systems?

2. Map the Jungle

What parts of your leadership or workplace feel overgrown, outdated, chaotic, or ignored?

3. Clarify the Garden

What would a values-aligned, thriving team ecosystem actually look like?

4. Prune, Compost, Plant

- What do you need to cut (outdated tasks, roles, habits)?
- What do you want to compost into learning (failures, stress patterns, systemic friction)?
- What do you want to plant, moving forward (new rituals, team agreements, responsibilities)?

How to Build a Resilient Team from the Start

A thriving garden doesn't grow on good intention alone. It requires consistency, care, and a thoughtfully cultivated environment. The same is true for building a sustainable team. Hiring and retention are not just operational tasks. They are foundational burnout prevention strategies. Who you invite into your organization, how you support them, and how you respond to challenges all shape who you are as a leader.

Hiring well is one of the most powerful ways to protect your team and your own capacity. Yet, many leaders find themselves swinging between two extremes: Perfectionism and desperation. On the one end, we search for the mythical unicorn, the candidate who has done it all, seen it all, and needs nothing from us except a start date. This person rarely exists. And even if they did, they might struggle in your system if emotional flexibility and values' alignment aren't also present (Bond et al., 2013).

On the other end, we're drowning. We needed someone yesterday, so we hired anyone with a pulse and a résumé. But desperation-based hiring often leads to deeper chaos, including misaligned expectations, unclear boundaries, and a constant drain on emotional and relational energy. Both ends of the spectrum can contribute to burnout.

The alternative is hiring for willingness. Look for a mindset rooted in curiosity, flexibility, and values alignment. You can teach skills. What's harder to teach is the ability to sit with discomfort, receive feedback with openness, and collaborate with care. You're not just hiring someone to do a task. You're bringing someone into a living system. You're not just filling a role, you're planting roots.

Think beyond résumés. Ask: Is this someone I'd want to navigate a tough season with? Is this someone who brings clarity, not just credentials? Is this someone who will make the culture better just by being in it?

Most interviews default to "biggest strengths and weaknesses" or "where do you see yourself in five years?" questions that reward polished scripts more than real insight. If we want to understand how someone will actually operate under pressure, we need prompts that unearth their psychological flexibility, values in action, and compassion. ACT- and CFT-informed questions can invite deeper insights (Hayes et al., 2012; Gilbert, 2010). Get curious how candidates notice threat, return to the soothing system, defuse harsh self-talk, set boundaries, repair after mistakes, and care for others without burning out.

1. *What daily habits or small rituals help you feel steady at work? When those habits get disrupted, how do you notice and reset?*

   Assesses: Self-awareness, regulation, and proactive burnout prevention

2. *When stress shows up, many of us avoid tasks or conversations. Can you share a time you noticed yourself leaning toward avoidance, and what helped you move back toward action?*

   Assesses: Avoidance patterns, willingness, and committed action

3. *Tell me about a situation that didn't go the way you planned. How did you work with your reactions in the moment, and what guided your next choice?*

   Assesses: Flexibility, emotional regulation, and values-based decision-making

4. *Share a mistake you made that taught you something important. How did you respond at the time, and what changed in your approach afterward?*

   Assesses: Growth mindset, accountability, and perspective-taking

5. *Burnout often shows up in relationships. How do you notice when a teammate is struggling, and what do you do to show up in a way that's supportive but not rescuing?*

   Assesses: Compassion, boundaries, and relational intelligence

6. *How does self-criticism show up for you? How do you address it?*

   Assesses: Self-compassion, resilience, and ability to work with difficult thoughts

7. *Tell me about a time when feedback felt hard, whether you were giving or receiving it. What made it difficult, and what did you learn about yourself in the process?*

   Assesses: Humility, repair, and emotional processing

8. *What kind of environment helps you feel energized and aligned with your best work? What signals tell you when you're starting to run low on energy or engagement?*

   Assesses: Burnout risk, cultural fit, and early warning signs

9. *What's a personal or professional goal that deeply matters to you?*
   When setbacks happen, what helps you keep moving toward it?

   Assesses: Values in action, persistence, and willingness

10. *Imagine your team or clients describing you at your best. What would*
    you hope they say, and what do you do to live into that description?

    Assesses: Strengths-based identity, intentional action, and leadership
    vision

Feedback Is a Burnout Prevention Tool

One of the most overlooked skills in leadership is effective feedback: Feedback that is timely and constructive. When team members don't get clear feedback about what they're doing well, imposter syndrome can set in. *Imposter syndrome* is a pattern where qualified and competent individuals internalize self-doubt and persistently fear being exposed as incompetent (Clance & Imes, 1978; Bravata et al., 2020). They start questioning themselves, striving harder, and over-functioning to compensate.

Imposter syndrome is often a feedback gap, rather than a self-esteem issue. The lack of feedback or imbalance of negative over positive feedback is interpreted as evidence of deficiency rather than as an absence of communication. Even if it doesn't accelerate imposter syndrome, it creates fertile soil for resentment, leaving associates feeling invisible, micromanaged, or harshly judged.

Positive feedback isn't about flattery. It's about reinforcing the behaviors that move your mission forward. When you're clear about what's working and why it matters, people feel seen, not just evaluated. It also promotes quality work. What gets acknowledged often gets repeated (Hattie & Timperley, 2007).

On the flip side, most people can handle tough feedback. What they can't handle is vague criticism, passive-aggressive hints, delayed input, shame-inducing commentary, or sweeping generalizations. Effective feedback is clear, timely, specific, and behavioral: Say what you saw, not what you assumed. Stay curious, invite context, and extend trust.

People almost always remember constructive or negative feedback more vividly than praise. That's not a sensitivity issue; it's neurobiology. Earlier in this book, we discussed the negativity bias, our brain's tendency to notice, remember, and give more weight to negative experiences than positive ones (Baumeister et al., 2001). That same bias shows up in the workplace, where even well-meaning leaders can unintentionally create fear-based environments if feedback skews negative.

That means, as a leader, you need to water more than you need to weed. If the only time someone hears from you is when something goes wrong, you're not cultivating growth, you're creating a fear-based environment.

Praise isn't a nice-to-have. It's a cornerstone of *psychological safety*, and when safety is strong, accountability becomes easier (Edmondson, 1999).

Beyond Burnout Practice: Water What Works, Weed What Hurts

Purpose: To give and receive feedback in a way that prevents burnout, builds trust, and reinforces clarity, not fear. When delivered thoughtfully, feedback becomes a tool for growth, alignment, and connection. When neglected or mishandled, it fuels disconnection, perfectionism, and burnout.

This exercise will help you reflect on your feedback habits, sharpen your delivery, and create a feedback culture that supports the ecosystem you're tending.

Step 1: Understand the Feedback Flow Positive Feedback

Great when specific. Also, powerful when generalized.

Give it privately and publicly.

Positive feedback helps people internalize what's working and why it matters. Specific praise reinforces exact behaviors. Generalized praise affirms someone's presence, steadiness, and unique contributions. Both are valid and important. Give feedback privately to build one-on-one trust. Give feedback publicly to normalize appreciation and highlight values in action. Examples:

- Private and Specific: "The way you handled that unexpected client question showed deep product knowledge and confidence. It built credibility in the room."
- Public and Generalized: "I want to acknowledge how steady and thoughtful you've been lately. It's made a great impact on the team."

Reflection Prompts

- Who's overdue for recognition?
- What values or behaviors do I want to water and help grow?

Constructive Feedback

Make it specific. Only generalize when naming a clear pattern with examples. Give it privately. If others are involved, be intentional and transparent. Constructive feedback is best done in private to protect psychological safety and prevent shame. If others need to be included for support, coaching, or transparency, make your intentions clear and the purpose of others' participation known. This is about shared accountability, not public bashing.

When naming a pattern, be specific about:

- Frequency: How often is this happening?
- Severity: What is the impact on the team, workflow, or client experience?
- Support: What expectations or resources are needed?

Examples:

- Private: "In yesterday's meeting, I noticed a few interruptions when others were speaking. It disrupted the flow, and I want to check in with you about how that moment felt."
- Pattern and Framing: "This has happened in 3 of our last 5 team meetings. It's starting to interfere with the agenda, and I want us to talk about it directly."
  Avoid generalized critiques like "You always . . ." or "You never. . . ."

Reflection Prompts

Have I been avoiding giving feedback because it's uncomfortable?
Is there a weed I need to gently but clearly pull?

Step 2: Practice Giving Feedback That Builds Trust

Use the prompts below to write both positive and constructive feedback. Practice grounding your language in observable behavior, shared values, and impact.

Positive Feedback Prompt

- What did they do?
- What value or strength did it reflect?
- What impact did it have?
"I want to acknowledge _____. It really reflected _____, and it helped _____."

Constructive Feedback Prompt

- What behavior or pattern needs to be addressed?
- What did you observe (be specific)?
- What support or expectation is needed?
  "I want to check in about _____. I noticed _____, and the impact was _____. I'd like us to talk about what support or clarity might help going forward."

Step 3: Align Feedback with Burnout Prevention

Final Reflection

- Do I use feedback regularly to cultivate growth or only to correct when something's wrong?
- When I give constructive feedback, do I focus on clarity or avoid discomfort?
- How would my team describe the feedback culture here?

When Feedback Gets Hard: Deliver Tough News Without Losing Trust

You've been practicing regular positive and constructive feedback. Sometimes, though, leadership asks more: Ending a contract, restructuring a role, or delivering feedback that will sting. Before these conversations, notice the urge to delay, soften, or skip them. Returning to experiential avoidance from earlier chapters: Notice if you're moving away from short-term discomfort in ways that create bigger long-term costs like confusion, resentment, financial or reputational fallout, and of course burnout (Hayes et al., 2012). Instead, choose clarity and care with this sequence.

Clear-and-Kind Playbook

1. **Prepare: Regulate and set intention.**
   Two soothing breaths. Silent aim: "Be clear and respectful."
2. **Open with dignity, then state the message (what + why).**
   "I know this may be hard to hear. This doesn't erase the effort you've put in."
   "Because of X, we need to make Y shift." (Be specific, direct, values-aligned.)
3. **Listen and reality-test.**
   "How is this landing for you?" "What might I be missing?"
   "Given our goal, what support or adjustments would help?"
4. **Decide, document, and hold boundaries.**
   Co-create next steps (timeline, resources, checkpoints).
   Close with care: "I'll follow up in writing. Here's what's nonnegotiable, and here's where we have flexibility."

Real leadership holds complexity with compassion: Clear and connected, firm and kind. Done well, these moments don't just minimize harm. They strengthen the team (Brown, 2018).

Early Signs of Toxicity

Everyone has hard days. But persistent patterns like chronic blame, disconnection, low empathy, and resistance to feedback often signal deeper misalignment. Distinguish burnout behaviors (withdrawal, irritability, fatigue) from toxic dynamics (entitlement, abusive conduct, erosion of psychological safety). One calls for support; the other calls for accountability. Before demanding personal responsibility, rule out system causes (unclear policy, unreasonable expectations, normalized dysfunction) and address those first (Skakon et al., 2010).

Part of compassionate leadership is holding space for struggle and protecting the ecosystem. Avoiding conflict may feel easier now, but it creates long-term damage.

Use the Support + Willingness Framework

- Clarify the issue and offer specific support.
- Assess willingness: Is the person taking accountability and engaging in repair?

  - *Yes*: Co-create a time-bound plan (goals, support, check-ins).
  - *No:* You may be facing a values or readiness gap. This requires different clarity.

Even with care, structure, and coaching, some team members cannot or will not align or, worse, they create safety risks to the team. Letting go is hard, and it can be an act of compassionate leadership. The main goal should be protection over punishment.

A principled exit can be respectful and clear. Done well, it affirms the values you're protecting and creates space for someone else to thrive elsewhere in many contexts. Leadership means knowing when to water, when to prune, and when to compost what no longer supports growth.

Model Accountability When You Miss the Mark

Leadership won't spare you from mistakes; it will simply make them more visible. What sets the tone for your team isn't flawless execution. It's whether you own missteps, repair the impact, and change behavior. When you model real accountability, you trade ego-protection for trust-building and give everyone permission to learn (Edmondson, 1999).

The Accountability Loop (Five Moves)

1. Pause and regulate. Get back in your window of tolerance so that you can respond, not defend.

2. Name the impact (not just intent). "My delay stalled your work," "My tone shut down the discussion."
3. Own your part with no qualifiers. Drop the "but." "That was my call, and it missed the mark."
4. Repair and support. "Here's what I'll do now," "What do you need from me to move forward?"
5. Change the conditions. Adjust the process, expectations, or norms so that the same mistake is less likely next time. Document, follow up, and close the loop.

Phrases That Help

- "I didn't model what I ask of you. That's on me."
- "Impact matters more than my intent. I'm sorry."
- "Here's the fix and the timeline. I'll report back Friday."
- "Next time I'll do X instead of Y; here's the new check we're adding."

If the pattern repeats, get curious, not defensive: Seek feedback, examine workload and systems, and ask for coaching. Accountability isn't self-flagellation; it's values in action. Your team doesn't need perfection. They need to see you take responsibility and realign with what you stand for.

Beyond Burnout Exercise: Accountability Audit

Take a few moments to reflect on your relationship to accountability, especially when things go off course.
1. When was the last time you made a mistake as a leader?
   How did it impact your team? What did you do next?
2. Did you take clear responsibility or did you deny it, explain it away, shift blame, or avoid dealing with?
   What would full accountability have looked like?
3. Is there a place where repair still needs to happen?
   What's holding you back from initiating it?
4. Are you modeling the kind of ownership you hope to see from your team?
   Where might perfectionism or pride be blocking the path?
5. Complete the sentence:
   "As a leader, I want to model _____ even when I make a mistake."

Leadership is never just about the individuals you manage; it's about the culture you shape. And culture, like a garden, needs constant tending. You've now learned how to hire with intention, give feedback that nourishes, and lead with fierce compassion. But what happens when the soil itself is depleted? When the burnout you're facing isn't just personal or team-based but systemic?

In the next chapter, we expand beyond individual or team dynamics. We'll explore how to apply *the Beyond Burnout Blueprint* to organizations, institutions, and collective spaces so that you're not just tending one garden but helping cultivate healthier ecosystems wherever you go.

References

Baumeister, R. F., Bratslavsky, E., Finkenauer, C., & Vohs, K. D. (2001). Bad is stronger than good. *Review of General Psychology, 5*(4), 323–370. https://doi.org/10.1037/1089-2680.5.4.323

Bond, F. W., Hayes, S. C., & Barnes-Holmes, D. (2013). Psychological flexibility, ACT, and organizational behavior. *Journal of Organizational Behavior Management, 33*(3), 207–228.

Bravata, D. M., Watts, S. A., Keefer, A. L., Madhusudhan, D. K., Taylor, K. T., Clark, D. M., Nelson, R. S., Cokley, K. O., & Hagg, H. K. (2020). Prevalence, predictors, and treatment of imposter syndrome: A systematic review. *Journal of General Internal Medicine, 35*, 1252–1275. https://doi.org/10.1007/s11606-019-05364-1

Brown, B. (2018). *Dare to lead: Brave work. Tough conversations. Whole hearts.* Random House.

Clance, P. R., & Imes, S. A. (1978). The imposter phenomenon in high achieving women: Dynamics and therapeutic intervention. *Psychotherapy: Theory, Research & Practice, 15*(3), 241–247. https://doi.org/10.1037/h0086006

Clegg, S. R., Courpasson, D., & Phillips, N. (2006). *Power and organizations.* SAGE.

Edmondson, A. (1999). Psychological safety and learning behavior in work teams. *Administrative Science Quarterly, 44*(2), 350–383. https://doi.org/10.2307/2666999

Gilbert, P. (2010). *Compassion focused therapy: Distinctive features.* Routledge.

Harvard Joint Center for Housing Studies. (2024). *The state of the nation's housing 2024.* https://www.jchs.harvard.edu/

Haslam, S. A., Reicher, S. D., & Platow, M. J. (2011). *The new psychology of leadership: Identity, influence and power.* Psychology Press.

Hattie, J., & Timperley, H. (2007). The power of feedback. *Review of Educational Research, 77*(1), 81–112. https://doi.org/10.3102/003465430298487

Hayes, S. C., Strosahl, K. D., & Wilson, K. G. (2012). *Acceptance and commitment therapy: The process and practice of mindful change* (2nd ed.). Guilford Press.

Kahneman, D., & Deaton, A. (2010). High income improves evaluation of life but not emotional well-being. *Proceedings of the National Academy of Sciences, 107*(38), 16489–16493. https://doi.org/10.1073/pnas.1011492107

Keltner, D. (2016). *The power paradox: How we gain and lose influence.* Penguin.

Keltner, D., Gruenfeld, D. H., & Anderson, C. (2003). Power, approach, and inhibition. *Psychological Review, 110*(2), 265–284. https://doi.org/10.1037/0033-295X.110.2.265

Killingsworth, M. A. (2021). Experienced well-being rises with income, even above $75,000 per year. *Proceedings of the National Academy of Sciences, 118*(4), e2016976118. https://doi.org/10.1073/pnas.2016976118

Killingsworth, M. A., Kahneman, D., & Mellers, B. A. (2023). Income and emotional well-being: A conflict resolved. *Proceedings of the National Academy of Sciences, 120*(10), e2208661120. https://doi.org/10.1073/pnas.2208661120

Mani, A., Mullainathan, S., Shafir, E., & Zhao, J. (2013). Poverty impedes cognitive function. *Science, 341*(6149), 976–980. https://doi.org/10.1126/science.1238041

Maslach, C., & Leiter, M. P. (2016). Burnout: A multidimensional perspective. In C. L. Cooper & P. L. Perrewé (Eds.), *Routledge companion to wellbeing at work* (pp. 35–49). Routledge.

Mullainathan, S., & Shafir, E. (2013). *Scarcity: Why having too little means so much*. Times Books.

Oncken, W., Jr., & Wass, D. L. (1974). Management time: Who's got the monkey? *Harvard Business Review, 53*(6), 75–82. https://hbr.org/1974/11/management-time-whos-got-the-monkey

Ryu, J. (2022). Subjective financial worry and psychological distress: Evidence from national survey data. *Journal of Mental Health, 31*(6), 867–874. https://doi.org/10.1080/09638237.2021.1919186

Senge, P. M. (2006). *The fifth discipline: The art and practice of the learning organization* (Rev. ed.). Doubleday.

Skakon, J., Nielsen, K., Borg, V., & Guzman, J. (2010). Are leaders' well-being, behaviours and style associated with the affective well-being of their employees? A systematic review of three decades of research. *Work & Stress, 24*(2), 107–139. https://doi.org/10.1080/02678373.2010.495262

TIAA Institute. (2024). *Financial wellness survey report*. https://www.tiaainstitute.org/

University of Georgia. (2025). *Financial stress and burnout among U.S. employees*. [Report].

Chapter 12

Scaling the Beyond Burnout Blueprint

Burnout is personal. But it never starts or ends there. As we try to understand who we are, it's humbling to remember how much of our identity has been shaped by time, place, and circumstances. Had you been born 50 years earlier or later, or a 1,000 miles in another direction, so much would be different—your accent, your interests, your stomping grounds. But beyond that: Your belief systems, your access to opportunity, your cultural norms, and the people you might call community. In a society that often celebrates rugged individualism, we must not lose sight of our intrinsic connection to the broader collective. None of us were formed in isolation; we are shaped in relationships, molded by systems, and linked across generations (Bronfenbrenner, 1979; Putnam, 2015).

Even your unique expression of burnout is not simply a personal experience, it is a manifestation of your human spirit reacting to environmental conditions and social constructs. It reflects your values, sensitivities, and desire for purpose and integrity. But it is also shaped by everything you've ever experienced directly or indirectly, consciously or unconsciously. The jobs you've held, the messages you've absorbed, the systems you've moved through, and the way your identity has been seen or unseen, supported or dismissed. Burnout is personal, yes, but it is also political, cultural, and historical (Maslach & Leiter, 2016).

The U.S. labor market reflects these complexities: A blend of resilience and exploitation, innovation, and inequality. While most American businesses are small, large corporations set the pace and dominate influence, often leaving smaller players to navigate rising costs, shifting regulations, and dwindling protections (Kalleberg, 2011). Many essential industries like agriculture, caregiving, construction, and hospitality quietly depend on undocumented labor, even as immigration laws remain unstable and punitive (Milkman, 2020). Artificial intelligence promises efficiency and innovation few could have imagined a decade ago, but it raises real concerns about job displacement, depletion of environmental resources, and the dehumanization of work (Susskind, 2020). Inflation, supply chain

DOI: 10.4324/9781003640592-16

volatility, and global policy decisions shape our everyday realities in ways that are felt but often go unnamed. These structural, invisible forces privilege some while deeply disadvantaging others (Harvey, 2005).

In an interconnected world, it is easy to feel overwhelmed. And I cannot pretend that the next chapter illuminates some magic, simple solution to the world's most complex problems. But I do believe that imagining what compassion and psychological flexibility might look like at scale is a worthy endeavor. Understanding the values embedded in our broader work cultures and the systems we are part of is essential if we want to create something better. This chapter is not a prescriptive blueprint for institutions. It is an invitation to think creatively, expansively, and collectively: What would it take to build not just burnout-resilient individuals but burnout-resilient communities, workplaces, and systems?

Earlier in this book, I named the impact of capitalism on the burnout phenomenon, and I want to return to that here with a wider lens. In Chapter 3, we touched on how many describe our current reality as *late-stage capitalism*, a phrase that functions more as social commentary than as a formal economic classification. It conveys the cultural sense of living in an era marked by widening inequality, corporate consolidation, ecological collapse, and the erosion of public systems meant to support the collective good (Fisher, 2009; Mandel, 1975/1999). It captures the lived perception of a system that feels increasingly unsustainable, both materially and psychologically.

It is understandable at times to feel defeated in the wake of these forces, and yet, within this fractured landscape, healing still happens. Communities still care for each other. People still grow and thrive. That's the paradox I want to hold space for in this chapter. It reminds me of the beautiful Japanese art of *kintsugi*. *Kintsugi* is the practice of repairing broken pottery with gold. The goal isn't to erase the cracks, but to honor them. The object becomes more beautiful because of its breaks, not in spite of them. Stronger at the very places where it was once most fragile.

To me, this is what systems transformation can look like. Not necessarily smashing everything to the ground and starting over, but filling the fractures with intention, with care, creativity, community, and gold.

One such "gold-filled" model is *Conscious Capitalism*, described by John Mackey, cofounder of Whole Foods Market, and business scholar Raj Sisodia (Mackey & Sisodia, 2014). Mackey built Whole Foods Market in the late 1970s, transforming a small natural grocery store into a major company by centering health, sustainability, and ethical sourcing at a time when those ideas were far from mainstream. His experience revealed both the possibilities and the pitfalls of trying to run a values-driven business within a profit-driven economy. Out of this tension, Mackey and Sisodia articulated the framework of Conscious Capitalism as a way to humanize economic life and push against the notion that shareholder profit must be a company's singular purpose.

At its core, Conscious Capitalism seeks to address some of capitalism's most pressing critiques: Short-term profit maximization, worker exploitation, environmental degradation, and organizational cultures that prioritize efficiency over humanity. It asks: What if business could be a force for flourishing, not just extraction? What if companies measured their success not only by quarterly returns but also by their contributions to human and ecological well-being?

The framework rests on four pillars:

1. *Higher Purpose*—businesses should serve a mission beyond profit, whether that means improving health and well-being, protecting the environment, or fostering community. Profit is still essential, but it is seen as fuel for the mission, not the mission itself.
2. *Stakeholder Orientation*—true success is measured by how a company treats all its stakeholders: Employees, customers, suppliers, communities, and the planet, not just shareholders. This approach acknowledges interdependence and rejects the zero-sum assumption that one group must lose for another to win.
3. *Conscious Leadership*—leaders are called to embody emotional intelligence, integrity, and service, cultivating trust and aligning decisions with both values and long-term vision rather than short-term personal gain.
4. *Conscious Culture*—organizational culture is recognized as foundational, not peripheral. Psychological safety, inclusion, transparency, and collaboration are seen as critical conditions for both people and businesses to thrive.

By naming and systematizing these principles, Conscious Capitalism offers a pathway for businesses to innovate without abandoning humanity. It does not erase capitalism's contradictions, but it offers a pragmatic framework for companies and leaders searching for ways to reconcile profitability with responsibility.

One visible expression of this shift is the rise of *social entrepreneurship*: For-profit companies that bake social or environmental goals into the core business model, not just side philanthropy (Battilana & Kimsey, 2017). Think TOMS Shoes (early "buy-one, give-one," evolving toward community impact investments) and The Honest Company (a mainstream brand built around safer products and transparency). These are examples of Conscious Capitalism in action: Revenue and impact pursued together, with real tensions and trade-offs to manage.

Around the world, alternative economic models are being imagined, tested, and lived, many grounded in justice, sustainability, and care. None are perfect, but each offers something worth learning from.

- *The doughnut economy*, developed by Kate Raworth (2017), reimagines economic success not as infinite growth, but as thriving within boundaries by meeting every person's core needs without surpassing the planet's ecological ceiling.
- *The solidarity economy* flips the script on competition and extraction, favoring cooperation, democratic ownership, mutual aid, and equity (Utting, 2015). It shows up in worker cooperatives, community land trusts, and time banks and centers collective well-being over individual profit.
- *The regenerative economy* takes its cues from nature, focusing on restoring what has been depleted environmentally, socially, and emotionally (Fullerton, 2015). It asks how we might leave places, people, and systems better than we found them.
- *The care economy* brings visibility and value to the labor that holds everything else up like caregiving, parenting, emotional labor, domestic work—roles traditionally dismissed or underpaid. It challenges us to build economies around care rather than convenience or consumption (Folbre, 2021).

These are not abstract theories. They are active blueprints, being lived into existence. We may not be able to fully opt out of capitalism, but we can take inspiration from these models, ask better questions, and redesign from the inside out, starting with the systems we touch.

When we start to take this broader view, many people get overwhelmed, perhaps feeling that our systems are broken beyond repair. And this is where *kintsugi* becomes more than metaphor for me.

I truly believe we can hold both: Grievance and gratitude. We don't need to pretend the bowl was never broken. But we also don't need to throw it away either. Like *kintsugi*, we can repair what's cracked, not to make it flawless, but to make it stronger. More beautiful at the places it once split open. We may not be able to build a perfect system. But we can build a more responsive one. One that acknowledges harm, practices repair, and dares to align with what truly matters.

Building a Responsive Work Culture

Even the most values-aligned systems can't shield us from the complexity of the world we live in. Conscious Capitalism may offer a path toward more integrity within our institutions, but it cannot eliminate the grief, uncertainty, and injustice that surround us. As we attempt to build better systems, we remain human beings with nervous systems constantly responding to turbulence (Porges, 2011).

Thanks to technology, we are more connected than ever, but that connection comes at a cost. Our nervous systems are flooded daily with images and stories of natural disasters, mass violence, political unrest, humanitarian crises, and systemic injustice. We were not built to carry this much grief, this constantly (Maté & Maté, 2022). And yet, we're expected to show up for meetings, hit deadlines, and respond to emails while the world feels sometimes metaphorically, sometimes literally on fire.

Scholar Alexei Yurchak coined the term *hypernormalization* to describe the eerie disconnect that occurs when systems are visibly failing, yet daily life continues as if everything is fine (Yurchak, 2006). First applied to the late Soviet Union, the concept resonates today: We go to work, pay bills, and meet expectations, even as the world around us feels increasingly unstable or surreal. This disconnect helps explain why so many people feel burnt out, numb, or overwhelmed while still performing "business as usual" (Han, 2015).

If we're serious about building burnout-resilient cultures, we have to acknowledge the conditions people are navigating both inside and outside of work. The forces that shape us, economic, political, cultural, environmental, do not pause at the office door. Employees are affected by mass shootings, anti-LGBTQ+ legislation, wars, climate disasters, devastating diagnoses, or family crises. Sometimes, these events happen directly to us; other times, they unfold around us. Either way, they reverberate in our nervous systems (van der Kolk, 2014). People do not stop being human at work, and they shouldn't be expected to.

That doesn't mean workplaces must become round-the-clock processing spaces, nor that every organization needs to issue constant political statements or pressure employees to share vulnerabilities. What it does mean is rejecting the idea that professionalism requires detachment. A responsive work culture is one where people are not punished, explicitly or implicitly, for being affected by their world.

This terrain is complicated. People bring different identities, histories, traumas, values, and coping strategies to work, and those differences become even more pronounced in times of stress. This is the emotional complexity of working in community. And it is precisely why organizations cannot leave the work of caring for their teams' well-being to chance or to a few overextended individuals.

Too often, the emotional labor of a team is absorbed by the most empathic, relationally attuned, or historically marginalized members, most commonly women. They are the ones who notice when a colleague is shutting down, who offer quiet check-ins, who hold space when others fall apart. But without recognition or structural support, this care remains invisible and unsustainable (Hochschild, 2012). When organizations fail to acknowledge, compensate, or redistribute this labor, they risk reinforcing the very burnout they claim to resist.

Care can be designed into the culture, not improvised or defaulted to employees based on personality or identity. Organizational systems can take collective responsibility for well-being. That means care is resourced, responsibilities are shared, and managers are trained not just in oversight but also in holding emotional complexity with skill, humility, and boundaries (Edmondson, 2019).

A responsive culture does not react to distress with panic or performance. It meets complexity with intentionality. The five principles given below are not a checklist, but a commitment to shaping workplaces where care, equity, and flexibility are woven into the foundation. They help ensure that people are supported not just as workers but also as whole humans and that the labor of support is shared.

Beyond Burnout Practice: Building a Responsive Work Culture

Purpose: Use this tool to assess, reflect, and identify next steps for building a culture that holds emotional complexity, prevents invisible labor, and distributes care equitably.

1. Make the Invisible Visible

Creating a burnout-responsive culture means building psychological safety, where people can share what they're holding if they choose to without fear of being judged, punished, or quietly excluded from opportunities.
Leaders don't need all the details. But they do need to make it explicit that real life is allowed here and that naming struggle isn't seen as weakness, but as part of being human. Whether it's a message acknowledging current events, a private check-in after a hard meeting, or a clear statement that people can take up space when needed—these moments matter.

Reflection Questions

- What global, communal, or personal events might be impacting people at work right now?
- How are we currently acknowledging (or avoiding) these realities?
- Is there a psychologically safe space where people can disclose personal or family crises without fear of penalty—formally or informally?

Prompt for Action
What's one way we could make it clearer that people are allowed to be human here?
(e.g., leadership modeling, policy language, team agreements, opt-in message templates, private outreach options)

2. Offer Flexible Containers for Support

- What pathways currently exist for people to ask for support or decompress?
- Are those options opt-in, emotionally safe, and inclusive of different processing styles?
- Who has access to those options and who might not?

   Prompt for Action: What's one additional, low-stakes support container we could offer or strengthen?
(e.g., anonymous needs form, affinity spaces, protected flex time)

3. Adjust Expectations During Stress

- Are we softening timelines, communication norms, or deliverables during times of personal, communal, or collective stress?
- Do our systems allow people to downshift without being penalized either formally or through team dynamics?
  Prompt for Action
- Where are expectations currently fixed that could be made more humane?
- Who's most impacted, and what accommodations could reflect true equity?

4. Align Action with Values

- What are our publicly stated or internal organizational values?
- How do we embody those values in moments of rupture or stress?
- Where might our current response be out of alignment?
  Prompt for Action
- What would it look like to operationalize our values in response to what's happening right now?
- How can we make this reality not just rhetorical?

5. Prevent Emotional Labor from Becoming Invisible

- Who is currently holding the emotional weight of the team (formally or informally)?

- Are we recognizing, supporting, and compensating for this labor, or are we letting it default to certain people?
- Are managers trained to respond to emotional needs or are they left unprepared?
  Prompt for Action: What's one step we could take to redistribute the emotional labor of care more fairly?
  (e.g., leadership training, care roles, peer check-in teams, rotating responsibilities)
  Next Step I Will Take This Week:

Don't Perform Care: Practice It

By now you might be wondering if all of this is really necessary. Maybe some internal objections are bubbling up: Isn't work just . . . work? Isn't this getting a little too touchy-feely? After all, many of us were taught to leave our feelings at the door. We learned that professionalism means keeping your head down, being efficient, and not making it personal. That mindset, *it's just business*, has deep roots.

Here's what I'd say in return: Until the AI overlords officially take over, teams are made of people. People with nervous systems. People with bodies. People with histories, some of them traumatic. People with families, identities, chronic illnesses, care responsibilities, ambitions, fears, and dreams. They are not code. They are not algorithms. They are not productivity machines.

Experts predict that artificial intelligence will soon surpass humans in many domains, from diagnostics to decision-making to complex problem-solving (Brynjolfsson & McAfee, 2014; Tegmark, 2017). But the one thing AI cannot authentically replicate is empathy. The ability to attune to another person's emotions, to connect through care, to respond with compassion. This is uniquely human (Decety & Cowell, 2018). Empathy is not a "soft skill." It is the skill that ensures trust, belonging, and resilience in teams (Boyatzis et al., 2012; Worline & Dutton, 2017). It is the one edge we will always have, so it's time to lean in.

Trying to silo humans from their humanity may buy short-term compliance, but it erodes trust, corrodes creativity, and accelerates burnout. Centering compassion and values isn't "soft." It's strategic. It's the long game. Because if you're building something that's meant to last, you need people who are well enough to carry it with you.

Values in the Storm

When values are truly centered in an organization, they don't just hang on the wall or appear in a mission statement. They guide behavior, shape culture, and influence how decisions are made, especially under pressure. When values become virtue signaling rather than authentic guidance, the gap between what's said and what's done becomes painfully obvious (Brown, 2018; Worline & Dutton, 2017).

These contradictions show up across sectors:

- Saying we prioritize mental health but refusing to adjust unrealistic workloads.
- Declaring people come first while treating staff as expendable.
- Talking about transparency while making decisions behind closed doors.

Such inconsistencies are not neutral. They erode trust and accelerate burnout (Maslach & Leiter, 2016). As of 2025, we're also living through an immense political and cultural backlash against Diversity, Equity, and Inclusion (DEI). DEI initiatives seek to promote the fair treatment and full participation of all people, particularly those who have been historically excluded or discriminated against. The backlash has been especially hostile toward efforts addressing systemic racism and supporting gender minorities, including transgender communities (Pager & Shepherd, 2008).

Psychologist Dr. Dana Crawford, creator of Crawford Bias Reduction Theory (CBRT), describes this backlash as *retrenchment*, the resistance that often emerges when equity gains disrupt entrenched power structures. Retrenchment occurs when progress in racial justice or equity is followed by losses through organizational or structural resistance to change (Crawford, 2025).

We see retrenchment across multiple arenas: Dismantling affirmative action in higher education, corporate boardrooms eliminating DEI roles, research grants for health equity being cut, tech companies slashing employee resource group (ERG) budgets, and rollbacks of pay-transparency laws.

Organizations are especially vulnerable to this pullback when their equity commitments were never structurally embedded to begin with. A clear example is Target, a major American retailer. After years of publicly championing equity and inclusive practices, Target abruptly pulled back on DEI in early 2025 under political pressure. Target began retreating from several of its equity initiatives under mounting political pressure in early 2025 (Meyersohn, 2025a). The pullback drew a swift public response: Reverend Jamal Bryant organized a 40-day "Target Fast," a boycott rooted in Black church traditions of economic activism, which gained national attention and further intensified scrutiny of the company (Meyersohn, 2025b). The company also announced a CEO transition later that year, adding to perceptions of instability during a period of reputational turbulence (Target Corporation, 2025).

By contrast, Walmart also scaled back DEI quietly, but without significant backlash, because its brand was never built on equity promises. Costco, meanwhile, stayed steady. It didn't market itself as progressive, but it didn't retreat either. It kept its policies in place; paid workers fairly; and treated inclusion as infrastructure, not advertising.

This isn't about praising one company and condemning another (though I am proudly Team Costco). It's about authenticity. Only through authenticity can values hold a strong foundation in an organization. When values are only visible during calm weather, they vanish in a storm. But when values serve as a blueprint, they remain intact even under pressure.

Beyond Burnout Exercise: From Declaration to Design—A Values Integration Audit

Purpose: Use the following prompts to assess how your values are showing up at the organizational level, not just in branding or newsletters but also in daily operations, culture, and decision-making.

1. Name Your Stated Organizational Values

Choose two to three values your organization claims to uphold (e.g., equity, sustainability, quality, safety, transparency, integrity, care, innovation):

_____

_____

2. Where Are They Visible?

- For each value, identify where it shows up clearly in practice.
- How is it reflected in policies, resources, time, or behavior?
- Would someone feel it without being told?

_____

_____

3. Where Are They Fragile?

Name areas where the value is:
- Conditional or inconsistently upheld
- Present only during public moments
- Disconnected from daily operations

_____

_____

4. Pressure Test

Ask: If this value became politically unpopular, financially inconvenient, or culturally challenged, would we still stand by it?
☐ Yes ☐ Maybe ☐ No
Explain:

_____

_____

5. Design Adjustment

- What's one way we can move this value from aspirational to operational in the next 30 days?
- A policy change?
- A structural investment?
- A new ritual or accountability mechanism?

_____

_____

Compassion Is Not a Liability

A persistent myth in business is that compassion in leadership is a liability and that putting people first somehow undermines growth. However, many organizations that prioritize dignity, fairness, and well-being are abundantly successful and outperform competitors in profitability (Cameron et al., 2004; Worline & Dutton, 2017).
Consider these examples:

- *Patagonia:* An outdoor apparel company founded in 1973 by Yvon Chouinard, Patagonia is as well known for its environmental activism as for its fleece jackets and climbing gear. In 2011, it ran a bold *Don't Buy This Jacket* ad in *The New York Times* on Black Friday, urging consumers to consider the environmental cost of overconsumption even if it meant buying less from Patagonia. Instead of hurting revenue, the campaign boosted sales and cemented trust in the brand (Chouinard & Stanley, 2012). Today, Patagonia is valued at around $3 billion and holds a B Corp score of 151.4, nearly triple the certification threshold, showing that business success and environmental stewardship can reinforce one another (B Lab, n.d.).
- *Microsoft:* Founded in 1975, Microsoft is one of the largest technology companies in the world, employing more than 220,000 people globally. Under CEO Satya Nadella, who took the helm in 2014, the company underwent a cultural transformation. Nadella replaced the internal competitiveness of the Ballmer era with a culture of curiosity,

empathy, and growth mindset. He encouraged leaders to shift from "know-it-alls" to "learn-it-alls," breaking down silos and promoting collaboration (Nadella, 2017). These cultural changes, combined with strategic investments in cloud computing, helped increase Microsoft's market value from about $300 billion to over $2.5 trillion, making it one of the world's most valuable companies.

- *Unilever:* Headquartered in London, Unilever is one of the largest consumer goods companies in the world, selling food, cleaning products, and personal care brands like Dove, Ben & Jerry's, and Hellmann's in more than 190 countries. When Paul Polman became CEO in 2009, he reoriented the company around the *Unilever Sustainable Living Plan.* This strategy aimed to decouple growth from environmental impact, while improving social value across the supply chain. Polman challenged the idea that sustainability undermines profitability, and during his decade of leadership, Unilever delivered a 290% total shareholder return, outperforming peers and proving that purpose and profit can scale together (Polman & Winston, 2021).

- *Chobani:* Founded in 2005 by Turkish immigrant Hamdi Ulukaya, Chobani reshaped the U.S. yogurt market by popularizing Greek yogurt. From its base in upstate New York, the company grew to become America's top-selling yogurt brand within a decade. Ulukaya distinguished himself by creating what he called an "anti-CEO playbook": Offering wages well above industry standards, paid parental leave (including for adoption and foster care), and generous profit-sharing and committing 10% of profits to philanthropy (Ulukaya, 2015). His approach demonstrated that treating employees generously could build both market dominance and brand loyalty.

- *Costco:* A membership-based warehouse retailer founded in 1983, Costco has grown into one of the largest global retailers while maintaining a reputation for employee-centered practices. Unlike many in retail, Costco offers above-average wages, robust health benefits (including for part-time workers), and clear pathways for promotion. Under CEO Craig Jelinek (2012–2023), the company consistently prioritized worker well-being, resulting in low turnover, high customer loyalty, and steady profitability. By August 2025, Costco's market capitalization surpassed $435 billion, underscoring that long-term financial success can coexist with a culture of stability and respect.

- *Mark Cuban Cost Plus Drug Company:* Entrepreneur Mark Cuban launched Cost Plus Drug Company in 2022 to disrupt the opaque and costly prescription drug market. The company sells generic medications at cost plus a 15% markup, with transparent pricing that bypasses traditional pharmaceutical middlemen. Cuban's goal was to make essential drugs affordable and accessible to more people, while still building a viable for-profit company (Cuban, 2022). Cuban himself has noted that earlier in his career, he led without much empathy, but he has since come to see compassion as essential to leadership. His venture shows how ethical disruption can be both mission-driven and financially sustainable.

These leaders show that compassion and business success are not at odds. When leaders design cultures that protect dignity and align with values, returns are measured in both profit and trust.

By contrast, some organizations achieve financial dominance while externalizing harm:

- *Amazon*: Founded in 1994 by Jeff Bezos, Amazon has grown into one of the largest global retailers and cloud computing providers, with a 2025 market value exceeding $2 trillion. Bezos's personal net worth is estimated at more than $190 billion (Bloomberg Billionaires Index, 2025). Meanwhile, many of Amazon's warehouse employees earn near the minimum wage and have long reported grueling productivity quotas, high injury rates, limited job security, and insufficient access to affordable health care (Kantor et al., 2021; Day & Soper, 2023).

  This disparity highlights the false promises of trickle-down economics, the theory that wealth concentrated at the top will eventually "trickle down" to benefit all. Decades of evidence show that this rarely occurs; gains at the top tend to stay at the top (Stiglitz, 2019). At Amazon, the contradiction is clear: If trillions in market value and one of the largest personal fortunes in history don't materially improve worker well-being, how much wealth does it take to trickle down?

- *Tesla*: Founded in 2003, Tesla revolutionized the auto industry by making electric vehicles desirable and mainstream. At its peak, Tesla's market capitalization exceeded $1 trillion, reflecting its mission to accelerate the world's transition to sustainable energy. Yet, the company has also faced repeated lawsuits and investigations over racial harassment, unsafe working conditions, union-busting tactics, and employee retaliation (Hawkins, 2021; Tabuchi, 2022).

  Tesla illustrates the paradox of a mission-driven company, seemingly lacking compassionate leadership. Elon Musk's highly visible and often confrontational leadership style, marked by public clashes with regulators, erratic communication, and a reputation for dismissing worker protections, has shaped not only Tesla's culture but also its public image and profitability. The lesson is that visionary innovation can be undermined when human dignity is not woven into the mission.

- *Shein*: Founded in 2008 in Nanjing, China, Shein has become one of the world's largest fast-fashion retailers, generating over $30 billion annually. Its success rests on speed: Thousands of new products are added to its site each week, driven by algorithms that track viral social media trends and churn out clothes within days (Barboza, 2022).

Behind the rapid growth are steep costs. Investigations have revealed workers sewing 16–18 hours a day for substandard pay in unsafe factories (Greenpeace, 2023). Environmentally, Shein epitomizes fast fashion's toll: Its disposable model contributes to the 92 million tons of textile waste produced globally each year, much of it synthetic and non-biodegradable (Ellen MacArthur Foundation, 2017). What looks like affordability for consumers is actually a transfer of costs to exploited workers, polluted ecosystems, and overflowing landfills.

Financial success alone doesn't equal holistic success. When profitability depends on squeezing the workers, degrading the planet, or evading accountability, it isn't innovation, it's extraction.

If you want to build something different, resilient, and excellent, you need a framework. That's where we return to *the Beyond Burnout Blueprint*. Originally designed for individuals, its six principles can be scaled to transform entire organizations. The next section will show you how to apply them to your team, culture, or system.

Reframing *the Beyond Burnout Blueprint* as a Systems Framework

The Beyond Burnout Blueprint began as a personal roadmap, a guide to help individuals reconnect with what matters, build resilience, and move through burnout with integrity and self-compassion. But my hope is that these principles can expand beyond your individual practice.

Each step in the Blueprint can shape how we design workplaces, lead teams, and build cultures. Below, you'll find a quick reminder of what each step means on a personal level—followed by how we might begin to apply that insight collectively.

The ten examples for each step are not exhaustive. They're a starting point. Let them spark your own thinking about what burnout-resilient systems might look like in your unique context.

Create a Compelling Vision (Chapter 5)

Individually: We explored how to create a compelling vision grounded in your values, one that energizes rather than depletes you. We emphasized the importance of holding that vision with compassion, allowing it to inspire you without becoming a source of pressure or perfectionism.

Collectively: Organizations need a compelling vision too, one that is co-created, clearly communicated, and meaningfully lived. When people understand why their work matters and how it connects to a shared purpose, burnout decreases, and engagement increases.

Ten Systems-Level Applications

1. Host an annual team retreat to co-create and re-center the organizational mission.
2. Involve staff across roles in setting strategic goals.
3. Map how each department's work connects to the overall vision.
4. Rewrite mission and values in clear, human-centered language.
5. Include vision check-ins in regular team meetings.
6. Share staff stories that reflect values in action.
7. Build rituals that reinforce purpose (e.g., weekly "why we do this work" moments).
8. Use vision as a filter in decision-making processes.
9. Develop personal mission statements tied to the team's goals.
10. Ensure that new hires understand not just what they'll do but why it matters.

Welcome the Unwanted (Chapter 6)

Individually: You practiced turning toward difficult thoughts, emotions, and experiences with openness rather than avoidance. This helped you stay grounded in the face of uncertainty and deepen your resilience.

Collectively: Organizations must also learn to make room for discomfort, whether that's internal challenges, moral injury, injustice, or systems failure. Creating space for the unwanted doesn't mean forcing disclosure or processing, it means acknowledging the challenges head on.

Ten Systems-Level Applications

1. Offer optional reflection or check-in spaces after collective or global crises.
2. Train managers and supervisors in trauma-informed support.
3. Normalize grief and transition rituals (for loss, layoffs, or staff changes).
4. Create forums for naming moral injury or systemic challenges.
5. Implement anonymous feedback channels for reporting harm or fatigue.
6. Include equity-centered dialogues as a regular cultural practice.
7. Pause productivity expectations during acute collective stress.
8. Schedule processing time after distressing workplace events.
9. Partner with affinity groups to hold space for collective processing.
10. Model honest acknowledgment of discomfort from leadership, signaling that emotional truth is welcome from the top down.

Watch Your Words as Your Burnout Buffer (Chapter 7)

Individually: You learned how language, both internal and external, shapes experience. You learned defusion strategies to hold more words and self-narratives more lightly. You practiced noticing judgmental self-talk and threat-evoking language and replacing it with more flexible, compassionate narratives.

Collectively: The language used in an organization reflects and reinforces its culture. Systems must intentionally shape how communication is handled: How feedback is delivered, how people are spoken about, and how policies are written.

Ten Systems-Level Applications

1. Audit documents (policies, procedures, job postings) for dehumanizing or punitive language.
2. Set communication norms that emphasize clarity, inclusivity, and respect in meetings, emails, and daily interactions.
3. Provide feedback training grounded in curiosity and growth, not control or fear.
4. Frame challenges as shared responsibilities, avoiding blame-based language that isolates individuals.
5. Replace urgency-driven rhetoric ("ASAP," "drop everything") with intentional pacing that respects human limits.
6. Use human-centered language in HR processes, performance reviews, and public materials.
7. Identify and eliminate coded language and microaggressions that mask bias or exclusion.
8. Build repair pathways, so when language causes harm, people know how to acknowledge, address, and move forward.
9. Address venting and complaining norms by distinguishing destructive spiraling from constructive processing; provide tools like debriefs and compassionate check-ins.
10. Celebrate humanizing language that recognizes effort, centers shared values, and makes people feel seen. Encourage leaders to model compassion in both formal and informal speech.

Identify Your Unique Gifts (Chapter 8)

Individually: You reflected on what lights you up, your values-aligned strengths, the roles where you feel most alive, and the activities that feel nourishing, not draining. You learned about amplification and noticing and naming the unique contributions of your colleagues to generate uplifting and collaborative environments.

Collectively: Burnout-resilient systems understand that people thrive when their strengths are recognized and nurtured. Healthy workplaces foster collaboration, not internal competition, and design teams around complementary gifts, not conformity.

Ten Systems-Level Applications

1. Use *CliftonStrengths* (an online assessment identifying an individual's top 5 talent themes; Clifton & Harter, 2003; Gallup, 2023) or the *VIA Character Strengths Inventory* (a free tool grounded in positive psychology that highlights 24 character strengths; Peterson & Seligman, 2004; VIA Institute on Character, 2023) to identify and honor employee strengths.
2. Build complementary teams that leverage diverse work styles, talents, and character strengths.
3. Shift performance reviews from "what's missing" to "what's working," focusing on amplifying strengths.
4. Redesign roles or workflows to align with individual strengths and values.
5. Offer job-crafting opportunities during check-ins or evaluations, allowing employees to shape tasks around their strengths.
6. Encourage team-led recognition of peer strengths to build a culture of appreciation.
7. Promote shared success and collaboration, rather than zero-sum competition.
8. Train supervisors to notice when employees' gifts are underutilized or exploited and adjust accordingly.
9. Provide diverse leadership pathways beyond one-size-fits-all promotion tracks.
10. Create a culture where collaboration and contribution to the collective good are rewarded as much as solo wins.

Be Kind to Yourself and Others (Chapter 9)

Individually: You learned how to offer yourself compassion during pain, failure, or stress and change your relationship with your inner critic. You also learned how to extend that compassion outwards to activate your soothing system and navigate your environment, feeling more supportive toward yourself and others.

Collectively: Compassion can be operationalized at work. That involves creating systems where kindness isn't exceptional, it's expected. Where people feel seen, supported, and safe, and where cruelty, cynicism, or indifference are actively interrupted.

Ten Systems-Level Applications

1. Include compassion as a core organizational value and measure it.
2. Train staff in compassionate communication and conflict resolution.
3. Build in grace periods for illness, grief, or life transitions.
4. Shift performance reviews from punitive to developmental.
5. Normalize rest as a valid productivity tool.
6. Offer coaching or support, not just discipline after mistakes.
7. Implement peer kindness acknowledgments as part of culture rituals.
8. Interrupt hostility or cynicism when it shows up, publicly and clearly.
9. Allow self-compassion exercises or microbreaks during the workday.
10. Have leaders' model consistent foundational self-care practices.

Let Your Values Take the Wheel (Chapter 10)

Individually: You reflected on how to take committed action not based on fear, people-pleasing, or perfectionism, but in alignment with your deepest values. You learned that clarity and consistency make change sustainable.

Collectively: When systems are led by values rather than fear-based urgency, optics, or convenience, people trust them more. Values become the compass for policy, hiring, conflict resolution, and strategic decisions, not just words on the wall.

Ten Systems-Level Applications

1. Use values-based decision-making frameworks in team and leadership meetings.
2. Revisit values during moments of disruption or rapid change.
3. Evaluate how time and money are being used, and whether that reflects what you say matters.
4. Let values guide hiring and promotion, not pedigree or personality alone.
5. Host "values in action" town halls to crowdsource accountability.
6. Audit procedures: Who is impacted by your choices, and how?
7. Reward behaviors that reflect core values, not just outcomes.
8. Include values-check moments in performance reviews.
9. Offer training to help teams apply values during moral complexity.
10. Recognize when compassionate prioritization comes up at work. Honor when someone needs to prioritize family, health, or another honored value.

What's Next

You just finished this book, and that's no small thing. Whether you read it in pieces or all at once, whether you were searching for a way out of burnout or simply curious about a different way forward, *thank you* for showing up.

Now let's zoom way, way out.

We live on a floating rock, powered by a star. In a hundred years or so, every meeting, every metric, every competitor, and every unread email will be dust. And that's not nihilism. That's freedom. Because in the finale paradox of the book, none of it matters, and it all matters so much.

I hope something in these pages resonated. I hope something sparked. I hope a sentence made you pause, made you breathe, made you remember who you are underneath all the pressures, daily demands, and roles.

I hope this isn't just a book you finish but a companion you return to. A toolkit you reach for when the world feels heavy again. A permission slip to live more fully, more honestly, more in alignment with what matters most.

Come back to the skills that serve you on your burnout recovery journey. Revisit the metaphors, the questions, the practices that were helpful. Let them expand with you. And most importantly: Keep showing up for yourself.

What's next? Whatever you choose with purpose, with courage, and, whenever you can manage it, with compassion.

References

B Lab. (n.d.). *Patagonia: Certified B corporation.* B Lab. https://www.bcorporation.net/en-us/find-a-b-corp/company/patagonia-inc/Battilana, J., & Kimsey, M. (2017). Should you pursue a hybrid strategy? *Stanford Social Innovation Review, 15*(3), 50–55.

Barboza, D. (2022, November 6). Shein's business model is reshaping the fashion world – And raising concerns. *The New York Times.* https://www.nytimes.com

Bloomberg Billionaires Index. (2025). Jeff Bezos net worth. *Bloomberg.* https://www.bloomberg.com/billionaires

Boyatzis, R. E., Smith, M. L., & Van Oosten, E. (2012). *Helping people change: Coaching with compassion for lifelong learning and growth.* Harvard Business Review Press.

Bronfenbrenner, U. (1979). *The ecology of human development: Experiments by nature and design.* Harvard University Press.

Brynjolfsson, E., & McAfee, A. (2014). *The second machine age: Work, progress, and prosperity in a time of brilliant technologies.* W. W. Norton.

Brown, B. (2018). *Dare to lead: Brave work. Tough conversations. Whole hearts.* Random House.

Cameron, K. S., Bright, D., & Caza, A. (2004). Exploring the relationships between organizational virtuousness and performance. *American Behavioral Scientist, 47*(6), 766–790.

Chouinard, Y., & Stanley, V. (2012). *The responsible company: What we've learned from Patagonia's first 40 years*. Patagonia Books.

Clifton, D. O., & Harter, J. K. (2003). Investing in strengths. In K. S. Cameron, J. E. Dutton, & R. E. Quinn (Eds.), *Positive organizational scholarship* (pp. 111–121). Berrett-Koehler.

Crawford, D. E. (2025). Healing bias: Your guide to individual, interpersonal, and institutional change. W. W. Norton & Company.

Cuban, M. (2022). *The problem*. Mark Cuban Cost Plus Drug Company. https://costplusdrugs.com/our-mission/

Day, M., & Soper, S. (2023, October 15). Amazon workers struggle despite wage increases. *Bloomberg News*. https://www.bloomberg.com

Decety, J., & Cowell, J. M. (2018). The complex relation between morality and empathy. *Trends in Cognitive Sciences*, *22*(5), 337–339.

Edmondson, A. C. (2019). *The fearless organization: Creating psychological safety in the workplace for learning, innovation, and growth*. Wiley.

Ellen MacArthur Foundation. (2017). *A new textiles economy: Redesigning fashion's future*. https://ellenmacarthurfoundation.org

Fisher, M. (2009). *Capitalist realism: Is there no alternative?* Zero Books.

Folbre, N. (2021). *The rise and decline of patriarchal systems: An intersectional political economy*. Verso.

Fullerton, J. (2015). *Regenerative capitalism: How universal principles and patterns will shape our new economy*. Capital Institute.

Gallup. (2023). *CliftonStrengths: Discover what makes you unique*. Gallup, Inc. https://www.gallup.com/cliftonstrengths/en/home.aspx

Greenpeace. (2023). Shein's throwaway fashion model and environmental harm. *Greenpeace International*. https://www.greenpeace.org

Han, B.-C. (2015). *The burnout society* (E. Butler, Trans.). Stanford University Press. (Original work published 2010)

Harvey, D. (2005). *A brief history of neoliberalism*. Oxford University Press.

Hawkins, A. J. (2021, December 14). Tesla accused of workplace racism and unsafe practices. *The Verge*. https://www.theverge.com

Hochschild, A. R. (2012). *The managed heart: Commercialization of human feeling* (Updated Ed.). University of California Press. (Original work published 1983.)

Kantor, J., Weise, K., & Ashford, G. (2021, June 15). The cost of Amazon's fast delivery. *The New York Times*. https://www.nytimes.com

Kalleberg, A. L. (2011). *Good jobs, bad jobs: The rise of polarized and precarious employment systems in the United States, 1970s–2000s*. Russell Sage Foundation.

Mackey, J., & Sisodia, R. (2014). *Conscious capitalism: Liberating the heroic spirit of business* (Rev. & Updated Ed.). Harvard Business Review Press.

Mandel, E. (1999). *Late capitalism* (J. De Bres, Trans.). Verso. (Original work published 1975)

Maslach, C., & Leiter, M. P. (2016). Burnout: A multidimensional perspective. In C. L. Cooper & P. C. Quick (Eds.), *The handbook of stress and health: A guide to research and practice* (pp. 351–369). Wiley. https://doi.org/10.1002/9781118993811.ch21

Maté, G., & Maté, D. (2022). *The myth of normal: Trauma, illness, and healing in a toxic culture*. Avery.

Meyersohn, N. (2025a, February 19). Target retreated on DEI. Then came the backlash. *CNN*. https://www.cnn.com/2025/02/19/business/target-dei-boycott

Meyersohn, N. (2025b, March 5). A 40-day Target boycott starts today. It couldn't come at a worse time for the company. *CNN*. https://www.cnn.com/2025/03/05/business/target-boycott-jamal-bryant

Milkman, R. (2020). *Immigrant labor and the new precariat*. Polity Press.

Nadella, S. (2017). *Hit refresh: The quest to rediscover Microsoft's soul and imagine a better future for everyone*. Harper Business.

Pager, D., & Shepherd, H. (2008). The sociology of discrimination: Racial discrimination in employment, housing, credit, and consumer markets. *Annual Review of Sociology, 34*, 181–209. https://doi.org/10.1146/annurev.soc.33.040406.131740

Peterson, C., & Seligman, M. E. P. (2004). *Character strengths and virtues: A handbook and classification*. Oxford University Press.

Polman, P., & Winston, A. (2021). *Net positive: How courageous companies thrive by giving more than they take*. Harvard Business Review Press.

Porges, S. W. (2011). *The polyvagal theory: Neurophysiological foundations of emotions, attachment, communication, and self-regulation*. W. W. Norton.

Putnam, R. D. (2015). *Our kids: The American dream in crisis*. Simon & Schuster.

Raworth, K. (2017). *Doughnut economics: Seven ways to think like a 21st-century economist*. Chelsea Green Publishing.

Stiglitz, J. E. (2019). *People, power, and profits: Progressive capitalism for an age of discontent*. W. W. Norton.

Susskind, D. (2020). *A world without work: Technology, automation, and how we should respond*. Metropolitan Books.

Tabuchi, H. (2022, February 10). California sues Tesla over alleged racial discrimination and harassment. *The New York Times*. https://www.nytimes.com/2022/02/10/business/tesla-racism-lawsuit.html

Target Corporation. (2025, August 20). *Target appoints Michael Fiddelke as chief executive officer*. https://corporate.target.com/press/release/2025/08/target-appoints-michael-fiddelke-as-chief-executive-officer

Tegmark, M. (2017). *Life 3.0: Being human in the age of artificial intelligence*. Alfred A. Knopf.

Ulukaya, H. (2015). *The anti-CEO playbook* [Video]. TED Conferences. https://www.ted.com/talks/hamdi_ulukaya_the_anti_ceo_playbook

Utting, P. (Ed.). (2015). *Social and solidarity economy: Beyond the fringe*. Zed Books.

van der Kolk, B. A. (2014). *The body keeps the score: Brain, mind, and body in the healing of trauma*. Viking.

VIA Institute on Character. (2023). *VIA survey of character strengths*. https://www.viacharacter.org

Worline, M. C., & Dutton, J. E. (2017). *Awakening compassion at work: The quiet power that elevates people and organizations*. Berrett-Koehler.

Yurchak, A. (2006). *Everything was forever, until it was no more: The last Soviet generation*. Princeton University Press.

Index

Note: page numbers in *italics* indicate a figure and page numbers in **bold** indicate a table on the corresponding page.

For Product Safety Concerns and Information please contact our EU
representative GPSR@taylorandfrancis.com
Taylor & Francis Verlag GmbH, Kaufingerstraße 24, 80331 München, Germany